Faith and Science at Notre Dame

JOHN P. SLATTERY

FAITH AND SCIENCE AT
NOTRE DAME

JOHN ZAHM, EVOLUTION, AND
THE CATHOLIC CHURCH

University of Notre Dame
Notre Dame, Indiana

University of Notre Dame Press
Notre Dame, Indiana 46556
undpress.nd.edu
All Rights Reserved

Copyright © 2019 by University of Notre Dame

Published in the United States of America

Library of Congress Cataloging-in-Publication Data

Names: Slattery, John P., author.
Title: Faith and science at Notre Dame : John Zahm, evolution, and the
    Catholic Church / John P. Slattery.
Other titles: Old science, new problems
Description: Notre Dame, Indiana : University of Notre Dame Press, [2019] |
    Revision of author's thesis (doctoral)—University of Notre Dame, 2017
    titled Old science, new problems : a theological analysis of John Zahm's
    attempt to bridge evolution and Roman Catholicism. | Includes
    bibliographical references and index.
Identifiers: LCCN 2019021568 (print) | LCCN 2019981572 (ebook) | ISBN
    9780268106096 (hardback) | ISBN 0268106096 (hardback) | ISBN
    9780268106126 (pdf) | ISBN 9780268106119 (epub)
Subjects: LCSH: Zahm, J. A. (John Augustine), 1851–1921. | Catholic
    Church—United States—Clergy—Biography. | University of Notre
    Dame—Faculty—Biography. | Evolution (Biology)—Religious
    aspects—Catholic Church. | Religion and science—History.
Classification: LCC BX4705.Z234 S53 2019 (print) | LCC BX4705.Z234
    (ebook) | DDC 231.7/652092—dc23
LC record available at https://lccn.loc.gov/2019021568
LC ebook record available at https://lccn.loc.gov/2019981572

To Kristen, my love.

CONTENTS

TABLES

ACKNOWLEDGMENTS

First, I would like to thank the countless archivists and librarians who assisted me on the long journey to completing this project, especially those at the University of Notre Dame and Saint Paul School of Theology. I will always have a deep appreciation for libraries and librarians, no matter how technological this world becomes. Second, I would like to thank the Nanovic Center, the Sciola family, and the Rome Research Program for funding my travels to the Archives of the Congregation for the Doctrine of the Faith in Vatican City. This book would have been impossible without the newly uncovered documents and ideas I found while in Rome.

Third, I would like to thank the many colleagues who assisted me in preparation of this book: Matt Ashley, Don Howard, Bob Krieg, and Celia Deane-Drummond at the University of Notre Dame; and Nancy Howell, Kris Kvam, and Logan Wright at Saint Paul School of Theology. While any mistakes in the manuscript are mine alone, I am extraordinarily grateful for the countless comments, suggestions, and edits that were suggested to me over the past few years.

Finally, this book would not have been possible without the loving support of my family, including my wonderful children, Lucy, Finn, Blaise, and Kittiarra, who keep my theology grounded with the innumerable adventures offered by parenting. And lastly, deepest thanks and love to my wife, Kristen, to whom I literally owe this entire journey of graduate school, and with whom I look to the future in hope.

ABBREVIATIONS

Archives and Collections

ACDF Archives of the Congregation for the Doctrine of the Faith. Vatican City.

APC Archives Province Canadienne de la Congrégation de Sainte-Croix. Montréal, Quebec.

CSCA Archives of United States Province of the Congregation of Holy Cross. Notre Dame, Indiana.

JCC Joseph Carrier Collection. Archives Province Canadienne de la Congrégation de Sainte-Croix. Montréal, Quebec.

JZA John Augustine Zahm Papers. University of Notre Dame Archives. Notre Dame, Indiana.

JZC John Augustine Zahm Collection. Archives of the United States Province of the Congregation of Holy Cross. Notre Dame, Indiana.

UNDA University of Notre Dame Archives. Notre Dame, Indiana.

Papal Encyclicals and Conciliar Documents

AP *Aeterni Patris*
Pope Leo XIII, Encyclical Letter (August 4, 1879), in *Acta Sanctae Sedis* 12 (1879): 97–115, http://www.vatican.va /archive/ass/documents/ASS-12-1879-ocr.pdf. English trans., http://w2.vatican.va/content/leo-xiii/en/encyclicals /documents/hf_l-xiii_enc_04081879_aeterni-patris.html.

DF   *Dei Filius*
       First Vatican Council, Dogmatic Constitution (April 24,
       1870), in *Acta Santae Sedis* 5 (1869–70): 484–90, http://
       www.vatican.va/archive/ass/documents/ASS-05-1869-70
       -ocr.pdf. English trans., *Dei Filius*, in *Decrees of the Ecu-
       menical Councils*, 2 vols. ed. Norman P. Tanner, SJ, 2:804–11
       (Washington, DC: Georgetown University Press, 1990).
QC   *Quanta Cura*
       Pope Pius IX, Encyclical Letter (December 8, 1864), in
       Acta Santae Sedis 3 (1867): 160–167, http://www.vatican
       .va/archive/ass/documents/ASS-03-1867-ocr.pdf. English
       trans. updated from Pope Pius IX, "Text and Translation
       of the Encyclical and Syllabus," *Dublin Review* 4, no. 56
       (1865): 500–511.

CHRONOLOGY OF JOHN ZAHM'S LIFE
AND MAJOR EVENTS, 1851–1921

1851   Born 14 June, the second of fourteen children, to Jacob and
         Mary Ellen Zahm in New Lexington, Ohio.
1863   Moves to Huntington, Indiana, with parents. Educated at
         SS Peter and Paul School.
1867   After receiving warm welcome letter from Fr. Sorin, moves
         to Notre Dame, 3 December, to begin studies to become
         priest.
1871   Publishes "Thoughts on Science" in Notre Dame's student
         magazine, *Scholastic*. Graduates with bachelor of arts de-
         gree, 21 June. Enters novitiate of the Congregation of Holy
         Cross, 11 September. Begins teaching.
1875   Ordained to the priesthood, 4 June. Promoted to professor
         of chemistry and physics.
1879   Fire at Notre Dame destroys nearly entire scientific collec-
         tion, sending Zahm on a new mission of recovery for uni-
         versity, including redesigning fire-prevention systems.
1883   Delivers lecture in Denver, Colorado, "Catholic Church
         and Modern Science."
1885–92 Named vice president of the University of Notre Dame.
         Begins speaking more about evolution and Catholicism.
1892   Cements reputation as scientist with publication of *Sound
         and Music*.
1893   Presents a course of five lectures, "Science and Revealed
         Religion," at the Catholic Summer School in Plattsburg,
         New York, skyrocketing him onto national debate.

1894–98	Publishes numerous articles and pamphlets on science and Catholicism. Receives pontifical doctorate in 1895.
1896	Publishes *Evolution and Dogma*.
1898	Receives notice from Congregation of the Index to submit and retract *Evolution and Dogma*. Fr. Gilbert Français, superior general of the Congregation of Holy Cross, and Zahm's friends, fight against official publication of censure. Appointed provincial of the Congregation of Holy Cross. Vigorously pushes for a grand vision of Notre Dame but meets internal conflict.
1899	Compromise with Congregation of the Index reached. Zahm redacts Italian and French translations of *Evolution and Dogma*, agrees never to write on subject again in return for censure not being promulgated and book not being placed on the index.
1906	Loses reelection as provincial and position of power in the Congregation of Holy Cross. Begins traveling and writing, never again teaching or administering at Notre Dame.
1907–21	Travels to South America several times, then to Europe and the Middle East, while writing nearly a dozen books on science and the physical world.
1921	10 November. Dies at a hospital in Munich, Germany, while researching next book.

Sources: Weber, *Notre Dame's John Zahm*; Morrison, "A History of American Catholic Opinion"; Cavanaugh, "Father Zahm," 577–88; Marieli Benziger, "The Last Journey," JZA, UNDA; Carroll, "Mind in Action"; and O'Connor, "John A. Zahm, C.S.C.," 435–62.

Introduction

My sole, ardent desire, has been to show that there is nothing in true science, nothing in Evolution, when properly understood, which is contrary to Scripture or Catholic teaching; that, on the contrary, when viewed in the light of Christian philosophy and theology, there is much in Evolution to admire, much that is ennobling and inspiring, much that illustrates and corroborates the truths of faith, much that may be made ancillary to revelation and religion, much that throws new light on the mysteries of creation, much that unifies and coordinates what were otherwise disconnected and disparate, much that exalts our ideas of creative power and wisdom and love, much, in fine, that makes the whole circle of sciences tend, as never before, ad majorem Dei gloriam.

—Rev. John A. Zahm, CSC,
Evolution and Dogma (1896)

While John Zahm's name is not well known, his story is a modern fable: a pious scientist in trouble with the Church for being too far ahead of his time. His story starts with a young boy born in mid-nineteenth-century Ohio who became a priest not long after enrolling in the newly formed University of Notre Dame. As a teacher and popularizer of science, he enthusiastically proclaimed the modern

1

sciences of the 1880s as perfectly compatible with the teachings of the Holy Roman Church, and he proudly named the Church an eternal supporter of the sciences.

By 1890, at the age of forty, Zahm had already transitioned from promising student to professor of chemistry and physics, to chair of the science department, to vice president of the small but growing university. His 1892 book on acoustical science brought him national recognition as a scientist, and his 1893 lectures placed him on the international Catholic scene as a great defender of the faith. Five years, five books, dozens of articles, and hundreds of lectures later, however, Zahm's great mission would come crashing down. In 1898 the Vatican's Sacred Congregation of the Index of Prohibited Books (hereafter Congregation of the Index) censured Zahm's most popular work, *Evolution and Dogma*, requiring not only that Zahm retract the book but also that he stay away from discussing evolution and Catholicism.

Ever a faithful priest, Zahm submitted, shifting his ambitions to other areas of political and social involvement. Zahm was named chief administrator of his province of the Congregation of Holy Cross the same year, a post that he held until 1906. He would write many more books on science and on faith, but never in combination. He died at a hospital in Germany in 1921, in the midst of researching a book on travels to the Holy Land. John Zahm accomplished much in the last twenty-three years of his life, but he never again wrote on the possibilities for evolutionary theory and Catholic dogma.

———

This book aims to accomplish four tasks. First, it tells a new and fuller story of the Reverend John Augustine Zahm, CSC, and his quest to prove the compatibility of late nineteenth-century evolutionary science and Roman Catholicism. While some accounts of Zahm's inquiry have emerged over the last fifty years, none provide a complete explanation of the theological, philosophical, political, and scientific factors that caused Zahm to be censured by the Congregation of the Index in 1898. Second, in the midst of telling Zahm's story, this book examines and uncovers the Vatican's own conception of the intersection between faith, philosophy, and science in the nineteenth century. The philosophical construction in the halls of the Vatican is a

story of intertwined theology, philosophy, and politics in the tumultuous years of the formation of modern Europe. Third, in order to accomplish the above two tasks, this volume provides new translations
from Latin and Italian of two key texts: the 1864 Syllabus of Modern
Errors, and the initial letter used to condemn Zahm to the Congregation of the Index, written by Archbishop Otto Zardetti in 1897. The
current English translations of both texts were out of date syntac-
tically, employing antiquated phrases and confusing sentence structures. They were also both incomplete, as none included the full list
of citations that exists in the Latin. Given that one aim of this book
is to more clearly understand the philosophical and theological debates of late nineteenth-century Catholicism, an updated, revised, and
complete English translation of the Syllabus is appropriate and helpful. The translation of Zardetti's letter is the first full transcription
of the document in its original languages and the first full English
translation.

Fourth, this book aims to exemplify a little-used methodology in
theology and histories of theology: the analysis of conceptions or philosophies of modern science when examining intersections between
Christianity and the sciences. It is my hope that the practice of analyzing a theologian's conception of science instead of analyzing, as is
more common, a theologian's views on the latest scientific theories,
can serve as a roadmap to fuller explanations of the complex history
between theology, philosophy, and science.

Finally, before we begin Zahm's story, it is important to understand that this book, by and large, is an exercise in complexification.
The oversimplified vision of "faith versus science" continues to be the
most accepted approach to discussing questions of evolution, dogma,
and progress. This book intentionally complicates the history of the
discourse to show its necessary dependence on the political, theological, and philosophical forces at play in the world at any given
moment. It is easy to oversimplify Zahm's case, just as it is easy to
oversimplify the case of Galileo, as the Church fighting against Science. But all such explanations are inherently anachronistic and unhelpful: science does not mean the same thing to us today as it did to
Zahm, much less as it did to Galileo.[1]

Even describing Zahm's story as one simply of debates over evolution misunderstands the importance of *why* Zahm would come to

such different conclusions about evolution than the members of the Congregation of the Index in the first place. For example, Zahm's vision of science saw something that should never be feared, only embraced. For many of those who censured Zahm, however, accepting the latest scientific theories would question many central aspects of Catholic dogmatic teachings. But even *this* is an oversimplification, as it fails to take into account the impact of Zahm's formation at the fledgling University of Notre Dame, the revolutionary spirit in nineteenth-century Europe, and the rise of Neo-Scholasticism in Roman Catholic circles in the late 1800s.

But as this book complexifies it also enlightens. It is far more interesting to understand exactly how Zahm came to be a faithful Catholic and fervent scientist than to simply write him off as another casualty in the evolution wars. So, while I offer a large web of complex events in my explanatory tale, deep within this web of complexities one can find the simple, central thesis of this book: that current attempts to explain why John Zahm faced a Vatican censure do not give enough weight to the philosophical, theological, and political factors of the situation. The present volume fills this explanatory deficit by examining the multidisciplinary factors that affected the conceptions of science on the part of both John Zahm and the key figures at the Congregation of the Index who decided his fate.

But before all of this—before the complexities, the explanations, the philosophy, and the theology—there is a story waiting to be told. And to get this story straight, to ensure we are all on the same page, we have to enter fully into the political, theoretical, and social contexts of all the characters involved. As such, we begin with some intellectual time travel to a different Notre Dame, a different America, and a very different Catholic Church.

CHAPTER 1

Setting the Stage

A Historical Background

Origins of the Modern Acceptance of Evolution

The biological evolution of all life on Earth is no longer a problematic scientific claim for the Catholic Church. The Church has always maintained the uniqueness of humans and the divine creation of each human's immortal soul, but the general scientific theory of evolutionary development has been widely accepted by the highest authorities of Roman Catholicism since 1950.[1] Well before Pope Francis assumed evolutionary theory as normative in *Laudato Si'* and well before Pope Saint John Paul II made headlines (and confused scholars) in 1996 by calling evolution "more than a hypothesis," Pope Pius XII published the encyclical *Humani Generis*.[2] For the first time since Charles Darwin's *On the Origin of Species*, the encyclical granted scholars explicit permission to debate the idea as long as they did not question the origin of human souls.[3] But while *Humani Generis* was the first recognition by the papal office that evolutionary theories were not wholly incompatible with Church teachings, it was actually the result of a growing acceptance of the theory in Catholic circles since the 1920s.

One of the first signs of changing attitudes can be found in a widely used textbook for religious instruction of Catholic secondary and college students published in 1923. Archbishop Michael Sheehan, the author of the popular textbook, wrote, "If the proof were forthcoming to-morrow that the body of the first man was evolved from the lower animals, it would not be found to contradict any solemn, ordinary, or official teaching of the Church."[4] Sheehan admittedly follows this claim with a dismissal of all such science, but his openness toward evolutionary ideas is perhaps the first in an approved book for training future clergy.

The effect of this broadening receptivity can be seen a decade later in 1933, when a Fr. John O'Brien of the University of Notre Dame published an explicit defense of John Zahm's evolutionary hypothesis, and "nothing happened." Historian John Morrison writes that "there was but little criticism, no charges of radicalism were hurled, and few thought to say that he was, by past standards, temerarious."[5] By the 1940s the matter was openly discussed in Catholic scholarly circles. In 1947, for example, the same Fr. O'Brien received both the *nihil obstat* and *imprimatur* for a teaching pamphlet titled *The Origin of Man*, in which he wrote:

> In regard to the soul of man, it is the common teaching of theologians that God creates directly and immediately the soul of each individual human being. In regard to the body of man, the evidence of evolution from antecedent animal life is most impressive, and in the judgment of most scientists, overwhelming. The Church leaves the individual free to accept or reject this view in accordance with his judgment as to the weight of evidence behind it.[6]

While it is common practice today for scholars to quote *Humani Generis* as the starting point for the Church's warming to the scientific theory of evolution, it would be more accurate to say that Pope Pius wrote *Humani Generis* as a response to an already widespread discussion and acceptance of many aspects of evolutionary science among the Catholic faithful.

This reorientation of how scholars *should* approach *Humani Generis* underscores the importance of having an accurate and full account of historical documents before studying such a hotly debated topic as the reception of evolutionary theories within Catholic theology. The present chapter provides exactly such an account by examining the broader historical time period, analyzing previous scholarship on John Zahm, and discussing the context of Zahm's case within the Catholic Church in the late nineteenth century. The historical discussion of evolutionary theory and Catholic theology is nothing if not extraordinarily complicated. Science, politics, theology, philosophy, and even Church bureaucracy all come into play when unraveling the story of John Zahm's censure and anything resembling an official Catholic teaching on the biological evolution of life. And as this book employs Zahm as the lens through which to view the entire debate, an examination of the many aspects of Zahm's social milieu must first be accomplished through an analysis of previous scholarly approaches to the life and thought of John Zahm.

Scholarly Reception of John Zahm, CSC

Nine scholars have seriously inspected the life and thought of John Zahm since Fr. O'Brien's defense of his arguments in 1933. The first two scholars, the aforementioned John Morrison and the historian Ralph Weber, both appeared in the mid-twentieth century.[7] Morrison wrote his dissertation at the University of Missouri in 1951 on the American Catholic evolutionist movement in the late nineteenth and early twentieth centuries. For Morrison, Zahm became the hero and martyr of the American evolutionist story. While Morrison's work was never published, it remains the first comprehensive study of the struggle to make evolutionary theory palatable to the Catholic Church in the United States. Weber finished his biographical dissertation on John Zahm at the University of Notre Dame in 1956, which was later published as Weber's well-known book on the topic in 1961. As opposed to Morrison, Weber paints Zahm as a loyal son of Notre Dame with Zahm's encounter with the Congregation of the Index appearing only as a bump in the road in an otherwise stellar and devout career. There is no evidence that Weber knew of Morrison's work.

Several decades later, after the groundbreaking documents of the Second Vatican Council, historian R. Scott Appleby entered the discussion.[8] Appleby was the first scholar both to bring together Weber's and Morrison's works and to argue for a more politically and philosophically rich telling of Zahm's tale. For Appleby, Zahm, whose writings on evolutionary theory and Catholicism reached international fame, was first a political actor and leader of the so-called Americanist program among U.S. Catholics. The Americanist movement largely argued for things that the Church has now accepted, such as freedom of religious expression, freedom of speech, freedom of the press, acceptance of democratic governments, acceptance of Protestants, acceptance of African Americans, abolition of slavery and second-class status of ex-enslaved peoples, acceptance of science/evolution, acceptance of historical-critical biblical interpretation, and others. In essence, the Americanists held to "the best ideals of American Puritanism, the Enlightenment, [and] incipient ecumenism."[9] Appleby argues that Zahm battled with and lost to the anti-Americanists, but the Second Vatican Council has shown that Zahm landed on the right side of history.

After Pope Benedict XVI opened the Archives of the Congregation for the Doctrine of the Faith for scholarly research in 1998, one major and one minor historical study appeared on Zahm's case. The major work, *Negotiating Darwin: The Vatican Confronts Evolution*, by Mariano Artigas, Thomas F. Glick, and Rafael A. Martínez, covers not only Zahm's case but also five others that dealt with evolution in the 1890s. The shorter work, an article by Barry Brundell, focuses on the political role of the journal *Civiltà Cattolica* in Zahm's trial.[10] Artigas, Glick, and Martínez argue that while the outcome of Zahm's case was unfortunate, the archives show that the Congregation of the Index was acting judiciously in its silencing of Zahm and other key figures. The congregation neither expressly condemned nor approved evolution, pushing the issue to a future generation. Brundell paints a more negative view of both *Civiltà Cattolica* and the Congregation of the Index. Members of both organizations, he argues, went after Zahm precisely for his views on human origins in *Evolution and Dogma*, and thus, intentionally or not, implicitly forbade future dialogue on the matter of human evolution.

The remaining two scholars to significantly examine Zahm's case were Edward Heinle and Phillip Sloan, both of whom place Zahm's scientific arguments within historical contexts. Heinle posits Zahm as an amateur philosopher of science, while Sloan argues for Zahm's place alongside the great Catholic evolutionist, St. George Mivart.[11] Neither of the two make a clear statement on the reason why Zahm was silenced, but both offer valuable pieces to the scholarly corpus.

The following sections weave together Zahm's story by examining each of the above author's retelling of it and thus show the overlapping and sometimes contradictory portrayals of Zahm's life and work. (For an overarching timeline of Zahm's life and major events, including his dialogue between Catholicism and science, see the chronology at the beginning of this volume.)

John Morrison: John Zahm, Champion of Evolution

The first extended study on John Zahm is John L. Morrison's unpublished 1951 dissertation, "A History of American Catholic Opinion on the Theory of Evolution: 1859–1950." As the title suggests, Morrison's story stretches from the publication of Darwin's *On the Origin of Species* in 1859 to just before the publication of *Humani Generis* in 1950, at which point, Morrison writes, there was almost unanimous scholarly approval for evolution in Catholic circles.[12] He begins by painting the tricky process of discerning an "official view" of evolutionary theory: "Evolution was not one problem but a multitude of questions to which a variety of answers were given. Indeed, the answers given by a single author were not always consistent."[13]

Morrison traces the beginning of American Catholic immersion in the discussion of evolutionary theory to an anonymously authored 1873 article titled "The Evolution of Life" published in the popular journal *Catholic World*.[14] This article approved the general evolutionary sentiments of two English Catholics, distinguished scientist St. George Jackson Mivart and future bishop John Cuthbert Hedley, while simultaneously echoing Hedley's warning that "the theory of human evolution was 'rash and proximate to heresy.'"[15] While the general idea of evolutionary transformation may have been acceptable to some, Darwin's specific version of evolutionary natural selection, especially his focus on human evolution, "became inseparably connected in Catholic thinking" to "the agnosticism of Thomas Henry Huxley and Herbert Spencer and the materialism of Ernst Haeckel."[16]

After the First Vatican Council (1869–70) said nothing regarding the matter of evolution, the debate grew unchecked in the United States.[17] The 1870s, Morrison writes, represented a low point in the dialogue between evolution and Catholicism as William Draper's infamous book, *History of the Conflict between Religion and Science*, was published and read widely in 1874.[18] Draper's book landed on the Vatican's index of prohibited books in 1876, which did little to quell the problem of aligning evolution with atheism and anti-Catholicism.[19]

With such conceptions of evolution in the Church, Morrison argues, the prevailing spirit of the late 1870s could be encapsulated by Fr. Camillius Mazella, who published an anti-evolutionary book in 1877 and was shortly thereafter named a cardinal by Pope Pius IX. In Mazella's work, "every effort was made to make the evolution of man appear as revolting as possible . . . Darwinism was spiritually degrading . . . [and] in contrast to Christianity, which exalted human nature to a supernatural plane."[20] The journals *Nature* and *Popular Science Monthly* were the evildoers, touting evolution alongside Draper's anti-Catholicism and Huxley's agnosticism. There was no good to be found in any scientific theory that produced such philosophical horrors.

The 1880s saw several key changes in the Catholic discussion of evolution in America. First, *Catholic World*, the leading Catholic journal in the United States, stopped publishing articles anonymously, forcing authors to be more cautious and precise in their discussions. Second, Pope Leo XIII, a scholar and intellectual, was elected after the death of Pius IX in 1879. Third, the first book by an American priest that spoke positively of evolution was published by Rev. John Gmeiner in 1884, who claimed that evolution could produce "a more exalted conception of God."[21] While Gmeiner would come short of explicitly supporting evolution, his book set the stage for a generation of clergy to warm to the idea.[22] Fourth and finally, the American bishops wrote specifically of the liberty of Catholics in scientific matters at the 1888 Council of Baltimore.[23] By the end of the 1880s, a large group of Catholics—deemed Americanists—were becoming more at ease with evolution, while the rest still held rather anti-evolutionary and anti-Darwinian tendencies.[24]

The 1890s saw the further demarcation between these two factions, brought about largely because while "the leaders of Catholic thought steadfastly rejected the doctrine of evolution . . . in the nineties they displayed considerable sympathy towards it."[25] But as more Catholic authors warmed to evolution, the voices against it became louder and stronger still, exacerbating the political divide that encompassed many issues beyond evolutionary theory and spread far beyond the United States. Morrison notes that "a determined attack against all aspects of liberalism, of which evolution was only one, was being conducted in America, England, France, and Italy. Rome rather than America was the focal point of the conservative campaign."[26] Upon this politically divided stage of the early 1890s, after two decades of struggle and discussion, John Zahm enters Morrison's story.

This American historical perspective gives Morrison his methodological uniqueness. To Morrison, Zahm became part of an American problem that crept into European Catholicism. Morrison sees Zahm's tenure at the helm of the evolution debate in American Catholic circles beginning with his 1893 lectures at the Catholic Summer School, a nationally known event that presented several days' worth of talks from well-known Catholic educators on a variety of topics.[27] These lectures, while not necessarily original in the grand scheme of intellectual thought, proffered, Morrison avers, "startling views" to the Catholic crowd of 1893: first, that the Great Flood may not have been universal; second, that evolution was now a "plausible, yet unproven, concept"; third, "that the venerable St. Augustine was the father of theistic evolution."[28] Zahm's 1893 summer lectures were quickly followed by numerous articles and further speaking engagements. The summer lectures themselves would become well known as the basis for both Zahm's *Bible, Science, and Faith* and his infamous *Evolution and Dogma*.

By 1895, Morrison writes, Zahm had become "one of the most prominent leaders" of the Americanist movement in American Catholicism. That summer, he once again lectured at the Catholic Summer School, promoting evolution directly and gaining both notoriety and adulation in the Catholic world of the 1890s. By the time he published *Evolution and Dogma* in early 1896, criticism came rolling in from all sides. Yet Zahm was quite sure he was safe from Vatican authorities, arguing that his books "showed that evolution merely meant the Creator acted through the agency of secondary causes instead of directly. Thus understood, there was absolutely nothing inconsistent with Christianity in the theory."[29] Morrison agrees, noting that *Evolution and Dogma*

> was written with enormous clarity and persuasiveness, but virtually everything in it had been said many times before by other Christians. In some respects, Fr. Zahm was a bit more cautious in his views than, say, Mivart or Seton. He simply stated current, if not commonly held, Catholic theories more fully, provokingly, and vigorously than any American had yet succeeded in doing.[30]

Because of Zahm's dependence on previously published theological ideas, Morrison writes, "the tremendous reception accorded *Evolution and Dogma* must be accounted for by other considerations than the subject matter of the book itself."[31]

Without access to Vatican records, Morrison discusses the censure of Zahm's *Evolution and Dogma* through letters, notes, and popular reception. He examines the back-and-forth book reviews in the press, Zahm's own travels to Europe in 1896 and 1887, and the development of Americanism. In the end, Morrison argues, "the condemnation . . . was mixed up inextricably with a whole series of controversies which went under the rather loose headings of liberalism or Americanism."[32] Instead of attempting to unravel this inextricable weave, Morrison highlights the actions of the major players in the censure and its aftermath, leaving us more in awe of Zahm's ability to keep the censure from being published than disappointed in the fact of the censure itself.

By the time the dust settled, Zahm did not receive a published prohibition, but, as Morrison recounts, he might as well have. Morrison argues that Zahm had been instructed "not to write of evolution again and to keep his name from being associated with that theory in the periodicals."[33] Furthermore, when Zahm was forced to request a withdrawal of all foreign language translations of *Evolution and Dogma* in 1899, his letter of request to the Italian publisher was leaked to the newspapers and published throughout the world. Even though Zahm left the English version in circulation, his attempts to withdraw the foreign language translations (Italian and French) were enough for the popular press to declare him beaten. Morrison concludes, "Thus was humbled America's most controversial Catholic evolutionist, the victim, from the conservatives' standpoint, of his own radical excesses; the victim, from the evolutionists' point of view, of the kind of reactionary thinking that led to the condemnation of Galileo."[34]

While Morrison quotes various pieces of correspondence, the reasons behind the censure are less important to him than the effect of the censure: evolutionary theory was off limits when applied to humans. There never was an official statement from the Vatican to this effect, but doctrines and dogmas do not always need to be published to be enforced. Besides citing the lack of Catholic scholars who supported human evolution in the decade after Zahm, Morrison also quotes a popular Catholic journal from 1906 that refers to Zahm's specific case in refuting an obscure English priest who attempted to publish an article on the evolutionary origins of humans.[35] As late as 1918, some Catholic writers were still referring vaguely to the censures of "certain theological writers" as precluding the Church's acceptance of human evolution.[36] In the 1920s, as we have seen, the tides began to turn, but the Zahm censure remained an obstacle to Catholic acceptance of evolution for a long time before it became a reason to commemorate a scholar who was far ahead of his time.

Morrison's Zahm was a hero, a martyr, of the American case for accepting evolutionary theory. Because of this approach his treatise suffers from a certain blindness to Zahm's life, interests, and concerns that go beyond the scope of Catholic arguments over evolution. What other factors spurred Zahm's actions in the 1880s and 1890s? What did Zahm do after the censure, and how does this reflect on Zahm's character? As if to correct this blindness, Ralph Weber wrote the second major treatise on Zahm a decade later, casting his book as a general biography, and naming Zahm not as a censured evolutionist but as a loyal son of Notre Dame.

Ralph Weber: John Zahm, Loyal Son of Notre Dame

Ralph Weber completed his dissertation on John Zahm in 1956 at the University of Notre Dame. Five years later it was published as the popular biography *Notre Dame's John Zahm: American Catholic*

Apologist and Educator.[37] Where Morrison throws Zahm's life into sharp relief against the backdrop of the reception of Darwinian evolution and Americanism in the late nineteenth century, Weber constructs the biography of Zahm as the story of a holy and devout son of the Church and devotee to the cause of the University of Notre Dame. The last two lines of Weber's text exemplify the tone: "Following funeral services in Sacred Heart Church on January 7, 1922, he was buried in the Community graveyard at Notre Dame alongside his friend Sorin and the other great builders of a Catholic religious congregation and University. At long last the weary traveler was home among the saints and scholars he had envisioned."[38]

By focusing more on the person of Zahm than on the debates over evolution, and by interviewing people who knew Zahm personally, Weber presents a clearer picture of Zahm's first involvement with evolutionary theory. Weber argues that as early as 1883, Zahm had already gained "international recognition" with a lecture published on the interrelations of Catholicism and science.[39] Between 1883 and 1893, when Zahm gave his summer school lectures, he traveled widely throughout the United States both to recruit students to Notre Dame and to popularize science among Catholic audiences.[40] Of particular importance to this period for Weber is Zahm's 1892 book, *Sound and Music,* which was so popular that it went into a second edition by 1900.[41] With *Sound and Music,* Zahm established himself as a scientist, despite not having an advanced degree in a scientific field. By 1893, Weber argues, thanks to *Sound and Music,* his immensely popular scientific lectures on and off campus, and his work to bring national recognition to Notre Dame's science program and museum collection, Zahm's reputation was sealed as a scientist, an orator, and a Catholic educator.[42]

Weber's focus on Zahm the *man* yields many interesting perspectives. Weber often speaks of Zahm as one who enjoyed the fame of recognition. Zahm played the popular presses as well as anyone and reveled in talk of heresy and disaster, as it served only to bring him greater audiences and his books more readers. Zahm's ambitions and political aspirations served him and Notre Dame well for a while but grew dangerous with the publication of *Evolution and Dogma.* Zahm was warned by several close friends *not* to publish the book, but he roundly ignored this advice, pushing ever forward, emphasizing that "he was not a Darwinist or a 'Huxleyist' and . . . had little faith in natural selection."[43] He would never be censured, he thought, simply for saying that one *could* believe in evolution!

Like Morrison, Weber relies on the plethora of correspondence to determine the causes behind Zahm's censure. Weber's focus on Zahm's persona, however, offers us insight beyond Morrison's picture of the man. Weber's ambitious, sometimes incautious John Zahm reveals how Zahm tirelessly encouraged his friends to prevent his book from being placed on the Vatican's index of prohibited books.

Weber's only analysis of the reasons for Zahm's censure, in fact, is borrowed from a letter from Zahm's superior, Rev. Gilbert Français, who tried to explicate the various reasons to a confused and frustrated Zahm.[44] First, Français writes, many critics took umbrage at the way Zahm interpreted Thomas Aquinas and Augustine to make them evolutionists. Second, Zahm "placed too much credence in evolution." Third, "the authorities did not oppose evolution in general but only when the Bible was endangered. Thus, they believed that the doctrine of the evolution of man's body could not be safely taught for that would make many say that the explanation for the body of woman was a myth." Fourth and finally, Zahm's good friendship with the well-known Americanist Monsignor Denis O'Connell was troubling, since "O'Connell was considered by the court of Rome as extremely imprudent in speech."[45]

Weber's account of Zahm's case in the Congregation of the Index ends shortly after his discussion of this letter, and Weber quickly closes this chapter of Zahm's life. The entire debate about evolution was quelled, Weber argues, first by Leo XIII's encyclical *Testem Benevolentiae*, condemning aspects of Americanism in 1899; and second by Zahm's aforementioned letter to the Italian publication company that was leaked to the worldwide press.[46] Zahm's "active concern with Americanism ended" after this time. He remained "a publicly silent . . . apostle" of Americanism but "concentrated his energies on developing the Holy Cross Congregation in the United States."[47]

Contrasted with Morrison's vision of Zahm the evolutionist, Weber's biographical portrait shows a fervent, ambitious Zahm whose love for science and the Church is only matched by his belief "that the

Catholic Church in America faced a future of glory within the framework of American institutions and law."[48] Where Morrison's account gives a much wider picture of the progress made by Catholic scholars regarding evolutionary sciences, Weber's account shows Zahm's evolutionary writings to be but one of many causes that was served by the devout priest from Notre Dame. This is the shortcoming of Weber's study, which could easily be described as a hagiographical account of a beloved son of Notre Dame. If Morrison's blind spot was in missing the wider context of Zahm's life, Weber's blind spot was in disregarding the negative impact of Zahm's ambitious behavior on institutions and persons that relied on his input. After serving as vice president of Notre Dame for six years, Zahm was all but exiled from the university after his quiet censure. Furthermore, he was voted out of his role as provincial of the Congregation of Holy Cross in 1906 due to his negligence of the Holy Cross community in his care, in his attempt to fulfill a vision for the grandeur of Notre Dame. Weber argues that this removal was due to "conditions over which he had no control" and "in reality a blessing, for Zahm's health had declined seriously."[49] Weber professes a vision of Zahm that Zahm's friends, family, and university might cherish but that lacks the objectivity desired for more accurate representations of the past.[50]

R. Scott Appleby: John Zahm, Americanist and Modernist

The two decades after the publication of Morrison's and Weber's books were transformative for Roman Catholicism. The Second Vatican Council (1962–65) changed the Roman Church in a variety of ways, such that by the 1980s a new generation of Catholic scholars was emerging from institutions of higher education. These scholars experienced Mass only in English, knew only an ecumenical outlook toward other Christians, and considered the late nineteenth-century set of philosophical and theological arguments known as Neo-Scholasticism a relic of an antiquated Catholicism that failed to meet the needs of a modern society. With this backdrop we turn to R. Scott Appleby, who entered the discussion of John Zahm through his dissertation on the history of American Catholicism at the turn of the twentieth century.[51]

Appleby focuses his attention on the rise of the modernist movement in the late nineteenth and early twentieth centuries. In the Catholic context, modernists "endorsed contemporary biblical criticism, accepted historical developments in Christianity, strongly opposed Neo-Scholasticism, and were thoroughly receptive to progress in science and philosophy."[52] In particular, Appleby examines how the modernist movement affected the American Catholic scene in the form of Americanism. While Morrison and Weber had already shown that the debate over evolutionary theory was waged amid a fierce ecclesial battle over the relationship of American Catholicism to its political, cultural, and social milieus, Appleby places the discussion of evolution at the forefront of the political stage: "Nowhere was [the] polarization of American Catholic purpose more evident than in the debate over the theory of evolution."[53]

With evolution at the center of Catholic political thought in the 1880s and 1890s, Appleby's John Zahm (whose case makes up the second chapter of Appleby's dissertation) becomes the focal point not only for discussions of evolution and Catholicism but also for the entire political battle for an "American" Catholic Church.[54] Appleby retells the story of Zahm's censure by focusing on its political consequences, including Zahm's decision to stay out of the fray after 1899. Zahm is painted as someone who brushes up against the deeper themes of modernism, only to be held back by practical concerns and a devotion to his Church and his order.

> Zahm's ultimate submission to authority may be interpreted as a sincere attempt to protect the status of his congregation and recent serious theological error, or as a calculated retreat designed to limit the damage to the liberal cause, or both. But the fact remains that Zahm's final serious apologetical work, *Evolution and Dogma*, was, to that date, the most radical American Catholic statement on the theological implications of modern scientific discoveries, and one that entertained and developed modernist themes. Before this modernist impulse [of Zahm's] could emerge more clearly and self-consciously, its author lapsed into an enforced silence.[55]

In Appleby's estimation, especially in his dissertation, Zahm's censure was as much about politics as it was about science, but not as some sort of side activity apart from his scientific work. Appleby's study weaves together the entire post-Darwinian discussion of science and religion with the philosophical debates of the late nineteenth century. Zahm did not consciously become a scientist, theologian, and politician. He entered a debate already fully intertwined in politics.

Appleby transformed his work on Zahm from his dissertation into several articles and book chapters, one of which merits special consideration here. In "Between Americanism and Modernism: John Zahm and Theistic Evolution," published in 1987, Appleby adds a consideration of Neo-Scholasticism to the discussions of Americanism and modernism in discussing Zahm's case.[56] "Here," Appleby writes, "is precisely where Zahm went wrong in the eyes of the conservative Catholic clergy and hierarchy: he had challenged the supremacy of the Neo-Scholastic paradigm as an encompassing worldview within which scientific research as well as doctrinal development must take place."[57] While he does not elaborate on it, Appleby's insight marks the first time a scholar placed Zahm within the Neo-Scholastic milieu of the late nineteenth century. Chapter 4 of this volume will delve into this milieu in considerable detail.

Appleby's work furthers the historical account of Zahm by situating him appropriately in the modernist and Neo-Scholastic currents of the late nineteenth century but is limited by Appleby's own role as a historian and not a philosopher or theologian. Indeed, one of the central goals of this book is to fill in the details of Appleby's insight: How actually did Zahm contradict Neo-Scholasticism? Who represented Neo-Scholasticism during the time of Zahm's trial? How was Zahm specifically influenced by modernism, especially in the case of the evolution debates?

Artigas, Glick, Martínez, and Brundell: Zahm's Unfortunate Case

Not long after the publication of Appleby's essays, a new development opened up volumes of previously unavailable material on the Congregation of the Index in the late nineteenth century. In 1998 a certain Cardinal Ratzinger opened the Archives of the Congregation for the Doctrine of the Faith for scholarly research, which set off a torrent of studies on the historical data, including Mariano Artigas, Thomas F. Glick, and Rafael A. Martínez's *Negotiating Darwin*. Barry Brundell also published findings based on the new archival data but focuses mostly on the connection between the Zahm case and the Italian journal *Civiltà Cattolica*.[58]

The authors of *Negotiating Darwin* argue that the Congregation of the Index deployed a soft, pragmatic approach to evolutionary theory in the latter part of the nineteenth century. "The archival documents reveal," they write, "that there were actions of the Holy See aimed at the concept of evolution, but also that care was taken not to give them an official public stamp."[59] They posit that the decades of reluctance to write on human evolution in Catholic theological circles in the United States after Zahm's censure confirms their thesis on the congregation's careful work:

From one perspective it could be said that the Holy See did not condemn evolution because it never issued any official publication condemnation. From a different perspective it could be said that it did condemn evolution, because evolutionist books were condemned, but these had no official, public character.[60]

In discussing Zahm's case specifically, *Negotiating Darwin* advances the previously mentioned Zahm literature by offering the first account from the point of view of the Congregation of the Index, including the original denunciation of Zahm by Archbishop Otto Zardetti, a well-known member of the anti-Americanist wing of American Catholicism. For the purposes of my approach to the Zahm case, *Negotiating Darwin* offers an analysis of four key documents from the Vatican archives: first, Zardetti's initial complaint to the Congregation of the Index in November 1897; second, the extended report by a member of the congregation, Dominican Enrico Buonpensiere, in April 1898; third, a follow-up smaller report and subsequent voting records by a subset of the congregation in August 1898; and fourth, the notes and outcome of the meeting of the entire congregation that decided Zahm's fate in September 1898.[61]

Following their discussion of these documents, *Negotiating Darwin* provides both the documents from the Congregation of the Index and the Zahm-related correspondence, in order to offer a detailed look at the complicated politics in Zahm's case. While helpful for the historical record, such level of detail leaves the reader with a mixed understanding of the causal factors for Zahm's case: between Zahm's populism, his seeming acceptance of the simian origin of humans, his friendship with Americanists, and the translation of his book into Italian, the authors proclaim the Zahm case to be "an exemplar of the kinds of complexities involved in the relationship between science and religion."[62] As such, the major limitation of this text is the failure of the authors to engage the stipulation intimated by Appleby: the conflict between Zahm's and the congregation's conceptions of science, which is precisely the lacuna that the present study fills.

Also discussing the Zahm case after the opening of the archives is historian Barry Brundell, who argues for the important place of *Civiltà Cattolica* in Zahm's censure. Writing in 2001 and then again in 2008, Brundell contends that after Zahm's *Evolution and Dogma* was translated into Italian, *Civiltà Cattolica*'s editors were displeased beyond measure:

They lamented that this publication was hailed as the most memorable event of 1896 and were especially upset that well-known Catholic journals gave it fulsome reviews. This was all typical, according to *Civiltà Cattolica*, of the spirit of mistaken conciliation shown by certain schools that had been forming in both the old and the new worlds in these years.[63]

Brundell points to the role that *Civiltà Cattolica*'s negative review of Zahm's book played in the denunciation sent to the Congregation of the Index by Zardetti. Brundell allows for wider political pressures, of course, but stresses that the influence wielded by the journal should not be underestimated. While Brundell's argument is valuable in highlighting aspects of the relationship between the journal and the Congregation of the Index, it is limited in its focus on one small area of Zahm's rather sprawling case.[64]

Edward Heinle and Phillip Sloan: John Zahm, Scientist

This brings us to the final two essays on Zahm's case, both of which bring to the fore conceptions and arguments of science. In 1987 Edward Heinle penned a master's thesis for the University of Notre Dame's History and Philosophy of Science Program, directed by the other scholar treated in this section, Phillip Sloan. While the thesis was never published (the copy only exists as a bound title in Notre Dame's Hesburgh Library), Heinle takes Morrison's and Weber's promptings into a different arena than Appleby. Heinle spends much of the essay arguing for the specifics of how Zahm's own thought evolved from 1883 to 1896. In Zahm's early works, Heinle writes, "science could not contravene Scripture because its claims were uncertain. At the end, religion was secured, because its domain was restricted to faith and morals."[65] Heinle examines Zahm's changing views on special creation, human creation, and the Great Flood to support this claim. By 1896, he argues, Zahm's "professed neutrality disappears," and he had become a "full-blown evolutionist" with the publication of *Evolution and Dogma.*[66]

This much of the essay is helpful in its detail, but Heinle's conclusion is nearly as interesting as the preceding pages. First, Heinle sees the merit in the methodological approach employed by the present volume:

The account of Zahm's intellectual development and later influence is not yet complete. His philosophy of science, for example, could be traced from a naïve Baconianism, which requires a complete collection of data before valid generalizations may be made, to a more mature inductive approach which recognizes the value of theories which are "merely probable."[67]

Second, Heinle predicts the success of Appleby's work on political causes for Zahm's case:

[Furthermore,] the importance of the conservative attack upon Americanism should be explored. Was Zahm's attempt to harmonize dogma with evolution doomed to failure because of his liberal connections? Or was his approach simply considered overly rash in itself?[68]

While Heinle's own arguments suffer from a lack of historical and philosophical knowledge of the debates surrounding late nineteenth-century discussions of religion and science, his vision of the possibilities of future work on John Zahm are acute and helpful.

Following this discussion on the particularities of Zahm's scientific arguments, Phillip Sloan, Heinle's thesis advisor and a long-standing historian of biology at the University of Notre Dame, published an article in 2009 analyzing Zahm's roots in the works of St. George Mivart and the post-Darwinian evolutionary debates within the scientific community of the late nineteenth century.[69] Sloan places Zahm squarely within those debates by arguing that Zahm neither advocated "a form of neo-Lamarckianism, nor . . . an inner vital force that directs evolutionary development, as was commonly encountered in other forms of theistic evolution."[70] Instead, borrowing much from Mivart, Zahm attempted a novel and peculiar approach to the topic, one that excluded most of Darwin's contribution but still allowed for discussions of evolutionary development.

Sloan argues that Zahm's evolutionary position could be generally called a saltationist approach, ceding minor biological developments (what might be called *microevolution* today) to Darwin's natural selection hypothesis, while pointing out the inconsistencies between the fossil record and the development between differing species. While this aligned Zahm with a certain strain of scientific arguments, Sloan suggests that Zahm incorporated divine action into evolution through a separate theory of "two origins" when it came to human beings: a Mivart-derived complement to the saltationist evolutionary hypothesis, which allowed evolution to direct the development of the body, and God to direct the development of the soul.[71]

Sloan's conclusion returns our discussion to the decisions of the Congregation of the Index, for he points to the fact that Zahm had not realized that Mivart's theories were under scrutiny at the congregation at the time of writing *Evolution and Dogma*. Zahm was thus comfortable founding his evolutionary-theological arguments on Mivart's, while such foundations landed Zahm in trouble, ending with his 1898 censure.[72] Sloan remains one of the only scholars to examine Zahm in light of the nineteenth-century scientific evolution debates. Combined with the previous studies, Heinle's and Sloan's round out half a century of scholarly literature on John Zahm that reflects the variegated interests of the science, politics, and theology of Zahm himself.

Scholarly Reception of the Congregation of the Index

At this point, it is helpful to turn the lens briefly to the other major figure in this study: the committee who censured Zahm, the Sacred Congregation of the Index of Prohibited Books. "Until January 1998," writes Hubert Wolf, "the activities of the Congregation of the Index and the Roman Inquisition were shrouded in a veil of mystery, as the archives of the two Roman dicasteries responsible for the censorship of books, which are currently under the charge of the Congregation for the Doctrine of the Faith, were not accessible to scholars."[73] Wolf was one of the few scholars allowed access to the archives, with special permission when they were first opened in 1998, and took upon himself the formidable task of indexing both works that were banned as well as those that were merely considered by the Congregation of the Index. Because of this, Wolf's indices—an impressive fourteen books in all—are invaluable to anyone hoping to do research on the archives in Vatican City.[74]

Before 1998, writes Wolf, "the activity of the Roman Inquisition and its 'little sister,' the Congregation of the Index, was characterized by literal secrecy, the renowned Secretum Sancti Officii [Secret of the Holy Office], transgression of which entailed severe ecclesiastical censures. This was the only way the Holy Office could keep its investigations secret, and by maintaining non-publicity of its procedures keep the accused in the dark."[75] In Zahm's case, such secrecy meant that neither those who accused Zahm nor those who investigated him nor even those who ruled on his censure could ever discuss any aspect of the case for fear of an ecclesiastical reprimand.

With this in mind, it should be easy to see the need for the current study. While the Artigas, Glick, and Martínez volume catalogued and discussed many of the documents pertaining to the case, the complexities of the situation require a closer look at the political, theological, philosophical, and historical milieus that produced *both* the members of the Congregation of the Index as well as the world-renowned speaker, author, scientist, and priest named John Augustine Zahm.

CHAPTER 2

The Rise and Fall of John Zahm, CSC

A New Biographical Sketch

Who was John Zahm, and how did he become such an influential person in the discussion of evolutionary theory and Roman Catholicism? More importantly, what were the events that inspired him to take on the bold task of relating science and faith? This chapter serves as a biographical introduction to Zahm, focusing on how he went from seminary student to internationally divisive figure in the heated discussion between scientists and theologians in the late nineteenth century. We look at Zahm's life chronologically in four parts; first, from birth to joining the faculty at the University of Notre Dame (1851–75); second, from faculty member to his entry in the national debate on evolution and Catholicism (1876–92); third, from his controversial lectures at the Catholic Summer School to the end of his encounter with the Congregation of the Index (1892–99); and fourth, from his tenure as provincial of the Congregation of Holy Cross to his travels throughout Europe until his death (1899–1921). For a timeline of John Zahm's life and major events, see the chronology at the beginning of this volume.

From Birth to Joining the Notre Dame Faculty (1851–75)

John Augustine Zahm was born on June 14, 1851, the second of four-teen children born into a devout Catholic family in New Lexington, Ohio.[1] When he was twelve, his parents moved to Huntington, Indi-ana, where Zahm attended a Catholic school for a few years as he con-sidered a vocation to the priesthood. In 1867 he wrote to his aunt, a Holy Cross sister, and asked her to give a letter expressing his keen desire to go to Notre Dame to Fr. Sorin, then president of the young university. After receiving a welcome letter from Sorin, Zahm arrived on campus to begin studies on December 3, 1867.[2]

Because of his desire to become a priest, Zahm entered the Clas-sical Course of Studies, which included several courses in Greek, Latin, German, rhetoric, history, algebra, philosophy, as well as courses in the sciences, including astronomy, physics, chemistry, and natural history.[3] After completing his bachelor of arts degree in 1871, he began dedicated seminary training, consisting largely of directed readings instead of listed coursework, resulting in a master of arts de-gree in 1873.[4] Subsequently Zahm began regularly teaching at Notre Dame. He is listed as an "Assistant Professor of Chemistry, Physics, and Natural Science" for the 1873–74 school year, and as a "Professor of Chemistry and Physics, Librarian and Curator of Museum" for the 1874–75 school year.[5] Zahm was ordained a priest on June 4, 1875, capping an exciting journey of over seven years since he first arrived at the fledgling university.

Ralph Weber offers a typical characterization of these years of Zahm's life:

> The youth from Huntington, Indiana, had matured quickly during these years. His deep interest in classical studies combined with fine ability in scientific work gave promise of a well-balanced teacher. Many extra-curricular responsibilities developed his ad-ministrative talents while the busy "jack-of-all-trades" seminary years prepared him for the future role of developing a young reli-gious congregation and an expanding American Catholic univer-sity. . . . Scholarly, outwardly quiet, enthusiastic, he was anxious to develop a congregation and university of saints and scholars.[6]

It is helpful to remember the state of the university at the time. Founded in 1842, Notre Dame accepted boys from elementary age (called *minims*) to modern college ages (called seniors). At sixteen years old Zahm was among the older students at the school when he first matriculated. Offering a wide range of studies to a wide range of ages in the new American Midwest, the university found itself expanding quickly.

When Notre Dame celebrated its twenty-five-year anniversary at the end of the 1867–68 school year, the student magazine *Scholastic* noted that "the number of students now at the University is nearly five hundred, an annual increase since 1846 of about twenty-four students. Almost every state in the Union is represented here."[7] Faculty members were up from seventeen in 1859 to thirty-four in 1865. Fr. Patrick Dillon, the second president of Notre Dame, installed a Scientific Course of Studies to go along with the already successful Classical Course in the 1860s. Furthermore, in 1869, Notre Dame opened its law school.[8] The school was growing, donations were rising, and the ground was laid for an ambitious young priest with a head for politics to rise quickly through the ranks.

The Influence of Joseph C. Carrier, CSC

While chapter 3 delves more fully into Zahm's conceptions of science during these early years, a key relationship during this period of Zahm's life sheds light on his intellectual formation. This relationship is between Zahm and his primary science teacher at Notre Dame, Rev. Joseph Carrier, CSC, who, according to Weber, "exerted a great influence" on the young man.[9] Joseph Celestine Carrier was born the youngest of ten children in France in 1833 and received the best of Catholic education before being appointed professor of physics at a small college in Switzerland at the young age of seventeen. Soon afterward, both because of the political upheaval in Europe in the 1840s and because he was enticed by a desire to minister to uninhabited lands, Carrier left for the United States in 1855. After his inviting bishop passed away in 1860, Carrier moved from St. Paul, Minnesota, to Notre Dame and entered seminary studies. He was ordained a priest in 1861 as a member of the Congregation of Holy Cross and soon began teaching Latin and Greek at the university. Only two years after arriving on campus, Carrier was sent off to join General Ulysses S. Grant's army as a chaplain during the Civil War.[10]

After witnessing death and parrying with generals, Carrier returned to Notre Dame and took the reins of its newly developed science program.[11] His first task upon returning was to travel to France to procure books for the library, items for the science museum, and scientific instruments for instruction.[12] Under Carrier, the museum and library grew and the science program, for the first time, gained solid footing.[13] Carrier's time at Notre Dame ended abruptly, however, when Sorin sent him to Texas in 1874 to become the new president of the growing St. Mary's College in Galveston, Texas. This seeming advancement would turn out to be a trial for Carrier, as St. Mary's College would close after just two years. In 1876, instead of returning to Notre Dame, Carrier was sent to be a professor at St. Joseph's College in Cincinnati, Ohio, where he stayed for several years before being sent to be curator of a scientific museum at the College of Saint Laurent near Montréal, Canada.[14]

Before this change in status for Carrier, however, he made quite an impact at Notre Dame. An analysis of his mentions in the university's *Annual Catalogue* between the years 1866 and 1875 alongside that of Zahm reveals the similar aims and successes of the two men.[15] Table 2.1 shows their close connection, especially for the final two years of Carrier's tenure at the university, during which time he and Zahm undoubtedly worked side by side for much of every day. When Carrier was sent to Texas in 1874, Zahm was just twenty-three years old. Despite this, he took Carrier's place as librarian, curator of the museum, dean of the Faculty of the Sciences, president of the Scientific Association, director of the Philodemic Association, and member of the board of trustees! This shows a kinship, a working relationship, and similar goals. But what about scholarly influence? How did Carrier's scholarly work impact Zahm?

At the outset, this question challenges the modern researcher, for Zahm makes no explicit mention of Carrier in either his earlier or later works on the relationship of science to faith. Besides simply having a working relationship, the young Zahm and Carrier shared an interest in the relationship between the natural sciences and Catholic

Table 2.1. From Carrier to Zahm: Handing the Baton of Notre Dame Science

Notre Dame Annual Catalogue Volume, Year	Joseph C. Carrier	John A. Zahm
23, 1866–67	1. First mention: librarian and professor of French	No mention
24, 1867–68	1. Librarian and professor of botany, mineralogy, and geology 2. Director, newly founded United Scientific Association	1. First mention, student
25, 1868–69	1. Librarian, curator of museum, and professor of natural sciences 2. Director, United Scientific Association	1. Student, with awards 2. Librarian, Archconfraternity of the Blessed Virgin Mary
26, 1869–70	Same	1. Student, with awards 2. Vice president, Archconfraternity of the Blessed Virgin Mary 3. Secretary, Philodemic Society
27, 1870–71	Same	1. Student, with awards 2. President, Archconfraternity of the Blessed Virgin Mary 3. Secretary, Philodemic Society 4. Secretary, Scientific Association
28, 1871–72	Same, plus 3. Director, Philodemic Society	No mention. Zahm graduates and enters seminary this year.
29, 1872–73	1. Member, board of trustees 2. Librarian and curator of museum 3. Professor of chemistry and physics, and the natural sciences 4. Member, Faculty of Arts 5. Dean, Faculty of Sciences 6. Member, Faculty of Theology 7. President, Notre Dame Scientific Association 8. Director, Philodemic Association	1. Assistant librarian and curator of museum 2. Assistant in chemistry, physics, and the natural sciences 3. Vice president, Notre Dame Scientific Association 4. President, Philodemic Society 5. Graduate, 1871 6. Recipient of master of arts degree, 1872
30, 1873–74	All but no. 6 repeated	All but nos. 5 and 6 repeated
31, 1874–75	No mention. Sent to become president of St. Mary's College in Galveston, Texas, in the fall of 1874.	1. Ordained: "Rev. Zahm" 2. Member, board of trustees 3. Professor of chemistry and physics, librarian, and curator of museum 4. Dean, Faculty of Sciences 5. President, Scientific Association 6. Director, Philodemic Association

Source: University of Notre Dame, *Annual Catalogue of the University of Notre Dame,* vols. 23–31 (Notre Dame, IN: Ave Maria Press, 1866–74), Digital Collections, UNDA, http://www.archives .nd.edu/bulletin/.

faith. Indeed, records show that Carrier was deeply engaged in his own work on the relationship between the natural sciences and Catholicism. Records in the *Annual Catalogue* and *Scholastic*, beginning with the 1869–70 school year, show a strong predilection by Carrier to lecture on and promote the advancement of the natural sciences. The *Annual Catalogue* notes lectures on "Natural Sciences" to be presented by Fr. Carrier, the first of which was titled "The Record of the Rocks and the Record in the Bible Not Conflicting, but Proving Each Other."[16] He gave this lecture twice in the fall semester of 1870, once at Notre Dame on November 16, and once at St. Mary's College in Galveston, on November 23.[17]

Three years later, on January 14, 1873, *Scholastic* notes that Carrier had just delivered the second lecture of a series titled "The Work of Six Days of Creation."[18] This lecture continued the work of the previous lecture series by refuting "the arguments hurled against the Church of God by atheists and unbelievers, as well as showing the necessity of a 'first Cause' and refuting the slander and atheistic arguments of such as Darwin and his followers."[19] "Man could not have created himself," Carrier argued, "God, and God alone, *creates.*" The editor of *Scholastic* notes that Carrier "most conclusively proved" that the Catholic Church did not "oppose education and the study of the arts and sciences." Carrier's lecture "was philosophical, yet simple; easily comprehended, yet deep." It seems highly likely that Zahm would have been present at least at this lecture, since "many of the Reverend Clergy as well as most of the Faculty were present."[20]

At this juncture, it is helpful to turn to a previously undiscovered source of Carrier's work—his personal archives, located at the French Canadian headquarters of the Congregation of Holy Cross in Montréal.[21] For the purposes of this study, the gem of these archives is a series of thirteen lectures, with only two lectures missing. Written in English, the series analyzes the place of God as creator and includes several lectures with the title "The Work of the Six Days."[22] Unfortunately, the archival document has no date or place attached to it, but 1873 seems the most likely year, as the only other document in English in Carrier's archives—a lecture series on chemistry—dates from 1873. As such, it further seems possible that this lecture series is precisely the one reported on by *Scholastic* from January of the same year at

Notre Dame, at which John Zahm was likely in attendance. A close analysis of *Scholastic* and the archival material confirm this possibility.

First, *Scholastic* notes that "in this lecture [Carrier] did not speak of the subject proper." The archival material shows that the second lecture is titled "The Existence and Perfections of God," whereas the explicit lectures on the nature of creation do not appear until the fifth lecture. Second, *Scholastic* notes that, "in this lecture," Carrier "refuted the arguments hurled against the Church of God by atheists and unbelievers." The second lecture from the archives focuses primarily on precisely this question, refuting atheistic claims throughout the text, including the following two passages:

The so-called atheist, who dares to deny the existence of God does not think that there is no God, but he wishes it, that he might be more undisturbed in the gratification of his shameful passions. There is no God!! Such horrible blasphemy is not, by any means, an error of the mind, but a desire of the heart. So saying, I dismiss atheism and atheists.

The existence of a God, cause supreme, principle and end of all things has been believed and thought so clearly, so constantly, so unanimously by the whole antiquity, all nations proclaim it with such perfect unanimity that it seems impossible . . . not to recognize in this accord the voice of nature.[23]

Third and finally, the editor of *Scholastic* notes that the course of lectures was titled "The Work of the Six Days of Creation."[24] The archival material, as noted, does not have an overall title to the thirteen lectures, but the individual lectures are titled as follows:

1st: The Dogmas of Mankind
2nd: The Existence and Perfections of God
3rd: The Perfections of God
4th: The Attributes of God
5th: The Creation of the World
6th: The Work of the Six Days
7th: The Work of the Six Days (continued)
8th: The Work of the Six Days (continued)

9th: Missing
10th: Missing
11th: The Creation of the Dignity of Man
12th: The Creation and Fall of Man
13th: The Creation and Fall of Man (continued)[25]

Given the central place of the lectures titled "The Work of the Six Days," it would not be unreasonable for the overall series to be titled as such.

Are they the exact lectures given by Carrier at Notre Dame in 1873? Perhaps. Even if they are not, they were undoubtedly written around that time with a similar construction and distribution of arguments. Because of this highly likely fact, it is also nearly certain that Zahm heard the arguments that Carrier presents throughout this lecture series. There is not enough space in this book to examine Carrier's arguments in full; it suffices for this study to focus on several central reflections of Carrier's approach to the dialogue between science and theology.

First, Carrier presents the Church as being in perfect communion with science, disparaging all atheistic attempts to pit scientific achievements against the theologies of Roman Catholicism. Second, Carrier has no patience for evolutionary theories, stating repeatedly that God alone creates, God alone sustains, and no other force can accomplish either. Third, Carrier interprets the words of Genesis through the lens of modern scientific understandings of the natural world, echoing Augustine's attempt to do exactly that in *The Literal Meaning of Genesis*.[26] Fourth, Carrier not only employs Augustine's methodology but he also copies some arguments directly from Augustine, including an argument in the eleventh lecture, where he declares the Trinity is proven from God's statement, "Let us make man in our image," from Genesis 1:26.[27] Fifth and finally, while Carrier appreciates the marvels of science, his focus remains primarily philosophical and theological, as seen above in the second lecture. Carrier does not, as Zahm will do, argue first from science and second from theology. Rather, Carrier starts and ends each lecture with philosophical and theological arguments about the attributes of God and humanity.

The archival materials from the Congregation of Holy Cross head-quarters in Canada paint a much clearer picture of Carrier's influence on Zahm. Zahm surely imbibed a sense of harmony between science and Roman Catholicism from Carrier, but, as chapter 3 will show, he would depart from this notion of harmony in the 1880s and 1890s. By the time of *Evolution and Dogma*, Zahm's arguments were a world apart from the philosophical treatises of Carrier in the early 1870s.

Despite this eventual distancing from Carrier's conclusions, it remains odd that there is no record of Zahm mentioning Carrier in his earlier writings, an oddity that Carrier himself noticed during the height of Zahm's fame in 1895. In reminiscing to a friend about his time at Notre Dame, Carrier wrote:

> I am afraid that Fr. Zahm is not over unselfish, nor over just in his appreciation of what he may owe to me—little as that may have been. The disciple is now made famous by the conspiracy of—no doubt, well deserved—world-wide publicity, while the master (magister, I should say,) is content to remain ignored, or well-nigh so.[28]

Whether the bitterness of missed opportunities colored his vision, or whether his frustration was based in details of his leaving Notre Dame that are not accessible to us, Carrier clearly felt he should have been mentioned by Zahm, or at least given credit for his role as teacher early in Zahm's career.

Not content to merely gripe about Zahm's fame, Carrier went on to request a favor that would forever bolster the appearance of his role in the founding of Notre Dame:

> I am glad to hear that Prof. (Judge) Howard is writing the Hist. of Notre Dame up to date. I wonder if the mere name of one who worked faithfully, if not eminently, during the years at N.D. for the advancement of the sciences, the formation of a library and a museum (which, before his time, were in embryo) will appear in such a history. I would certainly be flattered for that distinction from the pen of an old and valued friend. Would you kindly say so to him?[29]

Carrier's request did not go unheeded. The golden jubilee history of 1895, *A Brief History of the University of Notre Dame du Lac*, written by Thomas Howard, presents a detailed look at Carrier's contributions over several pages, in a fond and foundational light, whereas Zahm's contributions were summarized in a single sentence amid these pages.[30]

History does not give us further access to Carrier and Zahm's relationship. No record of letters written between the two men exists, just as there is no record of why Carrier was sent away from Notre Dame in the 1870s. Perhaps the relationship between Zahm and Carrier did not end amicably, or perhaps Zahm simply did not find Carrier's contributions unique in the field. Furthermore, why was Carrier sent to Texas in the first place? What seems most likely, especially given Carrier's clear frustration with the turn of events and Zahm's swift move as Carrier's replacement at Notre Dame, is that Sorin transferred Carrier because he saw in Zahm a continuation of his own vision of a grand American university and a bold and fearless leader for the decades ahead.[31]

From Faculty Member to National Figure (1876–92)

From the moment he replaced Carrier as a member of the board of trustees at Notre Dame in 1875, Zahm's popularity and power grew. Zahm worked assiduously as a science educator and popularizer, traveling the country and presenting numerous lectures on the grandeur and magnificence of science and scientific achievements. As Weber writes,

> In March, 1876, Zahm presented the first chemistry lecture in the Scientific Series, inaugurated by him, on "Water." In it, he demonstrated with an electric battery that water was composed of oxygen and hydrogen; moreover, he exhibited an oxy-hydrogen blowpipe, the electric arc, and suggested that machinery might be run off power from the latter. The audience termed his lecture brilliant and the *Scholastic* . . . urged its readers to procure their tickets to the next five lectures immediately.[32]

Besides popularizing modern science, Zahm continued Carrier's expansion of the library and museum, even traveling for several months in Europe in 1878 to procure next and exciting pieces for the growing collection.[33]

On April 19, 1879, however, disaster struck the university. A massive fire consumed nearly every significant building on campus, including Carrier and Zahm's beloved science museum and university library. Some would be defeated by such a tragedy, but Zahm was not among them. Side by side with a reinvigorated Fr. Sorin, Zahm took the destruction as a challenge.[34] Over the next five years, Zahm was given great leeway to collect scientific pieces for the museum, lab equipment, books, and funds from benefactors around the United States and Europe. Furthermore, Zahm personally reengineered the fire safety systems in the Main Building and purchased the first electric power plant for the campus so that gas lamps did not need to be employed on a regular basis.[35] The grand achievement of this phase of electrification, without doubt, was the 1884 installment of an "electric crown on the sixteen-foot statue on the Blessed Virgin on top of the Golden Dome"![36]

As his popularity and influence rose both locally and nationally, his confidence exploring new fields increased as well. On March 26, 1883, Zahm delivered his first public foray into the question of faith and science at a sermon while recruiting and fundraising for Notre Dame in Denver, Colorado. Nothing, he declared, is contrary between science and the teachings of the Catholic faith. This lecture was printed at Notre Dame and Saint Mary's College (Notre Dame, Indiana) shortly after its deliverance.[37]

In 1885 Zahm was made vice president of Notre Dame, mostly as a formal recognition of his years of giving lectures, recruiting, and fundraising. Sensing an area of growth on the evolution-Catholicism front, Zahm devoted himself to a study of the relationship between the two, producing several articles and lectures on the topic in the later 1880s, including an 1890 article titled "Catholic Dogma and Scientific Dogmatism" in *American Catholic Quarterly Review*. Arguably more important than these early entries in the field, however, was Zahm's first and only book-length publication in a scientific field. *Sound and Music* was published in 1892, representing for Zahm the culmination of years of study on acoustics and musical harmonics in relationship to physics. The book was popular among scientific journals and institutions around the world and, because of this, helped to cement Zahm's reputation as a scientist as well as a popularizer of science.[38]

The year 1892 also marked the end of Zahm's time as vice president of Notre Dame, which effectively ended his close relationship with the students of the university, since "the student trips which he had inaugurated in Ohio in 1880 and directed to the Southwest since 1882 were no longer under his personal command."[39] Others traveled the country and brought students to Notre Dame; others introduced them to the vision of the university; and others taught them what it meant to be an educated Catholic American. While 1892 established Zahm's national scientific reputation, it also marked the end of Zahm's most significant time of influence as a faculty member and administrator at Notre Dame.[40]

A decade of traveling the globe in support of the growing university, the popularity of *Sound and Music*, and a few national articles on evolution brought Zahm a level of recognition previously unknown by anyone from Notre Dame.[41] If there was added pressure, Zahm certainly did not let it show. If anything, the now forty-year-old priest happily accepted the newfound status and reveled in the possibilities it offered. In a letter to Fr. Sorin, he wrote:

> I am beginning to feel that I have a great mission before me in making known to the Protestant world the true relation of Catholic dogma towards modern science—this is surely a fertile field to labor in, & I trust I may be given the health & strength necessary for the work.[42]

These doggedly optimistic lines seem to take for granted this "true relation" of Catholicism and modern science. Such optimism was a character trait that, combined with Zahm's intelligence and charisma, had gained him much acclaim over the previous twenty years. But it was also the trait that would lead Zahm into discussions of philosophical theology in which he had neither the educational training nor competence to survive.[43]

An International Champion of Theistic Evolution (1892–99)

In 1893, when Zahm wrote the above letter to Sorin, he was visiting the known anti-Americanist leader Archbishop Michael A. Corrigan of New York City, who counted as an ally Archbishop Otto Zardetti, Zahm's future accuser. At this critical junction point in Zahm's life, John Cavanaugh, CSC, Zahm's friend and first biographer in 1922, provides the best description of the events to come:

> Up to this point, Father Zahm had a united Catholic backing to support him. As long as he stayed within the old fortresses and ventured not into fresh battlefields nor used strange weapons, he enjoyed not only a growing fame among the faithful, but the marked approval of all Catholic scholars as well. But at this time there sprung up in our country the interesting movement which produced the still vigorous Catholic Summer School at Plattsburg, the Western Catholic Summer School (now defunct) at Madison, Wisconsin, and the Catholic Winter School (never vigorous) at New Orleans. At all of these Father Zahm was invited to lecture, and he somewhat audaciously chose for his subject the most difficult, delicate and dangerous topics a Catholic apologist could elect.[44]

Given his ambitious character, it is not surprising that Zahm would utilize his position to advance what he considered the best and most advanced Catholic thought on the relationship of evolution and Catholicism during his five lectures at the Catholic Summer School in Plattsburgh, New York, in 1893. The five lectures, titled "Science and Revealed Religion," not only laid the foundation for his next three years of work, they essentially *were* his next three years of work. In the preface to *Evolution and Dogma*, Zahm writes,

> Part Second of this work covers substantially the same ground as my lectures on Evolution, delivered before the Madison and Plattsburgh Summer Schools and before the Winter School of New Orleans. Indeed, the chief difference between the subject-matter of Part Second, and that of the lectures as given at the

Summer and Winter Schools, consists in the foot-notes which have been added to the text, and in a more exhaustive treatment of certain topics herein discussed than was possible in the time allotted to them in the lecture hall. [Dated December 18, 1895][45]

Similarly, in the official pamphlet published by the Summer and Winter schools, Zahm admits the same:

The present little work embraces my recent lectures. . . . Aside from a few verbal changes, and a slightly different arrangement of the topics discussed, the subjects here treated retain their original form. The following chapters, it may also be remarked, cover essentially the same ground as Part II of my more extended work on "Evolution and Dogma."[46]

New Arguments, Same Science?

During the eight critical years between 1892 and 1899, Zahm's political turn was one fueled as much by a desire for scientific accuracy as by a fervor to sensationalize and astonish. Zahm was always a showman, but prior to these years his sensationalism had focused on the benefits of scientific progress itself: modern electricity, magnetism, chemistry, geology, etc. Seizing the moment and popularity of the Catholic Summer School, a movement seeking to bring together the best of American Catholic thought in the late nineteenth century, Zahm focused his tactics on the intersection of science and faith.[47] It is clear that he did not realize the dangers of a bold approach to such a controversial topic.

Zahm was convinced of both the popular and orthodox character of his lectures. "My audiences increased daily," Zahm wrote to a disciple and close friend, "and the last lecture was the occasion of quite an ovation. More than this a large number wanted me to repeat the course, or continue lecturing on a similar subject."[48] In an interview the same year, Zahm argued that people would only think him advanced if they lacked a proper knowledge of the field. "The conclusions of my articles and [my lectures] at the School have been familiar to me and to every Catholic Biblical 'scientist' . . . for many years. I have simply restated them and grouped old opinions and new illustrations about them."[49] Having established his reputation in the United States, Zahm now looked across the Atlantic.

International Fame

As his rapid set of publications show (seventeen in 1894 alone!), the wide reach and popular press coverage at Zahm's Catholic Summer School lectures in 1893 set off a domino effect on the rest of the decade. During the four years between 1892 and 1896, Weber notes, Zahm published "five books, four pamphlets, and twenty-one articles."[50] Zahm's fame in the Catholic world quickly expanded beyond the borders of the United States, ironically enough, a result of his need to travel there to rest from his prodigious labors in his native country. To rest, he toured France and Spain during the early autumn of 1893 and would return the following autumn.

Four significant moments in the development of Zahm's international stature occurred during this time with his attendance at the International Catholic Scientific Congress of September 4–7, 1894, in Brussels. First, he was elected as an official delegate from the United States due to the fact that "he was the leading Catholic scientist in the country."[51] Second, just prior to the congress, Zahm traveled to Rome and met in private with Pope Leo XIII, and from there "personally carried the Holy Father's benediction" to Brussels.[52] Third, Zahm delivered a lecture to the entire congress on the final day of the conference, arguing that seminaries were failing future priests by not including more science in their curricula. "If we were to devote as much time to science as we do to Classics," Zahm noted, "we could exhibit better results."[53] Fourth, six weeks after the conference, Zahm returned to Rome and presented to Leo a copy of his lecture, "beautifully printed in French and bound in white silk." Zahm praised the pope for the recently published *Rerum Novarum*, and the Holy Father praised Zahm for his work in religion and science.[54]

These interactions led to the final piece that would cement Zahm's international reputation: the conferral of an honorary pontifical degree of doctor of philosophy upon Zahm on February 24, 1895.[55] Upon returning to the United States in early 1895, Zahm moved to take full advantage of this heightened place on the world's stage. He would go on to publish over thirty articles and four books in the next three years on a wide variety of topics aside from evolution: a writing system for the blind, Pope Leo XIII's approach to science, Pope Leo XIII's social programs, a bibliography of many leading Catholic scientists, and a short biography of Catholic scientist Charles de Harlez.[56] Zahm seized upon his golden opportunity and published as widely and deeply as he felt possible.

Becoming Americanist, Becoming Explicitly Pro-evolution

One outcome of his international reputation as an evolutionary scientist was a necessary shift in political alliances. In the late-nineteenth-century Catholic Church anyone expressly supporting a general theory of evolution was decidedly considered in league with the progressive Americanist movement in the Catholic Church. It was not necessarily a heretical view, but it was certainly one that demanded a turn from the classical understanding of the development of life. Whatever ties Zahm previously held to the anti-Americanist movement (as noted above, he stayed as a guest of Archbishop Corrigan as late as 1893), he began to feel a cooling of these relationships as his views reached unprecedented numbers. Zahm's evolutionary leanings, and thus his explicit ties to Americanism, were made evident by his summer lectures in 1893. These lectures received praises largely from the Americanist Catholic elite, including several major Catholic magazines.[57] Cavanaugh's 1922 biography well describes the rancor caused by Zahm:

[After Zahm's lectures] certain Catholic scholars took alarm, and felt that the Church might need a defender against some of her defenders. Father Zahm immediately became a storm-centre of controversy within the Church; one influential and brilliant party attacking him with spirit, while another, not so large, but probably more brilliant, as ardently defended him.[58]

On this point, however, Zahm scholarship remains somewhat vague. When did Zahm first begin to side with the Americanist movement of the late nineteenth-century Catholic Church in the United States? Weber and John Morrison both argue that his outright Americanism began in response to his critics from the Catholic Summer School.[59] R. Scott Appleby contends, however, that Zahm was already well indoctrinated into the Americanist side of the Church in the late 1880s and early 1890s, citing letters from Zahm asking Monsignor Denis O'Connell, the rector of the North American College in Rome, to intercede with the pope on his behalf so that he might receive the honorary doctorate he was finally given in 1895.[60]

The historical record, unfortunately, fails to offer certainty on this transition. It seems most likely that, like so many intellectual transformations, Zahm's was a gradual one. In his dissertation, Appleby argues that two factors contributed to this turn. First, Appleby notes that Zahm was constantly in touch with the European scientific community, which "by and large" had endorsed evolution generally.[61] There is little proof of this constant contact during the 1880s, during which the transformation must have taken place. For this reason, it is more correct to explain his transformation by combining whatever contact Zahm had with the European scientific community with the general acceptance of evolution in the American scientific community in the same decade.

Second, Appleby notes that "he simply became a competent scientist," implying that as Zahm's own scientific prowess increased, his ability to see the possibilities of evolutionary theories increased as well.[62] A better version of this argument would seek to diminish neither the effectiveness of Zahm's studies at Notre Dame nor his many years of running a successful science department, science museum, and university library. It seems highly improbable that Zahm accomplished these tasks as an incompetent scientist. One should argue instead that, as a devoted empirical scientist from mid-1870s onward, Zahm accomplished what many scientists accomplish—he grew in knowledge, ever open to new possibilities. He did not, at least as the historical record shows, have a "light bulb moment," but instead, in the typical intellectual appropriation of novel ideas, he gradually came to understand that while Darwin's supporters' antireligious attitudes were certainly untenable, Darwin's science was not wholly dismissible. This thesis is not a very exciting one, but it helps to explain why Zahm became a leader in the Americanist movement.

In short, Zahm's passion for science drove him increasingly to accept a general evolutionary hypothesis, and Zahm's passion for politics and provocation, combined with a firm belief that he had the full support of the Church, drove him to share his newfound understanding with the world. The only sudden movement in the entire affair, it seems, was the astounding reception Zahm received after the Catholic Summer School lectures of 1893.

Zahm's aforementioned letter to Fr. Sorin about his "great mission" was actually written *after* the summer lectures, in late 1893. It seems clear that while Zahm was aware of the nature of the field generally, he did not anticipate quite the reaction he received. In fact, he was invited to give the lectures one year earlier, in 1892, but declined the invitation, citing previous engagements over the summer and noting that he could "serve as lecturer" for 1893 if his assistance in the Catholic Summer School project was requested.[63] This is certainly not a John Zahm who sees himself publishing unceasingly for the next six years.

After giving the lectures, Zahm's adoring public awakened an eagerness in him that pushed him perhaps beyond what he would have done otherwise. Zahm became famous overnight, and this fame had political consequences. Anti-Americanists found him an opponent, Americanists an ally and spokesperson, and Zahm willingly became swept up in the debates. After the lectures, and especially after his 1894 trip to Europe, he had a voice, and an audience, for whatever he wanted to write. This, more than anything else, explains the dramatic shift present both in the lectures and eventually in *Evolution and Dogma*. Zahm wanted a progressive Church, perhaps, but this was not why he joined forces with the Americanist crowd in the 1890s. Zahm truly wanted people to understand what he understood, and he wanted to use his voice in the best way possible to help people gain this understanding.

"My object," he wrote to his friend and Catholic editor, Augustine F. Hewit, a year before publishing *Evolution and Dogma*,

> is not to prove that the theories discussed are true, but that they are tenable, that they are not the great bugbear they are sometimes declared to be. I wish to show that Catholics have no cause

for alarm even should certain theories by which modern scientists set such store be proved to be true. . . . My desire is to quiet the doubts of many Catholics who are now sorely puzzled about certain questions to show them that there is no possibility of conflict between science & religion, & that in controverted questions the Church allows her children the utmost liberty.[64]

This desire, it seems, pushed him to ignore even the recommendations of trusted advisors such as Hewit in publishing the 1896 book.[65] Zahm may have been hopeful that the highest ranks of the Church would approve of the book, but he could not have been certain, even as early as 1895.

Chapter 3 will address the contents of *Evolution and Dogma* in detail, but it is sufficient at this point to note that the main differences between *Evolution and Dogma* and Zahm's previous publications (especially *Catholic Church and Modern Science*) lie in two areas: the immediate international fame of the book and the degree to which Zahm accepted pieces of Darwin's theories on the evolution of humans.[66] In *Evolution and Dogma*, Zahm spent half of the book covering science and the other half theology, so as to convince people of the tenability of both the scientific theories *and* the idea that these theories are compatible with Catholic dogma. The book was anticipated with a tidal wave of publicity, sold in droves, and, like any controversial book on science and religion—even today—met with strongly worded reviews both from the United States and around the world, with nearly as many critiques as praises.[67]

A Silencing, Not a Prohibition

The story of Zahm's silencing begins, of course, with the publication of *Evolution and Dogma* in 1896. Due to the predictable international acclaim for the book, French and Italian versions were already in press when the English edition was published, and both translations were soon printed thereafter.[68] Because I detail the theological arguments of the book's censure in chapter 5, this section only briefly outlines the events as they unfolded.[69]

As mentioned previously, Archbishop Zardetti, a friend of Archbishop Corrigan of New York, opened the case against Zahm with a letter condemning *Evolution and Dogma* to the Congregation of the Index dated November 5, 1897 (see appendix B in this volume).[70] The prefect of the congregation assigned the case to Dominican consultor Enrico Buonpensiere, who soon produced a comprehensive review.[71] Buonpensiere's April 14, 1898 report condemned the book, citing numerous errors of philosophy and theology throughout some fifty-five pages. He stated that the book should at least be removed from sale and that Zahm should issue a formal retraction.[72] Following Buonpensiere's report, the congregation commissioned an investigation on whether the Italian translation of the book was equivalent to the English, since the consultor's report was based on the former. This task was given to a Franciscan named Bernhard Doebbing, who in his report simply stated that the Italian version "is most faithful" to the English.[73] So much so, Doebbing notes, that he may call it *"ad litteram."*[74]

With the completion of these reports, the Preparatory Congregation (a subcommittee of the Congregation of the Index) began deliberating on Zahm's case on August 5, 1898. Three members of the Preparatory Congregation argued that Zahm should simply be warned; five argued that the book should be placed on the index, although one wanted to notify Zahm first; one argued that not only should the book be placed on the index but that a notice regarding the incompatibility of evolution and Catholicism should be published simultaneously; one argued that nothing should happen until the Holy Office considers and resolves the matter of evolution; and one simply supported the conclusions of Buonpensiere's report.[75]

The matter was then taken up by the General Congregation, which met on September 1, 1898, to review the results of the Preparatory Congregation and cast a vote. Besides Zahm's book, the General Congregation considered six other texts during this meeting. After discussing the books briefly in an audience with the pope on September 3, the General Congregation placed all of the other books on the index and published an official decree dated September 5, 1898.[76] With regard to Zahm's book, no difference of opinion among the members of the Congregation of the Index was recorded, although this was not unusual at this point in the proceedings. The General Congregation agreed with the opinion of the largest group of the Preparatory Congregation that Zahm's book should be placed on the index, but that the prohibition should be delayed until Zahm was given a chance to repudiate the book.[77]

This decision, dated September 1, 1898, had been brought before Pope Leo XIII on September 3, with a report that included the following two reasons for Zahm's prohibition, both taken directly from Buonpensiere's report. First, he should be condemned because

> Zahm supports the system of evolution not only for plants and lower animals, but also for the body of man: that is, man can be genealogically kin to some unknown simian or monkey species, and that in such a genealogical affinity there is nothing opposed to metaphysics and Dogma.[78]

Second, he should be condemned because Zahm connected this claim to "principles adduced by the two great luminaries of the Church, Saint Augustine and Saint Thomas." The report concludes, "The Cardinals decreed the prohibition, but that the Decree not be published until Father Zahm, through the mediation of his General, makes an act of submission."[79] Thus the prohibition against Zahm's book was *not* published on September 5 along with the others, but instead a letter was sent to Gilbert Français, the general superior of Zahm's order.[80]

Français quickly wrote to Zahm asking for submission, all the while assuring the Congregation of the Index, in a letter dated September 18, that Zahm would soon submit fully.[81] After receiving Zahm's official submission letter in late October, Français traveled to Rome to speak to the prefect of the congregation in person. On November 4, Français delivered two letters to the congregation, the first noting Zahm's full submission, and the second pleading with them not to publish the prohibition.[82] The reception of these two letters, and Zahm's capitulation to the decree, is noted in the official diary of the congregation on November 4, 1898.[83] The next, and last, entry in the diary concerning Zahm's case is a note dated February 3, 1899, indicating that during an audience Pope Leo "personally gave instructions to the Cardinal Prefect" not to publish the prohibition until Zahm could present himself in person.[84] But why did the pope give such an instruction? Four factors seem to have had the most impact: first, Zahm's personal relationship with the pope, as seen from his honorary doctorate and multiple audiences; second, Français's well-documented relentless petitioning on Zahm's behalf; third, the petitioning of many others on Zahm's behalf, especially Archbishop John Ireland of St. Paul, Minnesota; and fourth, the pope's dislike of embroiled political arguments.[85]

In the end, Zahm was never forced to go to Rome and the prohibition was never published. All parties involved seemed to be satisfied with a retraction, upon Zahm's request to his publishers, of the Italian and French translations of the book. After much prodding by Français, Zahm requested in a private letter dated May 16, 1899, that the Italian version be pulled from all shelves of bookstores. The letter was leaked to the press in Italy and attached to a similar letter, albeit one with a humorous tone, by the Italian translator, Galea, who wrote:

> I too join with the illustrious Dr. J. A. Zahm . . . and ask my sincere friends not to read nor give any further publicity to my miserable translation of the work mentioned, as a courtesy to the wishes of the Holy See, always ready to change my mind if I am asked.[86]

The retraction was picked up by the New York Daily Tribune and word quickly spread that Zahm had been chastened by the Church.[87] This, it seems, was enough. Although the public debate continued for a while, Zahm himself did not enter the scuffles. While his book was *considered* to have been prohibited by Rome, Zahm was relieved of the burden of the Congregation of the Index *actually* promulgating the decree.

The language of what happened with Zahm's book is, honestly, tricky. It seems acceptable to consider the book "censured" and Zahm "silenced" but not "prohibited," although this was certainly the original intention of the Congregation of the Index. In *Negotiating Darwin,* Mariano Artigas, Thomas Glick, and Rafael Martínez note many times that Zahm's case, among others, is proof that evolution itself was never condemned by the Vatican, even while books supporting various degrees of evolution were condemned, or nearly so.[88] But this argument fails to satisfy the historical record. While evolutionary theory was never pronounced upon by the Holy Office or the Congregation of the Index, and while the pope never officially condemned it, the censuring of books and silencing of people who wrote such books effectively acts in the same regard, at least temporarily.

While chapter 5 of this volume outlines the nuances of the philosophical differences between Zahm, Zardetti, and Buonpensiere, and thus helps to explain why his book was censured, the main reasons that the General Congregation gave were clear. Zahm argued that humans descended from apes, which, according to the Congregation of the Index, was undeniably against Catholic doctrine, and Zahm supported this argument by falsely employing the ideas of Augustine and Aquinas. If this is reason enough for the General Congregation, one must accept that evolutionary theory, especially applied to humans, was, for all intents and purposes, an implicitly condemned theory according to the highest authorities of the Catholic Church in the 1890s until proved otherwise. While the silencing of John Zahm may neither have defrocked him nor removed him from his elevated political post as provincial of the Congregation of Holy Cross (more on that in a moment), it certainly removed his voice from the conversation, proving to any and all following the same conversation around the world that the Vatican strongly disapproved of the idea.[89]

Provincial, Explorer, and Occasional Apologist (1899–1921)

The aforementioned appointment of Zahm as the provincial of the Congregation of Holy Cross in 1898 places this entire affair in a clearer light. Français, having just appointed Zahm as provincial of the order in the United States, was stunned by the letter he received from the secretary of the Congregation of the Index on September 10, 1898.[90] Français had appointed Zahm interim provincial on January 5 of the same year, and Zahm won the general election in August, just a few weeks before the edict would come from Rome.[91] Had the prohibition of Zahm's book proceeded as planned, Français's entire plans for the order would have been placed on hold: Zahm would likely have had to step down, or, at the least, he would have lost much credibility with the many institutions that he was appointed to manage. Thus, while several members of the Americanist wing advocated for Zahm in Rome, Monsignor O'Connell, Archbishop Ireland, and Archbishop John Joseph Keane among them, it was Français's dedication (for his own sake as well as for Zahm's) that persuaded all parties to keep the book off the index.

Knowing this pressure, Zahm would begin his tenure as provincial both mired in the political chaos of evolutionary debates and dreading the loss of liberty that the position would require of him.[92] As with his other ventures, however, Zahm dedicated himself completely to life as an administrator but ended up being voted out eight years later due to competing visions, essentially, for the future of the University of Notre Dame. Zahm began the 1870s heavily influenced by the idea of a great, renowned university, as envisioned by Sorin and Carrier, and he would enter the early 1900s pushing exactly this agenda during his time as provincial. Such a vision led Zahm to neglect the Holy Cross brothers, still numerous at the university, who eventually filed a petition railing against many injustices they experienced under Zahm's term.[93]

In January of his last year as provincial, under attack both from the Holy Cross brothers as well as from Français himself, Zahm penned a letter to his friend and superior, outlining the reasons for his sometimes brash actions and his vision for the future. Was he relentless? Was he brash? Was he incautious? It was only from necessity! To keep Notre Dame at the "forefront of the Catholic institutions of America" meant that he "could not permit a stand-still for even a single year." He continued,

> To do so would mean loss—it might be a very great loss. Our friends look for constant growth, never ceasing evidence of vitality and development in a material as well as in an intellectual way. . . . It means the erection of new buildings whenever called for; it means the equipment of new and large laboratories; it means a large and a better and more expensive staff of professors. . . .
>
> To be over cautious is to become stagnant; to endeavor to conduct such an institution as Notre Dame so as to incur no risks is to do what no sane business man would dream of doing. . . .

Notre Dame shall soon, like some of the great intellectual centers in the Church's past, be also a recognized home of saints and scholars.[94]

This letter did not quell Français's fears—indeed, it may have reinforced them and contributed to Zahm being voted out of office at the general congregation of the order that August.

After serving as provincial, and wielding so much power at the university, Zahm was effectively banished from the institution. Zahm would not be a part of Notre Dame from that point forward. But, of course, his spirit did not wane. He spent the next few years traveling through South America, at times with Theodore Roosevelt, eventually writing several books on his extensive travels under the pseudonym of H. J. Mozans, a reordering of letters in his name.[95]

He would spend the next ten years of his life researching, writing, and traveling, mostly around the United States. He became a strong advocate of women's suffrage, at least under his pseudonym, arguing in *Woman in Science* (1913) that women deserve a place in science and the arts, and gaining support from women's magazines and suffragette groups.[96] As if in response to an overenthusiastic reception of that book, Weber notes, Zahm's next book, *Great Inspirers* (1917), emphasized the "role women had played as gentle guides and sources of encouragement to great men."[97] During the same year, Zahm also published a collection of historical reflections on the story of El Dorado and the South American travels surrounding the folklore behind this figure.[98]

But Zahm still desired more. Specifically, he wanted to write a travel guide, similar to his popular South American books, while exploring Europe and the Middle East. He began his travels in 1918 and wrote *From Berlin to Bagdad and Babylon* as he journeyed across Europe, as well as through Iraq, Israel, and Turkey.[99] He had quite literally just completed the book and was beginning his journey home when he was struck with a fever in Dresden, which became severe bronchial pneumonia in Munich, Germany. He would not recover.

His extensive travels had finally caught up with him at the age of seventy, despite his perennially youthful spirit. He died on November 10, 1921, in Roten Kreuz Hospital in Munich.[100] After returning his body to the United States, his friends and family held a funeral Mass at Sacred Heart Church at the University of Notre Dame. Zahm's body was laid to rest in a burial plot next to Fr. Sorin, his longtime mentor and spiritual kin in his vision for the grandeur of the university, in the graveyard of the Holy Cross community on the campus of Notre Dame.

———

The adventures of Zahm's life were marked, quite distinctly, by his political and ambitious character. In some ways, one might liken his vision to the twenty-first-century phenomenon of the prosperity gospel, in which God not only wills salvation but material success for those on this earth. This concept, of course, is not new in Christian history. As early as the accounts of divinely willed military conquests in the Torah, there have always been those who believed that God desired their personal and national success as much as their spiritual salvation. Constantine's battle for the empire and subsequent conversion was one marked, throughout history, for Christian victory.

The nineteenth century was a harrowing one for Roman Catholicism. It was a century marked by wars, papal imprisonment, and the gradual and violent loss of nearly all political power. The concept of a divinely inspired monarchy, for example, which dominated the Catholic theological landscape at least until the First Vatican Council, was forced to give way to a pope who governed by moral and theological statements alone. In his own life, Zahm witnessed the American Civil War as a young teenager and during his time in university studies heard about the loss of the Papal States and the imprisonment of the pope. When Pope Leo XIII was elected, Zahm was filled with a renewed sense of purpose and ministry for the road ahead. His determination, combined with his naturally political character, made for an imposing figure in 1890s Catholicism.

Français appointed Zahm provincial of the Congregation of Holy Cross in 1898 precisely because of these characteristics, but Zahm's time in this office, predictably, did not go as desired for the superior general. Zahm's political character and vision for the grandeur of Notre Dame, likely fueled even more by his intense disappointment and resentment at the censure, drove him to overlook the personal well-being of many of the order's religious. Furthermore, as Weber notes, Zahm's ambitious drive was incompatible with the pressures of such an elevated office. He worked too many hours for too many years, giving himself little sleep and little rest.[101] His time after administrative life, while fruitful, was scattered and undisciplined.

It is difficult to look at this period and not wonder what could have been had he not been silenced. He would still have been made provincial, since this happened before the censure, but would he have pushed himself so hard in this role? Would he not have continued writing on the topic of evolution, studying the science of acoustics, physics, and biology? Undoubtedly he would have written more—given Zahm's prolific history, much more—on the subject. What contributions would he have made? How would the twentieth century be different? It is impossible to know. What is known, however, is that the censure from the Congregation of the Index, while stemming from good intentions, forever changed both the landscape of American Catholic theology and John Zahm's life. Given that Zahm's book would be considered remarkably conservative today, this turn of events is all the more tragic.

CHAPTER 3

The Scientific Mind of John Zahm, CSC

From Francis Bacon to Charles Darwin

John Zahm's complex and shifting conceptions of philosophy, science, reason, and faith begin with his first published essay on the nature of science in 1871 and the academic foundations that led to its writing. Zahm's early thought expands in the intermediate years between obtaining a degree and becoming an international figure (1872–92), during which he also struggled to disagree with a popular Catholic author whom he much admired, Orestes Brownson. Zahm's mature work in the field, beginning with his 1893 lectures at the Catholic Summer School and ending with his provocative scientific arguments in *Evolution and Dogma,* shows that, by the latter's publication, Zahm was a changed man on the concept of evolution. What was simply "based on assumptions" in 1883 would become "highly likely" and "universally acclaimed" in 1896.[1] But while Zahm would still demur on human evolution—even in 1896—and would still abhor Darwin's theory of natural selection, he would define the doctrine of special creation, the idea that all species were created simultaneously in their present states by a divine being, using the same words with which he defined evolution in 1883: a theory based on assumptions with a pronounced lack of empirical evidence.

Origins and Philosophies of Zahm's First Published Work, "Thoughts on Science" (1871)

On May 15, 1871, a nineteen-year-old John Zahm stood before the Notre Dame Scientific Association and read his essay "Thoughts on Science and the Age in Which We Live."[2] This work offers specific insights into Zahm's twenty-five-year development as a philosopher of science, and while in later years Zahm would significantly expand on his thought, he would also cling to kernels of wisdom expressed here. The essay begins with a reflection on the progress of culture:

> Our age has often, and we believe the truth, been denominated an age of progress and general enlightenment. To satisfy ourselves that such is the case, we need only consult the pages of history, compare the different ages of the world with "the living present," and all our doubts, if we have any about the question, will immediately vanish. We will find that in the primitive ages of the world all nations, with few exceptions, were hurried in ignorance and barbarism, living like the present nomadic tribes of Asia, or like the rude Indians of America.[3]

This crude racial bias was formed on the perception that successful culture is defined in terms of scientific or, more precisely, engineering successes.[4]

> Greece, the mistress of antiquity, was the seat of literature and science and in particular of the fine arts; or in the language of poets, "the fount of all knowledge." But had it not been for their assiduous cultivation of "these polished arts which have humanized mankind," their successful study of the sciences, which so preeminently distinguish a nation's superiority in power and mental culture, these nations, too, would, like nearly all others of antiquity have passed away without leaving even a remnant of their former existence.[5]

But cultivation of the sciences alone was not enough for cultural success, notes Zahm. "Archimedes," he writes, "might have done a great and lasting good to the world had he been more practical and experimental in his studies [but] he considered it a disgrace . . . to stoop from theory to practice." Archimedes lived at a time "that did not favor inventions or discoveries" but that lifted philosophy without instruments as the highest form of thought.[6]

"How different," Zahm notes, "this system of philosophy [is] from that of the moderns." Zahm proceeds with a comparison of the two systems using archetypes for each, choosing Plato for "the ancients" and Francis Bacon for "the moderns."[7] Bacon's focus, Zahm writes, was on the idea that cultural progress was grounded in scientific advances:

Instead of discoursing on the *summum bonum,* the origin of the world, the existence of good and evil, of indifference to pain and misfortune, as did the philosophers of the Portico and Academy; or of recognizing the absurd and contradictory principles and theories of the Stoics, Cynics, Pythagoreans and Epicureans, the moderns [like Bacon] have aimed at a mark less high, it is true, but tangible; they have adopted theories less imposing, less flattering to the pride of man, but practicable. Instead of teaching him to be indifferent in sickness and distress, to consider them as necessary evils, modern science and philosophy have made the greatest possible efforts to assuage his pains and comfort him in his afflictions.[8]

Zahm's juxtaposition of ancient philosophy with modern science finishes by claiming Aristotle's lack of inventions as a decided failure, despite his intellect:

Aristotle, who possessed a most extraordinary intellect, did much towards the furtherance of science, but he is known to us only by his writings, not by any inventions or discoveries. Some of the great mathematicians of antiquity, it is true, made a few useful discoveries, but they can bear no comparison to those of Watt, Morse, Newton, Bacon, Kepler, Laplace, Pascal, Fulton, Franklin and many others of scarcely less renown.[9]

After dispensing with the limits of philosophy, Zahm proceeds to describe why science is "the only talisman of wealth, prosperity and happiness" in the modern world. More than "Persia or Arabia," more than the "Empire of Rome," certainly more than "Hindoostan" and "the Orient," the United States and Europe have "annihilated . . . time and space" with the invention of the telegraph and marked the road for "true progress" in the future. Science, for the young John Zahm, is "the highest exponent of power and intellectual superiority . . . [and] the primary index of the material and social condition of mankind [*sic*], and . . . the most reliable touchstone of the progress and tendency of the age in which we live."[10]

In *Notre Dame's John Zahm*, Ralph Weber argues that the main feature of Zahm's essay is its embodiment of "late nineteenth-century American glorification of Progress."[11] Such a general argument, however, leaves much to be desired when attempting to situate this essay in light of Zahm's many later works. Instead, Zahm's essay is more accurately seen as a vision of science that would become the cornerstone of his twenty-five-year corpus. In short, Zahm's modern world of science is one where cultural progress stems directly from experimentation and empirical advances in the natural sciences, which must eschew theory and philosophy for the sake of practical application. Such a vision is exemplified for Zahm by Bacon, whom Zahm considered "one of the most acute and practical philosophers that ever lived."[12] To situate Zahm's early but seminal conception of science, one must determine how the concepts of Bacon came to Zahm in the first place, and how Zahm's understanding of them shifted throughout his career.[13]

Baconianism in Early Nineteenth-Century America

John Zahm was not alone in his praise of Francis Bacon. Indeed, the impact of Bacon's philosophy upon the early nineteenth-century American scientific scene cannot be overstated. "Baconian philosophy so dominated that whole generation of American scientists," historian George Daniels writes, "that it is difficult to find any writer during the early part of the nineteenth century who did not assume . . . that his readers knew all about it."[14] This assumption began in the same Enlightenment-fueled air that produced the American Revolution just a half century prior. Writing in 1789, for example, Thomas Jefferson called Bacon (with Newton and Locke) one of "the three greatest men that have ever lived, without any exception."[15]

This vision of Baconian importance, mentioned by presidents and scientists alike, became so popular that to be credible at all in the early nineteenth century, a scientist felt required to attribute his or her successes to "the method of Newton and Bacon," despite a variety of interpretations as to what exactly such methods entailed.[16] Daniels identifies three general principles typically employed by scientists to describe Bacon's method:

> First, it meant "empiricism," or the idea that scientific statements must rest solidly on observed facts. Secondly, it meant "anti-theoretical": that science must avoid "hypotheses" and not go beyond immediate observation. Finally, "Baconianism" frequently meant the identification of all science with taxonomy.[17]

Additionally, Daniels argues that American scientists generally considered Baconian methods as those of deduction and inference based on a set of observable data. They implied "a kind of naïve rationalistic empiricism—a belief that the method of pure empiricism consistently pursued would lead to a rational understanding of the universe."[18]

Error, in this understanding,

> could not possibly arise in the observation of facts. Error could only be introduced by false or too hasty inference from the never-to-be-doubted facts and could therefore be corrected by additional observations. The truthfulness of the testimony of the senses could not even be questioned, as one spokesman said, "without questioning the truthfulness of our constitution, nay, the veracity of God himself—without questioning everything, through whatever channel derived."[19]

This belief in the infallibility of observational sense data—that is, the information gathered about the world through our five senses—caused the popularity of Baconian idealization to fade during the mid-nineteenth century. It was not that people stopped believing in observation, but the time of unqualified praise for Bacon's impact on science was coming to an end. "Baconianism," remarks historian Herbert Hovenkamp, "was not really a tool; it was a symbol—something to use in the opening paragraphs of essays in order to show that one was on guard against rationalism, deism, speculative science, or anything else that might approach infidelity."[20]

Attacks on such uses of Francis Bacon came from both scientific as well as religious communities. While the war over Baconian thought was largely waged between different Protestant groups, Roman Catholics, Daniels notes, were among the accusers.[21] Anti-Baconian critics asked, Did God pattern all things? Can God be empirically defined? On account of the many criticisms of Bacon from all facets of society, those working in the sciences began to see the faults, more generally, in too-strict empirical approaches to science. If all scientific theories must be based on strict observation, how could one postulate general laws and mysteries of nature that cannot be observed? Should one cast away all hypotheses regarding the history of geological formation or chemical compounds because such things are not directly observable?[22]

By the 1860s, spurred by the divisive publication of Darwin's *On the Origin of Species* in 1859, these scientific methodological fights shifted into arguments over the place of religion in light of modern science. Three positions unfolded as the dust settled in the 1870s. First, philosophers and scientists such as T. H. Huxley and Herbert Spencer led the charge that modern science—exemplified by Darwin's theories—was the crowning achievement of an evolving humanity and would once and for all eliminate "metaphysical and theological language" from all descriptions of nature.[23] Edward Youmans, an influential disciple of Spencer, argued that "tension between science and religion . . . was the 'natural and inevitable' result of religionists' obdurate refusal to grant scientists a truly free rein in the investigation of nature."[24] There was only tension, in short, because religious leaders failed to give way to the cultural and political progress that is inevitable with scientific advances.

Against this argument, predictably, were many of the leaders of mainstream American Protestant Christianity, exemplified by the Presbyterian minister and professor of theology at Princeton Theological Seminary, Charles Hodge. Hodge was well known and respected throughout the Presbyterian Church: he published over 140 essays on Reformed theology in the mid-nineteenth century in addition to a three-volume work titled *Systematic Theology* in 1872–73. In 1874 he published a more popular version of the arguments that he had detailed in *Systematic Theology*, titling the book *What Is Darwinism?* In it, Hodge attempted to do for the Protestants in the United States what Zahm tried to do, early in his career, for Catholics, when Zahm opposed evolution.[25] Hodge presented the scientific and theological arguments and came to a clear conclusion: "the conclusion of the whole matter is, that the denial of design in nature is virtually the denial of God."[26] Since Darwin's methods and conclusions resulted in no less than the denial of God, Hodge argued, not only should Darwin's theories be condemned but his improper utilization of science should be condemned as well! Hodge's view was widely held in Roman Catholic circles, exemplified by the Catholic popularizer Orestes Brownson, who, as we will see below, was both extremely popular and extremely hostile to Darwin.[27]

Between the two extremes, some attempted to construct an intermediate theory that included religious truths and scientific methods, striving to balance a condemnation of atheism while defending Charles Darwin's science, at least partially. Such a view was exemplified by the preeminent American botanist, devout Christian, and Fisher Professor of Natural History at Harvard, Asa Gray. From the 1840s through his death in 1888, Gray tried to articulate a necessary space between the "implied" atheism of Darwin's books and the ability for Christian theological beliefs to withstand the scientific theories of evolution via natural selection.[28] As a renowned scientist himself, Gray defended Darwin's use of scientific empiricism even though he disagreed with some of Darwin's findings. But, Gray argued, such inadequacies should not lead us to discredit Darwin—or the empirical methods of science—as a whole.

Science Battles and Notre Dame Textbooks

As education creates scientists, textbooks create the bounds of acceptable science.[29] This is as true today as it was in the mid-nineteenth century, when Notre Dame was a small Catholic boys' school, educating students from elementary to college age. A particularly helpful practice during the first few decades of the university, for research purposes at least, was that the school's *Annual Catalogue* listed not only the general courses of study but also the specific textbooks that would be used in each course. For example, the 1865 catalogue, the last year in which every textbook was listed, sixth-year students—the highest grade level possible—studied Plato's *Republic* in Greek, Quintilian in Latin, and Asa Gray's *Botany* in natural history.[30]

Table 3.1. A Comprehensive List of Zahm's University Coursework

Academic Year	Courses Taken by Zahm
1867–68	Algebra (4th and 3rd)
	English Grammar (2nd and 1st)
	German (3rd: 1st and 2nd divisions)
	History (Ancient/Modern)
	Latin (7th: 1st and 2nd divisions)
1868–69	Algebra (1st)
	Latin (5th and 4th)
	Geometry (3rd)
	German (2nd)
	Greek (5th and 4th)
	Natural/General History
	Rhetoric (2nd and 1st)
	Zoology [Biology]
1869–70	Botany
	Conic Sections/Trigonometry
	Greek (3rd)
	Geometry (1st)
	Latin (2nd)
	Rhetoric (1st): English Literature
1870–71	Ancient Classical Literature
	Astronomy
	Chemistry and Natural Philosophy
	Greek (2nd and 1st)
	Latin (1st)
	Moral Philosophy and Metaphysics
	Physics

Sources: University of Notre Dame, *Annual Catalogue of the University of Notre Dame,* vols. 21–29 (Notre Dame, IN: Ave Maria Press, 1864–72), Digital Collections, UNDA, http://www.archives.nd.edu/bulletin/; and *Scholastic* 1–4 (1867–71).

Note: The ordinals 1st, 2nd, 3rd, etc. connote the level of course. For example, 1st Greek was the most advanced Greek course offered at the time, whereas 7th Latin would have been an introductory Latin course. Courses without ordinals did not have a sequence.

By the time of Zahm's entrance to Notre Dame in fall of 1867, there were three possible curricula at the university: classical, scientific, and commercial. Zahm began taking classes in the Classical Course of Studies in 1867 and graduated with his undergraduate degree in May 1871. From the *Annual Catalogue* and from the student magazine *Scholastic*, one can gather Zahm's specific course schedule (table 3.1) as well as the science textbooks he would have been assigned (table 3.2) during his undergraduate years.

By the time Zahm began his studies at Notre Dame, the debate over Baconian methods and their applicability to Darwin's theories of natural selection was lively and constant. While we cannot know for certain what was discussed in Zahm's classrooms, we do know the four textbooks from which he would have derived his earliest perceptions of scientific methods and scientific progress (see table 3.2). It is

Table 3.2. Zahm's Science Courses, Professors, and Textbooks

Academic Year	Science Course	Professor	Textbook
1868–69	Natural/General History	J. Carrier, CSC	Lyell's *Geology*
1868–69	Zoology [Biology]	J. Carrier, CSC	Tenney's *Manual of Zoology*
1869–70	Botany	J. Carrier, CSC	Asa Gray's *Botany*
1870–71	Astronomy	T. E. Howard	Silliman's *Physics*
1870–71	Chemistry/Natural Philosophy	T. Vagnier, CSC	Silliman's *Physics*
1870–71	Physics	T. Vagnier, CSC	Silliman's *Physics*

Sources: This table was compiled from close examination of lists printed in the Notre Dame's *Annual Catalogue* and *Scholastic* magazine. Sometimes the first issue of a volume in *Scholastic* gives the courses in detail, and sometimes such listings are only present in the final issues of the academic year in June. At other times, courses and professors are provided in the *Annual Catalogue*. See *Scholastic* 1–4 (1867–71); and University of Notre Dame, *Annual Catalogue of the University of Notre Dame*, vols. 21–29 (Notre Dame, IN: Ave Maria Press, 1864–72), Digital Collections, UNDA, http://www.archives.nd.edu/bulletin/.
Note: Zoology of the mid-nineteenth century constitutes the same general grouping of information as modern biology.

undeniably challenging to link Zahm's intellectual foundation with the books he was assigned as an undergraduate. Nevertheless, these texts are the best way to situate Zahm's own employment of scientific methods within the larger framework of nineteenth-century American scientific discourse, and simply by choosing these texts, the faculty of Notre Dame have presented us with their acceptable limits of discussing science in northern Indiana in 1870.

We begin with Charles Lyell's *Principles of Geology*, originally printed in 1828, which was already in its tenth edition by 1866. An immensely popular textbook, Lyell's *Geology* was both a manual in the history of the geological sciences as well as a survey course on the most recent advances in the field. Lyell did follow a particular method, but it differed strongly from the popular employment of Baconian empirical methods, as Lyell realized such empirical devotion could not apply to historical geological discoveries. As Steven Jay Gould writes, Lyell held that "geological truth must be unraveled by strict adherence to a methodology" that he would try to capture as "an attempt to explain the former changes of the earth's surface by reference to causes now in operation."[31] All past events, in other words, "could be explained by the action of causes now in operation. No old causes are extinct; no new ones have been introduced."[32] No Baconian scientist could have accepted such an anti-empirical theory as a guiding scientific methodology! The popularity of Lyell's methods points both to the steady decline of a strict Baconianism, as described above, and to the popularity of the idea that a wide variety of scientific methods could be employed to negate traditionally held theological beliefs.

On this latter point, in simplistic terms, Lyell's presence in the Notre Dame classroom confirms the rejection of any sort of biblical timeline of geological history. The idea of an ancient Earth was widely recognized by the scientific community by the time Lyell first wrote the textbook in 1828. Indeed, Lyell places the rejection of the five-thousand-year-old Earth to about 1800. This recognition and rejection is especially compelling given that this idea was controversial enough in the 1890s for Zahm to continue including it in nearly every one of his books.[33]

In terms of Zahm's intellectual development, Lyell's methodology for proving geological changes over time provided proof to a young

Zahm that a continuously applied scientific methodology was not only efficacious but necessary for progress in the natural sciences. Lyell's accepted geological studies set up "a strict dichotomy between vain speculation and empirical truth, defined, respectively, as belief that causes worked differently on an ancient earth versus conviction that our planet has remained in a dynamic steady state throughout time."[34] As Gould writes, even though "the reality of history is so more much complex" than Lyell's "steady state" hypothesis, "the irony of history is that Lyell won [and] his version became a semi-official hagiography of geology, preached in textbooks to the present day."[35] Lyell's arguments would not have convinced Zahm of the power of Baconian empiricism, but they would have driven him closer toward the idea that scientific methods, applied consistently, have remarkable power to drive knowledge and progress.

Sanborn Tenney's textbook was not as groundbreaking as Lyell's *Geology* but remained a widely used scientific text for a descriptive study of the animal kingdom. Today Tenney's *Natural History: A Manual of Zoology for Schools, Colleges, and the General Reader* would be classified as a biology textbook, a descriptor not commonly used in the mid-nineteenth century. Over five hundred illustrations populate the 535 pages of the book, helping the university student to identify all varieties of animal life from around the world. Tenney bookends his text with general reflections on the subjects of science and evolution. Discussing the nature of the geographical distribution of animals, he writes,

> It would seem that climate has no power to mould or shape the species of animals,—and the same is true in regard to plants—or to change one species into another. Were it so, any given climate would produce, in the course of time, the same species of animals in all the countries within its limits. . . . On the contrary, careful observers have been led to believe that animals as well as plants have been created by an Omniscient Being, in the places, and for the places, which they now occupy.[36]

Written several years after Darwin's *On the Origin of Species*, Tenney's claims would have been seen as directly opposed to the theory of a common ancestry of plants and animals, popularized by but not unique to Darwin.[37]

Notre Dame's use of two such different philosophical approaches to evolutionary theory helps us understand the faculty's desire to employ the best scientific texts of the time. Although we cannot know how these texts were employed in Zahm's courses, it is clear that they represented different sides of the ideological spectrum. For example, the closing paragraph of Tenney's text is not to be found in Lyell's similarly comprehensive book:

When we consider the classes, the orders, the families, the genera, the vast number of living and perhaps much greater number of extinct species, and that probably no two individuals even of the same species are exactly alike in every particular, and yet that each one of all these uncounted millions bears within itself the stamp of a Radiate, or a Mollusk, or an Articulate, or a Vertebrate, so clearly, that, by patient study, the student of nature is able to refer every one of to-day, and of bygone ages, to its appropriate type, we are impressed with the great truth that in the Animal Kingdom—and it is so in all nature—there is the greatest possible diversity, and that in all this diversity there is perfect unity; and hence we are forced to believe that all the animals of the past, and all those of the present, have been created according to a plan wrought out in the Divine Mind before the foundation of the world.[38]

As this chapter searches for the bridge between Zahm's hesitant early writings and his more bold work in the 1890s, it is helpful to realize that Zahm's undergraduate education included works from all sides of the political spectrum, including that of the aforementioned public scientist and outspoken Christian, Asa Gray.

Despite Gray's public influence in the debate surrounding Darwinism, his *Manual of the Botany of the Northern United States* does not explicitly discuss philosophy throughout the seven-hundred-plus-page text.[39] However, Zahm's use of Gray's textbook does show *where* Zahm likely first encountered the world-class botanist whom he would cite numerous times in the 1880s and 1890s.[40] One can sense a connection between the younger and older Zahm from Zahm's own words in *Evolution and Dogma:*

> But all evolutionists have not entertained, and do not entertain, the same [atheistic] opinions as those just mentioned. America's great botanist, Prof. Asa Gray, was not so minded. One of the earliest and most valiant defenders of Darwinism, as well as a professed Christian believer, he maintained that there is nothing in Evolution, or Darwinism, which is incompatible with Theism.[41]

Gray was perhaps the first person Zahm encountered who was a strong public Christian, a world-renowned scientist, and outspoken defender of Charles Darwin. If Zahm cared more about the methods of science in the 1870s than the debate over evolution (which he would not enter until 1883), as I contend here, Gray's work may have been less compelling to Zahm than his final textbook, Silliman's *Physics.*

In three courses during his last year as an undergraduate—and immediately before his May 1871 address—Zahm would have used Benjamin Silliman's *Principles of Physics or Natural Philosophy.*[42] Silliman, then professor of general and applied chemistry at Yale College, discusses a broad range of subjects in this important work, including astronomy, meteorology, chemistry, and, of course, physics.[43] Most relevant here, however, is Silliman's extended introduction on the nature of science and the scientific method:

> When individual experience is enlarged by the experience of other inquirers and other times, and the combined knowledge of many is so arranged as to be comprehended by one, the system becomes a *science* or philosophy of nature. Because its principles are founded upon a comparison and analysis of facts, a system of this kind is also called *Inductive* Philosophy.
>
> Inductive philosophy is of modern origin. Galileo . . . was the first to commence a course of experimental researches; and Bacon . . . in his immortal work, *Novum Organum,* showed that this was the only road to an accurate knowledge of nature. The ancients were ignorant of the principles and methods of inductive science. Their explanations of natural phenomena were based on

assumed causes; they are therefore confused and contradictory, and often in direct opposition to experiences.[44]

Silliman's account of science seems nearly identical to Zahm's May 1871 address: both express clearly that modern science alone shows a path to knowledge; both lift up Bacon as exemplary; and both denigrate the methods of the ancients—including their abstract philosophical inclinations—so as to show the vast superiority of "experimental" and "inductive" science.

Zahm was exposed to a wide variety of scientific methods at Notre Dame, each of which offering something slightly different to the young man. Silliman's *Physics* argued for the rejection of theoretical approaches and the importance of empiricism. Gray's and Tenney's texts exemplified the potential of taxonomic approaches to science, a branch of Baconian methodologies but certainly not limited to Bacon. Lyell's *Geology*, contrarily, unflinchingly advocated for his own theory-laden scientific methodology, but one that allowed him to successfully negate the biblical theories on the origin and timeline of the world. While Zahm's love of science was surely due to ideas derived from each of these authors, his 1871 address can be directly tied to Silliman's clear Baconian progressivism.

Before leaving Zahm's undergraduate career, we must refer back to the influence of Joseph Carrier during this time. As the previous chapter discussed, Carrier was a devoted scientist and theologian from the first days of Notre Dame and often taught about the intersection of scientific theories and doctrines of faith. Portions of Zahm's work are reflective of Carrier's teachings, especially Zahm's early disavowal of evolution and his adherence to the Church's infallibility in relation to science. However, Zahm's adherence to a progressive interpretation of Baconianism seems to have separated the teacher from the student, and would prove the decisive factor in Zahm's change of heart in the 1890s.

Defending Science, Defending the Church (1872–92)

From 1872 to 1890, Zahm was first and foremost an educator and university administrator. As described in the previous chapter, he rose quickly through the ranks, becoming professor, museum curator, and chief librarian after Carrier was sent to Texas in 1874. Due to the fire at Notre Dame in 1879, Zahm spent the next several years rebuilding an entirely new science museum, university library, and state-of-the-art laboratory. Zahm made himself invaluable to the university and, in due course, was appointed vice president in 1885, a post in which he would serve until 1892.

Zahm did not publicly enter the ongoing discussion of evolution and Christianity until 1883, when he delivered his lecture, "Catholic Church and Modern Science," in Denver, Colorado, and subsequently published it to broad acclaim.[45] Seeing his success in this venture, he focused on his newfound popularity, producing multiple lectures and articles on questions of evolution, Catholicism, and science. While Zahm's arguments betray his earlier commitment to a type of Baconian scientific method, a new influence is clear from his time and priestly studies at Notre Dame: that of the famous Catholic apologist Orestes Brownson.

The Anti-Darwinian Philosophies of Orestes Brownson

As mentioned in chapter 2 and touched on above, Joseph Celestine Carrier, CSC, was influential in Zahm's early career, introducing Zahm to the discussion of evolution and Catholicism and sharing with the young priest his lifelong passion for science education and outreach. Carrier's devotion to the Church above and beyond all scientific advances may have influenced Zahm's approach to the relationship between science and the Church in the 1880s. However, Carrier's greatest impact on Zahm may have been through Carrier's personal friend and the popular Catholic apologist Orestes Brownson.

"I can say without flattery," Zahm wrote to Brownson in late 1875, "that during my philosophical and theological studies I derived more profit from the study of your writings than from those of any other author."[46] Before 1875, Zahm's appreciation of Brownson was undoubtedly encouraged by his undergraduate and graduate studies at Notre Dame, where Brownson was a regular guest and close friend of the university's founder, Edward Sorin, as well as many of the faculty members.[47] Carrier, it seems, was particularly devoted to Brownson's work in the late 1860s and early 1870s, referring to himself as "a constant and admiring reader" of Brownson's corpus.[48] In a letter to Brownson, Carrier remarked that he had read "every work or page" Brownson had ever produced, had been a close friend of Brownson's son John before he died, and would like to be considered as a lifelong subscriber to Brownson's magazine.[49]

Three aspects of Brownson's thought appear to have had a large impact on Zahm. First, Brownson closely linked Darwin to outspoken atheists who used Darwin's theories to prop up their arguments. Although he had no scientific training, Brownson, a Catholic convert since 1844, was critical of evolutionary theory from the beginning. "The spirit as the tendency of the age is at enmity with God, and must be fought, not coaxed," Brownson wrote in 1873, "no concord between Christ and Belial is possible."[50] The article from which this quote arises condemns first William Draper and his infamous book, *History of the Conflict between Religion and Science*, which was published and read widely in 1874.[51] However, it also condemns the Catholic evolutionist St. George Mivart, whom Zahm would greatly admire in the 1890s. In the 1870s, however, Zahm was far more comfortable with the animosity of Brownson than with the evolutionary conciliations of Mivart.

Second, Brownson held a view of the Catholic Church as infallible in matters of word and deed when it came to science. This idealization of the Church's past would be echoed by Zahm in the 1880s but occurs regularly throughout Brownson's work. Brownson's exaltation of the Church was often done in tandem with a chastisement of those who misuse modern science:

It is false to say that the Church ever opposes light, science, liberty, or social progress. . . . She undoubtedly does not accept all your [scientific] theories, all your mad speculations and airy dreams; but you have no light she rejects,—have made no discovery in science she does not accept. But you talk of your light, as if you were the lights of the age,—of science, as if you had amassed an amount too vast to be compressed within the narrow inclosure of the Church. Quite a mistake, Gentlemen. If you set aside your guesses, your dreams, your mere theories, your unsupported speculations, and reserve only what you have really established, what may be said to be demonstrated, you have nothing not known to the Church long ages before you were born. The Church accepts all your light, and can find room to stow away all your truth; but she has no fondness for your darkness, and no space for your error and falsehood. With your doctrines and speculations she is quite familliar, for they are nothing but old errors and heresies, which she discarded and condemned many ages ago, and which the real movement party has long since outgrown. You are no creators, no inventors. With all your genius, you cannot even invent a new blasphemy.[52]

Zahm's notes from the 1870s are littered with rapturous praise for Brownson's work, including the argument that "science without faith" was exactly what the nineteenth-century philosophers offered, exemplified by Darwin's theories. Because of this, argued Brownson and highlighted by Zahm, the science of the nineteenth century was far below the science of the medieval doctors. In other words, "St. Thomas [Aquinas] had more science than Sir Charles Lyell, or Professor Owen."[53]

A third aspect of Brownson's work that had an impact on Zahm was his vilification of the inductive and empirical nature of modern science. For example, in an essay from 1844, Brownson argues that

there is not, and never was, any such thing as a Baconian Philosophy . . . . But we shall be told, that he has given us a method, that there is a real Baconian Method. Not at all. Nothing seems to us more vague, inconclusive, less scientific, than what Bacon says about Induction, unless it be what Englishmen and Americans say after him, and professedly in his spirit. The Inductive Method of philosophizing was no new discovery of Bacon's, but, so far as sound, is the method of the human mind itself, and has been practised by every philosopher in every age. . . . We doubt whether modern science in any department has as yet come up to the ancient. The more we penetrate into the concealed sense of this old world, the more convinced are we that science was not born with Francis Bacon, the more and more do we feel that the world has forgotten more than it knows.[54]

Brownson's concept of induction was largely synonymous with the other aspects of Bacon's methods we have been discussing. The philosophical concept of induction aligns well with arguments for empiricism and the preference of practice over theory, since induction is commonly seen as the argument from below, or, the production of an overarching philosophical principle based on a multitude of individual facts that have been observed by the philosopher. Brownson is arguing here that this philosophical method was practiced "by every philosopher in every age," which is not true, but it is unclear whether Brownson argues this point from ignorance or obstinance.

Whatever the cause of Brownson's argument, as we will see, Zahm disagreed. However, since Zahm would have been lecturing to Catholic audiences also influenced by Brownson's popularity, Zahm's employment of a Baconian vision of science would have raised questions among those who appreciated a stricter implementation of Brownson's ideas. Zahm would almost definitely have been aware of this challenge when he entered the field in 1883, which explains why his first major lecture employed a rather peculiar rhetorical argument.

Early Lectures on Science and Catholicism (1883–90)

Zahm produced one book and six essays on the subject of science and Catholicism between 1883 and 1890. In *Catholic Church and Modern Science*, Zahm's first foray into the field, Zahm illustrates his approach to the difficult subject. He employs what I call an argument of definitions and dichotomies in that he defines science in two ways, ancient and modern, and then proceeds to show Darwinian evolutionary theories as unsuited to either version of science. In this manner, Zahm attempts to walk the line between the classical Catholic argument exemplified by Brownson and the intellectual scientific argument exemplified by Gray. His argument succeeds in popularity but fails in its long-term efficacy. What happens, Zahm will ask in the 1890s, when ancient beliefs seem to conflict with well-reasoned and evidenced modern scientific ideas? Until 1890, however, this argument grounds Zahm's entire approach to the delicate field.

In *Catholic Church and Modern Science*, the argument unfolds as follows. First, following "the illustrious Dr. Brownson, one of the greatest philosophers our age, or any age, has produced," Zahm defines science as the "highest exercise of reason," and thus one can never find "a single conclusion of true science inconsistent with any article of faith."[55] This is a proposition "that every Catholic regards as self-evident."[56] Second, Zahm defines science as empirical and antitheoretical. We can infer this because of his critiques of aspects of Darwin's theories that are based predominantly on theories rather than empirically determined facts. Evolution, he writes, "is simply an assumption, and an assumption too that rests on other assumptions."[57] Empirically, evolution rests too much on assumptions and not enough on empirical data. It assumes, first, Pierre-Simon Laplace's "mechanical explanation of the formation of the universe"; second, "that organic matter was derived from inorganic matter"; third, "the truth of the theory of spontaneous generation"; fourth, the "the transmutation of species."[58] Since all assumptions must be true for evolution itself to be true, and since none of the assumptions have a "demonstrated foundation in fact," evolution is "a theory that, as it is now taught, would seem to be unprovable."[59]

By employing these two definitions, Zahm sets up a clever dichotomy. On the one hand, he defines science as the highest ideal of rationality, the handmaiden of Catholic faith, which of course it can never contradict.[60] On the other hand, he defines science as empirical and contrary to overtly theoretical approaches. By holding both positions with equal fervor, Zahm can argue that "every new conquest of science is a new argument in the natural order confirmatory of the verities that God has been pleased to reveal."[61] He can condemn atheistic and agnostic science because good science cannot be done without a belief in God.[62] Simultaneously, he can condemn individual scientists for theorizing outside the realm of empirical facts, since progress only occurs with the strictest of empirical standards.[63]

This dichotomy allows Zahm a third logical step: following Brownson, he can defend the Church's historical interactions with science as above reproach. "I do not come as an apologist for the Church," he argues in an 1889 lecture, for "the past history of her good works is all the apology needed. All that is good, grand and sublime in humanity is due to her. Without her, the world would be no better than nineteen centuries ago, when Christ came upon the earth. The

Church has no retraction to make."[64] Because science is simultaneously a handmaiden to theology *and* a modern empirical approach, and because *good science* will never undermine true faith, Zahm argues, there is not now nor ever has there been a mistake of the Church in its approach to science.

A Commitment to Inductive Science

Zahm's dichotomous approach undeniably placed him in contrast with Brownson, despite Zahm's multiple appeals to Brownson's genius. As a devout priest, Zahm appears to have appreciated Brownson's fervor for the Catholic faith and followed him in both his condemnation of atheistic strands of Darwinism and his praise for the infallibility of the Church. Zahm even followed Brownson's lead in terms of understanding *good science* to be equivalent to the science of Thomas Aquinas, an argument that leads to the above dichotomy of *Catholic Church and Modern Science*. Zahm did not follow Brownson, however, when it came to the "inductive sciences."

While his commitment to empirical methods can be seen in 1883, he explicitly spells out his ideas in an 1890 essay titled "Catholic Dogma and Scientific Dogmatism." In it he argues that the origins of empiricism come from within the Church itself and discusses the relationship of empiricism to philosophical sciences:

> One of the great glories of the Church is the introduction, by her children, of the experimental or inductive method into the study of natural and physical science. It was by studying nature in accordance with the principles of induction that the great Catholic scientists, from Galileo and Pascal to our own time, have been so successful in their investigations, and have been able to do so much genuine work in all the branches of science.[65]

Not only did the Church introduce the experimental method into science, but the Catholics who introduced the method also walked carefully within the bounds of proper scientific discovery:

But, while recognizing the value of the inductive philosophy as an aid to the study of nature, and to coordinating the countless facts and phenomena which came before them, these illustrious sons of the Holy Church knew well the extent of its availability as an instrument of research. They were ever conscious that the sphere of its application was circumscribed, and was limited to the discussion of facts and phenomena fully observed and classified, and to conclusions legitimately drawn from such facts and phenomena. They recognized all along the existence of higher and more trustworthy guides—a Christian metaphysics and a divine revelation—to which their inductive philosophy was always made subservient. Over and above their knowledge of facts and their inductions therefrom, they ever retained a science of principles which, corroborated and supplemented by the truths of revelation, prevented them from falling into error.[66]

Zahm's treatment of the history of inductive philosophy—that is, philosophers who believe in the scientific promise of inductive arguments—differs sharply from Brownson's, who believed that philosophers have always practiced inductive philosophy. Zahm sees a definite beginning to the use of induction and experimentation *and,* as a seeming homage to Brownson, argues for the "always . . . subservient" nature of inductive philosophy from the beginning.

Because of his commitment to the validity of the experimental sciences, Zahm is forced early on to leave the door open for evolutionary theories when Brownson would not hear of it. In 1885, for example, after thoroughly questioning the assumptions of said theory, he allows for the possibility of future studies: "Is there anything in the theistic idea of evolution contrary to the declaration of Scripture or to the teachings of Catholic faith? I trust you will not consider me as proclaiming a novelty, or as giving expression to a heterodox opinion, when I state it as my belief that there is not."[67] Zahm goes on to follow the argument of Mivart, that *if* evolution were true, God's creation *could* be maintained as happening through an evolutionary process, since there is no biblical or dogmatic mandate for instantaneous creation. Zahm is careful to distance himself from a *belief* in evolutionary theory at this point, but his affection for the *possibility* of Mivart's hypotheses, should the theory of evolution become demonstrated, is clear.[68] Zahm's devotion to the constant possibility of new scientific discoveries forces him to have an open mind to novelty at a time when the minds of others, like Brownson, firmly remained closed.

Controversies and Provocations (1892–97)

The year 1892 marked both the end of Zahm's time as vice president of Notre Dame and his entry into the professional scientific world with his internationally acclaimed book, *Sound and Music*.[69] While the introduction to the book is important to our study for reinforcing Zahm's commitment to the empirical methods of science, the real value of *Sound and Music* is its cementing of Zahm as a world-class scientist and educator to the national and international Catholic communities.[70] "No one will question that 'Sound and Music' is the most elaborate and exhaustive work of its kind American musical scholarship has yet produced," wrote a reviewer in the *Chicago Tribune*.[71] A reviewer in the *North-Western Chronicle* of St. Paul, Minnesota, foresaw the wider significance of *Sound and Music* for Zahm:

> The work reflects honor on the author, the well-known University of Notre Dame, and the Catholic priesthood; especially in our advanced age and country, it is of great consequence that Catholic priests should in all departments of science be found in the foremost ranks of the leaders of true modern progress.[72]

Sound and Music set Zahm's career on a new path and paved the way for his invitation to give a series of lectures at the 1893 Catholic Summer School, upon which his subsequent publications and reputation would rest.

The following sections examine both the theological and philosophical arguments of the summer lectures, as well as those of *Evolution and Dogma*, the censured text based on the summer lecture material.[73] These arguments illuminate Zahm's continued belief in the possibilities of novelty inherent to the empirical nature of modern science. While Zahm's theological arguments expand in their historical breadth, it is his commitment to the empirical sciences that both endears him to the public and sets him on a path of conflict with the Vatican.

Summer Lectures of 1893

After Zahm presented the lectures in the summer of 1893, they appeared in various publications over the next three years. First, they were printed as a series of essays in the *American Catholic Quarterly Review* in 1894; second, as part 3 of his 1894 book, *Bible, Science, and Faith*; and third, as an official publication of the Catholic Summer School in *Scientific Theory and Catholic Doctrine* in 1896.[74] Furthermore, while Zahm himself confirms that the second part of *Evolution and Dogma* is generally composed of the same arguments found in these lectures, Zahm extended and annotated them for the controversial book, such that they should be considered distinct from the multiple reprintings of the lecture text.[75] As *Scientific Theory and Catholic Doctrine* is the official publication of the Catholic Summer School Library, I reference this version.[76]

While Zahm insisted that the lectures offered little new from his previous material,[77] his detractors maintained that they overstepped the acceptable bounds of the dialogue between evolutionary science and Catholic doctrine.[78] The truth seems to be that the lectures are a culmination of Zahm's progression of thought in the 1880s, and while they do not express any controversial arguments that were not already published (such as Mivart's), Zahm misunderstood their level of acceptance in the Catholic hierarchy in 1893. The lectures offer many improvements over his 1883 *Catholic Church and Modern Science*, but the fundamental arguments remain the same: empirical, inductive science is a good and positive thing in the world; the Church has nothing to fear from science; scientific truths can never negate dogmatic truths.

First, Zahm focuses on the empirical nature of science more vehemently in 1893 than in 1883, perhaps because he was more comfortable condemning the opposition to science on the part of Brownson and those like him. Zahm writes:

It is found, and I think generally conceded, that certain of the representatives of science were the ones who brought on the imbroglio for which there was not the slightest justification. But it is the old story over again; hatred of religion concealed behind some new discovery of science or enveloped in some theory that . . . was raised to the dignity of an indisputable dogma.[79]

Zahm realizes this ground is dangerous: the safer route is to condemn all of modern science and modern scientific methods. Zahm cannot do this, however, given his unwavering commitment to Baconian methods. As such, Zahm uses the first four lectures to explain how some scientists and philosophers deliberately conflate philosophy and science, exacerbating fears of believers and confusing terms. Zahm spends much of these lectures defining concepts such as "materialism," "atheism," "agnosticism," and "monism" over against Catholic doctrines of "creation" and "nature." Misconceptions of these terms, Zahm laments, cause most of the trouble in the discussion of Christianity and evolution. "One of the chief causes of Agnosticism," he writes, "is ignorance of Christian philosophy and theology."[80]

After defining the terms, Zahm spends the next four lectures showing examples of the benefits of his specific definitions by defining Christian doctrines in light of specific scientific theories, including the immutability of species, spontaneous generation, the human soul, and the common evolution hypothesis. For example, in one short paragraph, Zahm highlights the need for limits in science, reaffirms the efficacy of a theory-eschewing modern science, and discusses evidence for a single evolutionary origin for all plants and animals:

[Current theories in] science, I mean experimental science, can tell us nothing more about the origin of life than it can regarding the origin of matter. These are questions which, by their very nature, are outside the sphere of inductive research, and their answers, so far as observation and experiment are concerned, must ever remain in inscrutable and insoluble mystery.[81]

Note how Zahm carefully navigates a defense of Church doctrines alongside a defense of the "experimental" and "observational" nature of science. He employs the same dichotomy in *Catholic Church and Modern Science* but with more emphasis on making the implicit defense of science explicit.

As a further example of this dichotomy, when discussing the possibility of human evolution from apes, Zahm cites an extended passage from Rudolph Virchow's "Anthropology in the Last Twenty Years": "Natural science, as long as it remains such, works only with real, existing objects. A hypothesis may be discussed, but its significance can only be established by producing actual proofs in its favor, either by experiments or direct observations."[82] In other words, not all scientific theories proposed by the best minds are actually proven. No one, Zahm states, has yet found the missing link between humans and apes, nor is anyone likely to do so.[83] However, in case people do find proof, Zahm argues, this would not negate the Catholic doctrine of creation or of the soul, for example, "As to the soul of man we can at once emphatically declare, that it is in nowise evolved from the souls of animals, but is, on the contrary, and in the case of each individual, directly and immediately created by God Himself."[84] Concurrently defending good science and good dogma, Zahm once again points out the possibility of novelty in scientific advances. Such lines undoubtedly hackled his anti-Americanist listeners, but they are entirely consistent with Zahm's assiduous devotion to the latest defendable scientific theories in evolutionary biology. Zahm is, in many ways, simply being honest.

On this point, for perhaps the first time, Zahm slips. He turns to Mivart, author of *Genesis of Species* (1871), a book which, "contrary to expectations of all . . . was not condemned" by Rome.[85] If it were dangerous or heretical to discuss the theory of evolution, or the evolutionary origins of humanity, Zahm argues, would Mivart's book have been publicly discussed for more than twenty years? But whether one accepts Mivart's argument for evolution through secondary causality or other accounts of divine creation, future scientific progress in this area, no matter what it shows, will never be "at variance with the declarations of the sacred text, or the authorized teachings of the Church of Christ."[86]

Apparently unknown to Zahm, Mivart was, in fact, under review for heresy by the Congregation of the Index in the 1890s.[87] To be precise, several of Mivart's articles on the nature of hell were under review and were placed on the index on July 19, 1893, in the midst of Zahm's summer lecture series. Mivart's condemnation on this front did not discredit his evolutionary ideas, but it placed him in a rancorous dispute with the congregation that would end with Mivart leaving the Church in 1900.[88] Because of Mivart's connection to evolution, this dispute was often misunderstood to be about evolution but such was not the case. Whether or not Zahm ever got wind of Mivart's troubles before publishing *Evolution and Dogma*, Zahm's reliance on Mivart shows a clean break from Brownson's influence, as Brownson had earlier condemned Mivart on several occasions for evolutionary ideas.

Zahm finishes his lectures with a rhetorical flourish that reinforces his dual commitment to science and faith with a three-tiered commitment to the relationship between science and the Church. First, empirical science means the inevitability of scientific progress:

And, as the evolutionary idea shall be more studied and developed, the objections which are now urged against it, will, I doubt not, disappear or lose much of their cogency. New theories will be promulgated, new explanations of present difficulties will be suggested, and a clearer knowledge will be vouchsafed of what are the real, if not the chief factors, of the vast evolutionary processes which are at the bottom of all forms of organic development. As in physics so also in biology; continued investigation of facts and phenomena is sure to issue in a clearer and truer view of nature, and of the agencies which have been instrumental in bringing animated nature from its primordial to its present condition. And every new discovery, every new fact brought to light and correlated with facts already known, will mean a step forward; will betoken progress, knowledge and enlightenment.[89]

Second, as science is not the enemy of faith, science and faith can never and have never come into conflict. Instead, Zahm writes, *bad science* condemned Galileo and *bad science*, not anti-science theists, condemns good science (i.e., Baconian, empirical, inductive, experimental science) today:

It is often said, even by those who should be better informed, that the greatest obstacle in the way of the general acceptance of the Copernican theory was the Church, and that the cause of all of Galileo's woes was the ignorant officials of the Inquisition. The fact is, however, that it was not churchmen, as such, who were opposed to the views which Galileo so ardently and so successfully championed. It was rather the old peripatetic system of philosophy, which, after dominating the world of thought for two thousand years, saw itself finally face to face with what, it was felt on all sides, was destined to prove the most formidable adversary it had yet encountered. . . . For we must bear in mind that it is not mistaken theory that retards the progress of science, but rather erroneous observations. All working scientists are aware, often to their cost, that it is inaccurate or mistaken observations which lead men astray, while erroneous theories have often a most stimulating effect. They suggest and provoke new and more exact observations, and thus lead up to true theories and ultimately to a true knowledge of nature.[90]

Third and finally, modern science (as well as modern philosophy) is not on the same level of theological explanations and can never be equal to theological arguments. Evolutionary theory helps to explain how the world works, but neither does it plumb the depths of creation nor raise humanity to something greater than itself:

Science and Evolution tell us of the transcendence and immanence of the First Cause, of the Cause of causes, the Author of all the order and beauty in the world, but it is revelation which furnishes us with the strongest evidence of the relations between the natural and supernatural orders, and brings out in the boldest relief the absolute dependence of the creature on its Maker. It is faith which teaches us how God "binds all together into Himself"; how He quickens and sustains "each thing separately, and all as collected in one."[91]

In other words, science may bring us to a realization of the necessity of God as "First Cause" of the world, but only revelation can help us understand our "absolute dependence" upon said creator. Science may be able to show us God's existence, but only faith can show us how God interacts with the world, and, especially, with us.

Evolution and Dogma

To Zahm, his 1896 book *Evolution and Dogma*, like the summer lectures before it, was less a vessel of new ideas than a popular re-packaging of his message. "The chief difference between the subject-matter ... and that of the lectures as given at the Summer and Winter Schools," he writes, "consists in the foot-notes which have been added to the text, and in a more exhaustive treatment of certain topics herein discussed than was possible in the time allotted to them in the lecture hall."[92]

The book is divided into two parts. The second part contains a slightly modified reprinting of the 1893 lectures, as previously mentioned, and needs little further discussion. Zahm added a few paragraphs and a few more quotations, but the main arguments are identical to those quoted above. The first part, however, is a review of the latest evolutionary science of the late nineteenth century. While it was ignored by the Congregation of the Index in its evaluation of the book, it serves as the main purpose for Zahm writing the book. In essence, the first half of *Evolution and Dogma* represents the pinnacle of Zahm's commitment to the empirical nature of modern science. If scientific theories are true inasmuch as they are demonstrated to be true, Zahm argues, then the entire case for the possibility of generic and human evolution rests not upon theological dogmas but upon a close examination of the scientific studies that postulate whether or not such evolutionary movements have happened. "Excluding the philosophical theories which have been built on Evolution, and the religious discussions to which it has given rise," he writes, "let us proceed to examine the evidences for and against it as a scientific theory." He continues:

> Let us inquire what are the grounds for the almost universal acceptance of this theory by contemporary scientists, and see

whether the arguments advanced in its support are in accord with the canons of sound logic and principles of true philosophy. The question is entirely one of the natural science, not of metaphysics, and hence one of evidence which is more or less tangible. What, then, are the evidences of organic Evolution to which modern scientists usually appeal? This is the question to which all that precedes is but little more than a preamble, and a question, too, that well deserves our closest and most serious consideration.[93]

Having situated the source of his argument as the "universal acceptance of this theory by contemporary scientists," Zahm offers a detailed discussion of what he considers the four classes of arguments for evolution: "classification, morphology, embryology, geographical distribution and geological succession."[94] His conclusion? General evolutionary theory, including human evolution, holds the "highest degree" of probability: "we may not be prepared to admit that the theory has the force of a demonstration . . . [but] it nevertheless possesses for the working naturalist a value that can be fully appreciated only by those who have labored in the museum and in the laboratory."[95]

In contrast, Zahm wholeheartedly discredits any anti-evolution arguments for the immediate creation of species by means of *the same methods by which he discredited evolution* in 1883: "special creation, as an explanation of the multitudinous forms of life with which the earth teems . . . is but an assumption, and an assumption, too, that has no warrant outside of the individual opinions of certain commentators of Scripture."[96] In 1883 Zahm wrote: "At the outset, I must tell you that evolution is, at best, only a theory—only an hypothesis. It is simply an assumption, and an assumption too that rests on other assumptions. . . . Evolution, so far, is, at best, a conjecture, a theory, not only unproven, but a theory that, as it is now taught, would seem to be unprovable."[97] Zahm's opinions of the science of evolutionary theory have clearly changed, but his scientific methods, just as clearly, have not.

He continues the argument in *Evolution and Dogma* with virtually the same language from *Catholic Church and Modern Science*, only the objective has changed: "Special creation is not a scientific theory but a metaphysical assumption, and does not hold ground against the vast evidence for evolutionary theories." The theory of evolution "unquestionably occupies a high rank among the best accredited theories of contemporary science," and rests "on as firm a basis as did the Copernican theory in the days of Galileo and Tycho Brahe."[98]

Nevertheless, Zahm argues, the questions have not all been answered. While the general theory of common ancestry seems highly likely, "all the theories of Evolution connected with . . . Lamarckism and Darwinism, Neo-Lamarckism and Neo-Darwinism, involve numerous and grave difficulties, which, so far, have not been satisfactorily answered."[99] "It is clear that, as yet, we have no theory of Evolution which is competent to coordinate all the facts that Evolution is supposed to embrace. . . . All of them, doubtless, contain an element of truth, but how far they can be relied upon as guides in research it is still impossible to say."[100] He concludes by cautioning that "the lack of this perfected theory . . . does not imply that we have not already an adequate basis for a rational assent to the theory of organic Evolution."[101]

Given that the second half of the book was composed of the 1893 lectures, one must assume that the first half, summarized above, was the impetus for writing *Evolution and Dogma*. The fact that both Zardetti and Buonpensiere, Zahm's accuser and the official reporter for the Congregation of the Index, entirely ignored the first half is all the more devastatingly ironic because of its importance in the volume. *Evolution and Dogma* likely stands as the most complete argument for evolutionary theory that any Catholic author in the late nineteenth century had written, a fact that undoubtedly helped to propel the book to immense popularity.

Defining Zahm's Evolutionary Position

It seems fitting to briefly reflect on what precisely Zahm believed and did not believe about evolutionary biology. While these precise details end up mattering very little to his accusers, they do help us twenty-first-century evolutionists understand the scientific mind of this enigmatic man in late nineteenth-century America. According to Phillip Sloan, whose recent study stands as by far the most complete on

Zahm's evolutionary position, Zahm's specific stance closely followed St. George Mivart, who argued for a concept of creation that was both "from nothing" (ex nihilo) and a continual act of the divine.[102] As Zahm himself wrote, "the action of God in the order of nature is concurrent and overruling... but is not miraculous in the sense in which the word 'miraculous' is ordinarily understood. He operates by and through the laws which He instituted in the beginning, and which are still maintained by His Providence."[103]

This divine action, Zahm and Mivart both argue, differs from William Paley's concept of a "watchmaker God" in that God grants the potentiality for nearly unlimited changes to all creatures on earth and throughout the universe. The creatures' changes, via evolution, are thus instances of "derivative" creation, distinct from God's original creation. This concept gives Zahm a way to support a notion of both God's Providence and the lack of need for miracles in evolutionary development.[104] This notion of derivative creation also differs, argues Sloan, from a form of neo-Lamarckianism that "appeal[ed] to an inner vital force that directs evolutionary development."[105] Sloan continues:

> There is, to be sure, for both Zahm and Mivart, an inner-directed purposeful development of the natural world as a larger system, and in this sense evolution is a teleological process. . . . But this neither depends on an inner will of the organism, nor does it mean there can be no mistakes, extinctions or dead ends in the process. . . . The critical issue for Zahm is that the system works by natural laws, and it is the *existence* of the laws themselves, rather than their specific mode of action in time, that is at the center of Zahm's theistic evolution.[106]

In terms of humanity's place in evolution, Zahm follows Mivart and continues with another facet of the argument for derivative creation, noting that the human soul must have arrived via a "different source" of divine creative action.[107] This became known as the "dual origin" position in theistic evolution, and a version of this position remains widely held in Catholicism today.[108] It is important to remember that both Zahm's general theory of derivative creation and his position on the evolution of humans sharply reject Darwin's theory of natural selection, especially as it applies to humanity.[109] He admits in *Evolution and Dogma* that Darwin's thoughts hold some value, but he is just as clear that Darwin's notions of evolutionary progress are severely flawed. Nevertheless, the general process of evolution seemed to him beyond any doubt, and Mivart's derivative concept of evolutionary progress, combined with the dual evolution of humanity's body and soul, seemed the best scientific and theological explanation for the phenomena.[110]

———

From his 1871 student lecture to his 1896 *Evolution and Dogma*, many things changed in the life of John Zahm, but his Baconian vision of modern science remained consistent throughout his career. How he applied this vision for science depended on circumstances and his own understanding of the best science of the time. From Brownson to Mivart, Zahm's commitment to the inductive, empirical, experimental, and theory-eschewing nature of modern science propelled him to author both a successful scientific text in 1892 as well as a rather provocative series of lectures on theology in 1893. His ability to popularize an idea allowed him to transform this simple commitment into a world-renowned argument for the endless possibilities of modern science under the guidance of the Catholic Church.

As the next chapter will show, Zahm's overarching devotion to the Baconian nature of modern science was precisely the opposite of what the Catholic hierarchy of the nineteenth century labored to create, first through the lens of monarchy, then through the lens of cultural rejection, and finally through the lens of Aquinas. Contrary to Zahm, the Neo-Scholastics who dominated the end of the nineteenth century would argue that one can only find a judge of good knowledge by rejecting the popular philosophies such as Baconianism and Kantianism and by accepting the dogmatic truth and philosophical insight of Aquinas. As such, Pope Leo XIII and his theological followers would find a strong footing for a floundering Catholic hierarchy but would leave the modern scientific world, including John Zahm, behind.

Portrait of student John A. Zahm, ca. 1867–1870s.

All images in the gallery are reproduced with the kind permission of the University of Notre Dame Archives.

University of Notre Dame,

Notre Dame, Ind., Nov 14 1867

Master J. A. Zahm.

Dear friend

As you seem so anxious to come & try Yourself here, I am willing to accept Your offer viz: on Your paying $50 to keep you for five months in the College. You may come anytime your parents will deem it expedient

Yours in haste

E. Sorin.

Letter from Rev. Edward F. Sorin to John A. Zahm starting school at Notre Dame, dated November 14, 1867.

Portrait of Rev. John A. Zahm, CSC, ca. 1870s.

Professor Rev. John A. Zahm, CSC (seated, with hat), with a group of students, posed outside with scientific instruments, ca. 1870s.

Professor Rev. John A. Zahm, CSC (seated, center left), with a group of male students, posed outside with scientific instruments, c1870s.

Aloysius Philodemic Association group photo with Professor Rev. John A. Zahm (front row, third from right) and students, 1875.

Notre Dame Ind. Apl 25 1893

Rev dear Father

I received your 2 interesting letters & felt delighted with your success in the course of your lectures. I hope the end will be as gratifying as the opening. God be praised for it. Mr. Drwyer is gone.

When will you be home again? We will be happy to welcome again the great & beloved President on monday

In haste for the mail
Your devoted wellwisher
E Sorin csc

Rev. J. a. Zahm csc

Letter from Rev. Edward F. Sorin to Rev. John A. Zahm congratulating Zahm on the success of his lectures and hoping that he will be home soon, April 25, 1893. The letterhead features an engraving of the Main Building.

Physics class with Rev. John A. Zahm, CSC (standing, center), posed on the steps of Science Hall (now LaFortune Student Center), 1893.

Rev. John A. Zahm, CSC (fourth from the left) with the students of his physics class posed on the staircase inside Science Hall (now LaFortune Student Center), ca. 1895.

Full-length portrait of Rev. John A. Zahm, CSC, ca. 1890s. [modern copy print]

Prot. 11411.

Ex Audientia SSmi habita die 29 Ja: 1895.

Cum ex indubiis testimoniis compertum fuerit Ph. D. Ioannem Zahm presbyterum Congregationis S. Crucis, Religionis zelo, morum integritate aliisque ecclesiasticis dotibus praeditum, in tradendis philosophicis discipli- nis valde esse commendabilem, SSmus Dominus Noster Leo divina providentia P.P. XIII, referente me infrascripto Sacrae Congnis de Propaganda Fide Secretario, eumdem in Philosophica Fa- cultate Doctorem creare ac declarare benigne dignatus est cum omnibus honoribus et iuribus quae Philosophiae Doctoribus propria sunt, ea ta- men lege ut consuetam Fidei professionem iuxta formulam a fel. rec. Pio IV et Pio IX praescri- ptam coram Ordinario suo emittat.

   Contrariis quibuscumque non obstanti-

Front and back page of a letter in Latin from Rev. Agostino Ciasca, Archbishop of Larissa and Secretary of the Congregation of the Propagation of the Faith, to Rev. John A. Zahm, CSC, conferring a doctorate degree from the Vatican, January 29, 1895.

Datum Romae ex Aed. S. Congnis de Propagan
da Fide die et anno ut supra

    A. Archiep. Larissen. Secr.

Angers 11 7bre 1898

Révérend et bien cher Père

J'ai reçu votre lettre ici, où
nous venons de terminer
la retraite.
Je regrette toute cette suite
de circonstances qui viennent
retarder le départ du
P. Linneborn, mais personne
n'en est responsable, et il
faut bien les subir jusqu'à
nouvel ordre —
Je remercie donc le P. départ
à Rome, ainsi que vous
le dites —
Je pense que Rome tolérera
encore un peu ce provisoire.
En tout cas, faites en sorte
que ce provisoire soit le
plus court possible —
J'ai toujours peur de déplaire
à Rome —

Front and back page of letter in French from Rev. Gilbert Français to Rev. John A. Zahm, CSC, expressing frustration with decision from Rome—

Ne songeons même pas à
pour la question de Washington.
— Elle est officiellement et
légalement décidée — Quant
Mg sera résolue par un
établissement définitif,
toutes les voix opposantes
seront bien forcées de se
taire.

J'espère que le père Cavanaugh
va se remettre vite et bien —
C'est une santé qui nous
est bien précieuse — Je prie
pour lui de cœur — Veuillez
donc le lui dire —

Ayez courage, mon cher Père —
Le bon Dieu est avec vous, et
vous Mg faire grande et
utile besogne, malgré toutes
les difficultés qui peuvent
vous attendre.
Je suis toujours l'homme
le plus prêt à vous aider par
tous les moyens en mon pouvoir.

Croyez moi bien vôtre en N. S.

C. Français
Sup. Gén. C. S.

Je retourne à Neuilly demain ou
après demain —

published the day before Français wrote the letter—and asking Zahm to
have courage and quickly submit, September 11, 1898.

Portrait of Rev. John A. Zahm, CSC, examining plants outside of a building, ca. 1910s.

Rev. John A. Zahm, CSC (*far left*), Theodore Roosevelt (*center*), and others at a train station in South America, ca. 1913–14.

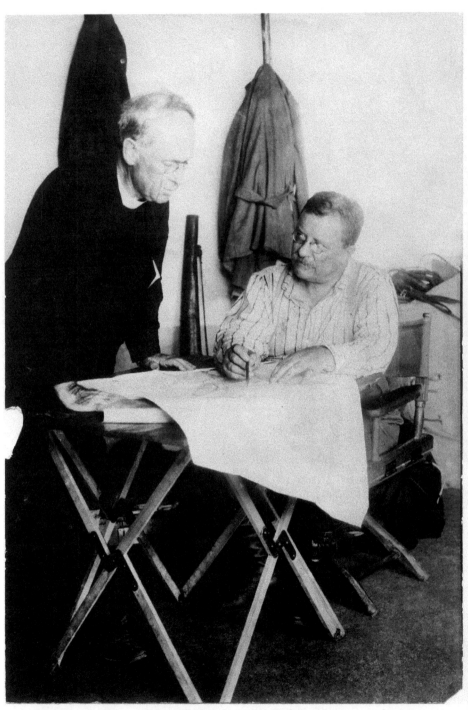

Rev. John A. Zahm, CSC, and Theodore Roosevelt looking over a map on their travels in Brazil, ca. 1913–14.

Rev. John A. Zahm, CSC, and Theodore Roosevelt sitting outside during their travels in South America, ca. 1913–14.

Zahm Hall exterior taken with infrared film or filter, ca. 1950s.

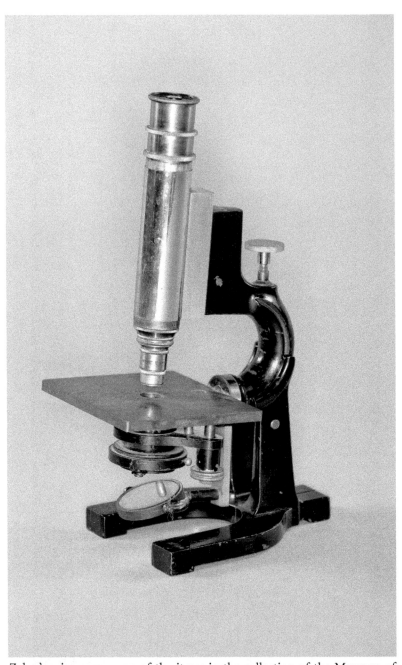

Zahm's microscope, one of the items in the collection of the Museum of Biodiversity in the Jordan Hall of Science.

CHAPTER 4

The Development of Catholic Teachings on Science, Faith, and Reason in the Nineteenth Century

After considering Zahm's philosophy of science in the previous chapter, we now shift our focus to the philosophical positions on science, faith, and reason that governed the official voice of the Catholic Church. Specifically, we look at the chronological framework of politics, theology, and philosophy that sets up a textual analysis of the specific writings from those involved in Zahm's censure, especially the members of the Congregation of the Index. This chapter centers around four pivotal moments in nineteenth-century Catholicism, placed historically in table 4.1: the publication of the 1864 Syllabus of Modern Errors by Pope Pius IX (appendix A in this volume); the promulgation of the document *Dei Filius* by the First Vatican Council of 1869–70; the papacy's 1870 loss of temporal power with the capture of Rome; and the promulgation of the encyclical *Aeterni Patris* by Pope Leo XIII in 1879.

These events relate to the scholarly conceptions of science within the Catholic Church in the late nineteenth century because they either directly affected the official relationship of Catholic theology to reason, and thus to modern science, or represented a drastic political

Table 4.1. The Pope versus Modernity: From the French Revolution
to *Aeterni Patris*

1789	French Revolution begins.
1790	Decree prohibiting monastic vows (13 February) and Civil Constitution of the Clergy (12 July) published, effectively removing the authority of the Vatican from all clerics and federalizing Catholicism in France. Clergy become state employees. Monasticism is illegal. Bishops are elected, not appointed. Civil Constitution of the Clergy in place until 1795.
1796	Napoleon invades Rome, declares Roman Republic.
1798	Pope Pius VI taken prisoner, brought to France. Dies 1799 in captivity.
1800	Pope Pius VII elected. Papal States restored.
1804	Pope Pius VII crowns Napoleon.
1808–9	France captures Rome and Papal States, again. Pius VII taken prisoner.
1814–15	Pius VII returns to Rome following abdication of Napoleon. Congress of Vienna returns Papal States to Vatican rule. Pius restores Jesuit order (out since 1773).
1823	Pope Leo XII elected.
1824	Return of the Roman College to Jesuit control and direction.
1829	Pope Pius VIII elected, dies shortly after.
1830	Pope Gregory XVI elected. An academic and a monk, Gregory has never before held a pastoral office.
1830s	Against liberalism: Gregory XVI publishes *Mirari Vos* and *Singulari Vos* against the liberalism and democratic values of French priest Félicité de Lammenais.
1840s	Against traditionalism: Abbe Bautain's epistemological explication of Friedrich Heinrich Jacobi's *Verstand* (understanding) and *Vernunft* (reason) culminate with a declaration that reason alone can never reach God. Bautain is brought to Rome and "convinced" of his errors. Gregory XVI says that "he sinned by too much faith."
1846	Gregory XVI dies, wildly unpopular, and Pius IX—a moderate alternative—is elected pope.
1848–50	Exile of Pope Pius IX. The 1848 French Revolution forces his exile until 1850. His politics switch, and he remains a staunch defender of the temporal/political power of the papacy until it is taken from him in 1870.
1850s	Against Rationalism and advancing Scholasticism: popular philosopher Anton Günther's work is placed on the index of prohibited books. *Civiltà Cattolica* is founded at the request of Pius IX (against the wishes of the Jesuit general).

Table 4.1. (continued)

1854	In *Ineffabilis Deus*, Pius IX "declares, pronounces, and defines" the Immaculate Conception of the Blessed Virgin Mary. Leads to questions of papal primacy (mostly in political and non-Catholic circles).
1864	
6 December	Pius IX announces his intention to call a general council.
8 December	Pius IX publishes the encyclical *Quanta Cura* and the attached Syllabus of Modern Errors.
1868	Pius IX publishes apostolic letter "Aeterni Patris" (not to be confused with Leo XIII's encyclical in 1879), calling for the council to begin in December 1869.
1869	Johannes Franzelin's "Definition Doctrinae Catholicae contra multiplices errores" becomes "schema I" for what will become *Dei Filius*. Goes through two explicit versions in committee. Joseph Kleutgen assists in further drafts.
1870	
January–March	Third and fourth drafts of *Dei Filius* (schemas III, IV) presented to the First Vatican Council. They include some significant changes concerning the "autonomy" of reason and science. Document limited from eleven-plus chapters to four.
24 April	Final draft of *Dei Filius* approved (unanimously) and published.
17 July	Doctrine of papal infallibility, *Pastor Aeternus*, approved.
19 July	France declares war on Prussia. Unrest begins in Italy.
19 September	Rome falls to Italian and Prussian troops. Pius IX: "I surrender to violence. From this moment on I am prisoner of the King." Italian independence begins.
20 October	Pius IX officially "adjourns" the First Vatican Council for a date to be fixed later. This, clearly, does not happen.
1878	Pius IX dies, much bereaved and loved by the people. Pope Leo XIII elected.
1879	
4 August	*Aeterni Patris* published.
15 October	Pontifical Academy of St. Thomas Aquinas created by Leo XIII as a practical exemplar of the desires of *Aeterni Patris*.

Notes: "he sinned by too much faith" (Gregory XVI), from Edgar Hocedez, *Histoire de la théologie au XIXe siècle*, vol. 2. (Paris: Desclée de Brouwer, 1952), 73, quoted in McCool, *Catholic Theology*, 54; "I surrender to violence. . . ." (Pius IX), quoted in Chadwick, *History of the Popes*, 217.

shift that affected the Church's opinions on the hierarchy of philosophy, modernity, and modern science. The Syllabus, I argue, was both political and dogmatic: it placed strict boundaries around accepted Catholic scholarship while setting the theological and philosophical stage for the First Vatican Council. *Dei Filius*, in comparison, should be seen as almost entirely dogmatic, filling out specifics in the boundaries of the Syllabus while offering a foundational layer of Catholic philosophy and theology, especially as it pertains to reason and science.

The fall of Rome in 1870 was clearly a political event, but one with profound philosophical and theological effects on the Church. The removal of all political power from the papacy not only immediately transformed the responsibilities of the pope but also engendered an abrupt end to the ecumenical council in full swing. I argue that it was precisely this political disaster, along with the feeling of an incompleteness to the council, which led to the election of Pope Leo XIII and the publication of *Aeterni Patris*. Leo XIII's pivotal encyclical—both dogmatic and highly political—is the final layer of this complex chronological framework of politics, theology, and philosophy. Reiterating the central points concerning faith and reason implied in the Syllabus and codified in *Dei Filius*, the 1879 encyclical declared that the exemplar of Catholic scholarship, of all kinds, is Thomas Aquinas.

Syllabus of Modern Errors (1864)

The Syllabus of Modern Errors was neither a stand-alone document nor one published in a hasty attempt to quell the dangers of liberalism in the mid-nineteenth century.[1] Containing a list of eighty "errors" condemned by Pope Pius IX, it was published as the postscript to his encyclical *Quanta Cura*, which gave the rationale behind the Syllabus. The encyclical, like so many in the decades before it, did not mince words when it came to the problems of the current society.[2]

> Our Predecessors have, with Apostolic fortitude, constantly resisted the nefarious enterprises of wicked men, who, like raging waves of the sea foaming out their own confusion, and promising

liberty whereas they are the slaves of corruption, have striven by their deceptive opinions and most pernicious writings to raze the foundations of the Catholic religion and of civil society, to remove from among men all virtue and justice, to deprave persons, and especially inexperienced youth, to lead it into the snares of error, and at length to tear it from the bosom of the Catholic Church.[3]

In the next eleven paragraphs, Pius proceeds to describe exactly what he intended the Syllabus to be, a reminder:

We raised Our voice, and in many published Encyclical Letters and Allocutions delivered in Consistory, and other Apostolic Letters, we condemned the chief errors of this most unhappy age, and we excited your admirable episcopal vigilance, and we again and again admonished and exhorted all sons of the Catholic Church, to us most dear, that they should altogether abhor and flee from the contagion of so dire a pestilence. (*QC*, para. 2)

But people have not listened, and the right following of religion has fallen away:

Since where religion has been removed from civil society, and the doctrine and authority of divine revelation repudiated, the genuine notion itself of justice and human right is darkened and lost, and the place of true justice and legitimate right is supplied by material force, thence it appears why it is that some, utterly neglecting and disregarding the surest principles of sound reason, dare to proclaim that "the people's will, manifested by what is called public opinion or in some other way, constitutes a supreme law, free from all Divine and human control; and that in the political order accomplished facts, from the very circumstance that they are accomplished, have the force of right." (*QC*, para. 4)

Because of the "great perversity of depraved opinions," Pius writes, "we reprobate, proscribe, and condemn all the singular and evil opinions and doctrines separately mentioned in this letter, and will and command that they be thoroughly held by all children of the Catholic Church as reprobated, proscribed and condemned" (*QC*, para. 6).

Quanta Cura was not simply a castigation of evils, but a call for unification. After a universal appeal to "approach with confidence the throne of grace, that we may obtain mercy and find grace in timely aid," Pius declares that all bishops should grant one month of 1865 as "a Plenary Indulgence in the form of Jubilee" (*QC*, para. 10). With castigation and reprobation, Pius writes, comes mercy, love, and faithfulness. The pope, while staunchly aligned against the modern world, was a devoted pastor to his flock and sought to castigate only to bring people closer to that precise fold of Catholicism defined by "auctoritate Nostra Apostolica" (our apostolic authority).

This is not to say that the documents were received in any such manner. As with any papal document, today or two hundred years ago, the reception of Pius's *Quanta Cura* and Syllabus produced more than a few attitudes of derision and comments on his obvious detachment from the modern world.

The *Syllabus* left Europe with a poor image of the Pope: as of the extreme right, an obscurantist about the development of thought or politics, an unwise person who could not predict the effect of his words. This impression had a touch of caricature. But partly it was the right image. There was a sense in which the Pope did choose to live dangerously. But the more resolute he was—and the more dangerously he lived—the more the protective instinct of Catholicism gathered round his person and his throne.[4]

The eightieth and final error of the Syllabus exemplifies this protective instinct: "The Pope can and should reconcile himself to, and agree with, progress, liberalism, and new modes of government."[5]

Indeed, the most remarkable part of the Syllabus, appearing in an era of violent revolutions and emerging capitalistic enterprises, is the brazen language that holds it together. The eightieth error, however laughable from our present context, marks a document meant to be nothing less than the most potent form of Catholic dogma since the last ecumenical council, the Council of Trent, in the sixteenth century. These errors, in fact, would become the basis for the unanimously approved constitution *Dei Filius* of the First Vatican Council and would cement the Syllabus as a turning point in nineteenth-century Catholic thought. While the errors may have been a source of ridicule when they were written, they unquestionably set the stage for the next century of Catholic theology and philosophy.

Outline of the Syllabus

The Syllabus is divided into ten sections, nine of which have specific errors attached to them (see table 4.2). The fourth section includes only a reference back to four previous encyclicals where "pests" have been "rebuked in the severest terms." As each of the other nine sections also reference errors reprimanded in earlier encyclicals, we can remove section IV from our detailed analysis due to the lack of emphasis on it in the Syllabus. Furthermore, the last six sections have little in common with the discussion between faith and reason and thus only tangentially help construct the theological-philosophical framework by which scholars of the 1890s related Catholic dogma to science. However, as they make up a majority of the document and aid to the political entrenchment, it is helpful to spend a few moments discussing their reach and aims.

Table 4.2. Syllabus of Modern Errors, Section Headings

I.	Pantheism, Naturalism, and Absolute Rationalism (1–7)
II.	Moderate Rationalism (8–14)
III.	Indifferentism, Latitudarianism (15–18)
IV.	Socialism, Communism, Clandestine Societies, Biblical Societies, Liberal Clerical Societies (only a note)
V.	Errors about the Church and Her Rights (19–38)
VI.	Errors about Civil Society on Its Own and in Relationship with the Church (39–55)
VII.	Errors about Natural and Christian Ethics (56–64)
VIII.	Errors about Christian Marriage (65–74)
IX.	Errors about the Civil Supremacy of the Roman Pontiff (75–77)
X.	Errors Which Reference Modern Liberalism (78–80)

Errors 19–80: Church and State

Sections V–IX, in one view, begin and end with error 19. If this error were repented, the rest would follow quickly thereafter:

19. The Church is not a true and perfect society of equal liberty, nor does it enjoy special and immovable rights conferred upon it by its Divine Founder, but, instead, the civil power can define the rights and limits within which the Church may exercise its authority. (Pius IX, Syllabus, § V)

The rest of section V, as well as sections VI–X, deal with specific rights and authorities granted, or not granted, to the Church in modern society. They include such things as:

30. The immunity of the Church and ecclesiastical persons derives its authority from civil law. . . .
40. The doctrine of the Catholic Church is opposed to the well-being and interests of human society. . . .
55. The Church should be separated from the State, and the State from the Church. . . .
63. One may refuse obedience to legitimate leaders; indeed, one may even revolt against them. . . .
76. The abolition of the political power possessed by the Apostolic See would be of greatest advantage to the liberty and prosperity of the Church.

These errors, and others like them, spoke directly to the political situation facing Pius. They represent a further hardening against democracy and nineteenth-century liberalism, and their approach is unequivocally negative: good and properly ordered Christian society is falling apart, and these errors are contributing to its downfall.

If a scholar desired to both discuss a new approach to modernity *and* remain faithful to the pope, the only choice would be a novel construction of political, theological, and philosophical ideas, a new Catholic way of thinking to combat the changing times. However, while errors 19–80 provided the political and social guidelines, it was the first eighteen errors that provided the theological and philosophical bounds within which Catholic theology would be formed during the next half century.

Errors 1–18: Faith and Reason

"During the two decades between 1846 and 1866," writes Gerald McCool, "Pius IX and the Roman congregations intervened repeatedly to influence the course of Catholic theology."[6] Beginning with the 1846 encyclical *Qui Pluribus,* directed against "the growing rationalism and agnosticism among European intellectuals," Pius labored to support and define the proper relationship between faith and reason.[7] He desired moderation but found himself consistently at odds with views that he felt would undermine both the papacy and the Holy Catholic Church. This feeling led to the first three sections of the Syllabus, which are best seen as, quite simply, reactions.[8] Pius published the Syllabus to set a precedent and to create a wall around proper Catholic doctrine, within which, once accepted, one can confidently construct sound doctrinal statements that would be ratified by the upcoming ecumenical council. In order to place the Syllabus into context and thus properly understand the philosophical boundaries set by Pius, this section analyzes the errors by giving examples of the philosophers that may have inspired them. Such a methodology illustrates that the Syllabus provides a clear explanatory groundwork for Catholic doctrine during the last forty years of the nineteenth century.

The first section begins with an argument against pantheism and Rationalism, two popular philosophical positions that were exemplified by Georg Hegel in the early nineteenth century. For example, note the third error:

> 3. Human reason, with entirely no regard for God, is the sole arbiter of truth and falsehood, of good and evil; it is its own law to itself and is inherently sufficient in providing for the well-being both of people and of nations. (Pius IX, Syllabus, § I)

And this passage from Hegel's *Phenomenology of Spirit*:

Reason is Spirit when its certainty of being all reality has been raised to truth, and it is conscious of itself as its own world, and of the world as itself. The coming-to-be of Spirit was indicated in the immediately preceding movement in which the objection of consciousness, the pure category, rose to be the Notion of Reason.[9]

It is helpful to remember that the errors in the Syllabus are not logical debates, but philosophical refutations. Pius is not debating with the likes of Hegel, but rather refuting Hegel and the like by stating the Church's undisputable truth. This use of refutation instead of argumentation, however, failed to serve the philosophical theologians of the nineteenth century. Hegel did not simply replace God with Reason, Hegel attempted to redefine the conceptions of Reason, God, and Morality altogether. Error 1 belies this careful delineation:

1. There exists no supreme, most wise, and most provident divine being distinct from the universe, and God is none other than nature, and is therefore subject to changes. In truth, God is created in man and in the world, and all things are God and have the very substance of God. Thus God is one and the same thing as the world, and, in the same manner, spirit is the same as matter, necessity as liberty, true as falsehood, good as evil, and justice as injustice. (Pius IX, Syllabus, § I)

Within this error one finds a plethora of philosophical distinctions, many of which contradict one another. Indeed, it would seem difficult to find someone who actually *agreed* with all facets of this error!

For example, Hegel may have agreed that God and the world could be one and the same, but one would have to read Ludwig Feuerbach's *The Essence of Christianity* to understand how humanity could have created the idea of God:

What man calls Absolute Being, his God, is his own being. The power of the object over him is therefore the power of his own being. Thus, the power of the object of feeling is the power of feeling itself; the power of the object of reason is the power of reason itself; and the power of the object of will is the power of the will itself.[10]

Feuerbach began lecturing and publishing openly on atheism and the anthropomorphic nature of religion in the 1850s, and it is not hard to imagine that the ideas he represented had a clear influence on the first section of the Syllabus.

Errors 4–7 follow the same pattern. They decry philosophical ideas commonly associated with the rationalistic school of Hume, Kant, Hegel, and many others, while avoiding any sort of philosophical argumentation:

> 4. All truths of religion derive from the inherent strength of human reason. As such, reason is the foremost standard by which humans attain knowledge: all truths, of every sort and kind, can and should follow from it.
>
> 5. Divine revelation is imperfect and therefore subject to a continual and indefinite advancement which corresponds with the advancement of human reason.
>
> 6. Christian faith opposes human reason. Furthermore, divine revelation not only fails to benefit human perfection, but it, in truth, injures it.
>
> 7. The prophecies and miracles set forth and narrated in the Sacred Scriptures are the fictions of poets, and the mysteries of the Christian faith are the result of philosophical investigations. The books of the Old and New Testaments contain mythical inventions. Jesus Christ is himself a mythical fiction.
>
> (Pius IX, Syllabus, § I)

There are many ways one could adhere to these errors, but along with the first three, they represent the furthest extremes from the Christian faith. While the errors may seem obvious and repetitious to some today, a historical placement helps one to see how they functioned as the boundaries within which one could have free reign to practice proper Catholic philosophy and theology.

The second section of errors is titled "Moderate Rationalism" and has the same characteristics as the first seven: they are pronouncements, not arguments, and they cannot all be held simultaneously without contradiction. These errors are directed at many philosophers, but Immanuel Kant could probably represent their figurehead, whether or not philosophers who held these errors would have agreed with Kant. Kant firmly believed in God and saw great value in Christianity but simultaneously relegated theology to a specific line of philosophical arguments to be proven or disproven. As such, errors 8–14 seem quite pointedly attacking ideas surrounding Kant's legacy, which could be said to include Hegel and Feuerbach as well as many others:[11]

> 8. Because human reason is equaled to religion, theological disciplines must be treated in the same manner as philosophical ones.
> 9. All the dogmas of the Christian religion are, without exception, the object of scientific knowledge or philosophy. Human reason, historically developed thus far, can perceive, by its inherent strength and principles, true understanding of even the most obtuse dogmas, as long as such dogmas had been proposed in terms of rationality.
> 10. While the philosopher may be one thing, philosophy is another. While it is the right and duty of philosophers to submit to the authority he considers true, philosophy neither can nor should submit to any authority.
> 11. Not only should the Church never judge philosophy, but it should also tolerate the errors of philosophy, relinquishing correction to philosophy itself.
> 12. The decrees of the Apostolic See and of the Roman Congregations impede the unconstrained progress of knowledge.
> 13. The method and principles by which the antiquated scholastic doctors developed sacred theology are no longer adaptable to the needs of our age and the progress of knowledge.
> 14. Philosophy should be discussed without taking any account of supernatural revelation.
>
> (Pius IX, Syllabus, § II)

Like the first seven, these errors could be interpreted in a variety of ways. For example, error 12 could be seen as either an outright attack on Christianity, like Feuerbach, or a simple negation of the impact of Christianity and Christian doctrines through the realization of the ideals of Reason, like Kant or Hegel.

The fourteenth error, which seems to follow quite readily from the others, has a footnote attaching itself to the errors of Catholic philosopher Anton Günther, who was condemned twice by the Vatican in the seven years preceding the Syllabus. It is helpful to note why Günther is specifically mentioned when so many others could be. Anton Günther's post-Kantian theological-philosophical system gained many, many adherents in Catholic Austria and Germany in the 1830s and 1840s, as he presented a full rebuke of Kantian rationalistic metaphysics through a Catholic philosophical lens.

Unlike the Vatican, Günther did not reject the Enlightenment but sought to remedy it. Instead of forcing the intelligent believer to make a choice between faith and reason, Günther argued for a third path in a progressive philosophy of historical revelation that mimicked "Christ's inner experience":[12]

The philosophy of revelation is not a timeless, unhistorical deduction of obvious conclusions from first principles which are equally evident to all men at all times. Philosophy must progressively increase the content of the intuitions given to intelligence in its receptive act of faith, and it must progressively clarify their content through reflective systematic thematization. The passage of time and society's growth in scientific knowledge and culture profoundly influence the depth and extent of intelligence's receptive intuitions and the clarity, rigor, and coherence of their reflection thematization.[13]

This outlook was too progressive for the mid-century mindset of the Vatican, and Günther's arguments that "theology must be given greater freedom" by the pope to combat modernism did not win him any favors.[14] As the Syllabus notes, Günther's works were condemned several times, with this mention in the document being only the most recent. Directly after error 14, the Syllabus reads:

NB—To the system of rationalism belong, for the most part, the errors of Anton Günther, condemned in the Letter to Card. Archbp. of Cologne, *Eximiam tuam*, June 15, 1857, and in the Letter to Bishop of Breslau, *Dolore haud mediocri*, Apr. 30, 1860. (§ II)

The specific mention of Günther, perhaps the best known of Catholic philosophers in the mid-nineteenth century, reinforces the status of the Syllabus as a boundary document for future Catholic scholarly work. The mention of Günther also assures the reader that his work is quite explicitly *not* an example of the future of Catholic philosophy.

Finally, it is helpful to consider the relationship of these particular errors to modern conceptions of science and scientific research. Error 13, in particular, seems relevant in discussing "the progress of knowledge." There does not seem to be any evidence that this statement was taken to diminish the importance of scientific research, but "philosophy" covered most of what one would consider "science" in the mid-nineteenth century, especially in the non-English-speaking world at the Vatican. One can thus assume that the authors of the Syllabus intended the errors to apply equally to scientists who declared themselves free of theological influences.

While the first two sections of the Syllabus address stringent and moderate forms of rationalism, the third section addresses the application of such ideas with regards to religious adherence. They represent what might be called an early combination of universalism, pluralism, and ecumenism:

> 15. Everyone is free to embrace and profess the religion which he believes true as guided by the light of reason.
> 16. People of any religion can discover the way of, and gain, eternal salvation.
> 17. At the very least, we should rightly hope for the eternal salvation of all those who in no way dwell in the true Church of Christ.
> 18. Protestantism is nothing more than another form of the same true Christian religion, in which it is possible to be equally pleasing to God as in the Catholic Church.
>
> (Pius IX, Syllabus, § III)

To negate or lessen the importance of the Catholic Church for eternal salvation is to negate the importance of doctrinal theology, and thus negate a central purpose of the Church as teacher.

While the errors from the third section (errors 15–18) appear to represent minor infractions compared to the first and second sections (errors 1–7; 8–14), their inclusion in the Syllabus places them in the same realm as outright atheism or rationalism. They are of the same cloth, these errors of rationalism, atheism, modernity, liberty, democracy, and pluralism. As such, anyone who wished to define a Catholic philosophical theology while working successfully within the boundaries constructed by the Syllabus would be forced to look somewhere other than the dominant strains of philosophy in Europe.

———

In conclusion, it is helpful to recall that the Syllabus was not addressed to "all the people of the world" or even sent to heads of state but to the bishops. It was not meant to persuade the world but to outline an idea, an idea that is Catholic doctrine. In the twenty-first century, barely a half century after the life-changing event known as the Second Vatican Council, it is hard to imagine what it felt like to rely on conciliar treatises several centuries old. The Council of Trent, which ended in 1563, was the last ecumenical council for over three hundred years. When Pius announced a new council on December 6, 1864, just two days before the publication of *Quanta Cura* and the Syllabus, the Catholic world was understandably shocked.[15]

Dei Filius (1869–70)

Writing less than a decade after the events that he attended, Cardinal Edward Manning deftly captures the feel of the First Vatican Council and the years leading up to it, and it seems appropriate to quote him at length:

> Few centuries since the Christian era have seen events of great magnitude or more far-reaching in consequence, than the age in which we live. It has seen the extinction in 1806 of the Holy Roman Empire, the heir and representative of the Caesars; the rise and fall of two Empires in France; the setting up of two French republics; the overthrow of more dynasties, and the abdication of more kings, than any former age. It is, characteristically, the century of revolution.

It has seen great wars which shook the whole of Europe from Madrid to Moscow; and lately two great empires overthrown in a few weeks or in fewer months. It sees now a German Emperor and a king of Italy. Once it has seen the head of the Christian Church carried away prisoner into France, once driven by bloodshed out of Rome, and now we see him stripped of all the world can clutch; twice it has seen Rome seized and held. These are not common events.

Finally, after a lapse of three hundred years, it has seen an Ecumenical Council, and it has occupied itself profusely and perpetually about its acts, its liberty, and its decrees. Few events of the nineteenth century stand out in bolder relief, and many will be forgotten when the Vatican Council will be remembered. It will mark this age as the Council of Nicaea and the Council of Trent now mark in history the fourth and the sixteenth centuries.[16]

Several points in Manning's introduction are worth noting. First, the air of tumult and revolt, as has been already described, was well imprinted on the minds of the bishops. The nineteenth century was a period of revolution and uncertainty in Europe. Second, one cannot discuss the Vatican Council without mentioning its aftermath: "we see him stripped of all the world can clutch." The theological statements of the council breathed the same breath as revolution and chaos, but as a response, not a folding.

Finally, as is clear from Manning's final lines, the council was seen as definitive and final by many, if not all, involved. The Council of Trent stood unchanged for three hundred years, so why should not the Vatican Council? Understanding this is particularly helpful when studying the council in the post–Vatican II world, where conciliar documents may or may not be employed to prove a necessary point. Nevertheless, the sense of finality after Vatican I gives context to the sense of purpose that the bishops clearly felt when attending the council. They were giving the contours of the Catholic faith a much-needed tuning in an age of new philosophies, new sciences, and new theological constructions.

Translating the Syllabus into a Conciliar Document

On December 6, 1864, Pius IX was presiding over a session of one of the many papal congregations when, after opening prayers, he asked all the officials to leave the room, leaving only the cardinals behind.[17] In this private meeting, Manning writes, Pius "had made known to the cardinals that for a long time the thought of convoking an Ecumenical Council as an extraordinary remedy to the extraordinary needs of the Christian world had been before his mind. He bade the cardinals to weigh the matter each one by himself, and to communicate to him in writing, and separately, what before God they judged to be right. But he imposed rigorous silence upon them all."[18]

When Pius published *Quanta Cura* and the Syllabus two days later, the cardinals saw an immediate and purposeful connection. "From the outset," writes Hermann Pottmeyer, "the convocation of the Council was seen in close connection with the most sensational and sharpest condemnation of all that the majority of public opinion praised as unquestioned intellectual and political progress."[19] To the cardinals, to the bishops, and to the public, it was clear that the intention behind the council was to solidify the attitude toward culture given in the Syllabus.

It was no surprise, then, that the same theologian who drafted section II of the Syllabus, errors 8–14, was selected to compose the first draft of the document that would become *Dei Filius*. Johannes Baptist Franzelin, a professor of theology at the Gregorian University in Rome, presented his *Definitio Doctrinae Catholicae contra multiplices errores* to the Dogmatic Theology Preparatory Committee in charge of preparing a dogmatic constitution on the Catholic faith.[20]

The committee appreciated Franzelin's theological arguments but judged his style too harsh and negative for a conciliar document.[21] After some deliberation, the task of redrafting the document went to Archbishop Dechamps of Mechelen, Belgium, Bishop Pie of Poitiers, France, and Bishop Martin of Paderborn, Germany. Bishop Martin "assumed the lion's share of editing," and appointed a theologian named Joseph Kleutgen as his assistant. At first, Franzelin's eighteen chapters were whittled down to nine, but time and political pressures pushed the number down further: only four chapters were approved by the general council of bishops in March of 1870.[22]

There were many reasons for this trimming of the original document, but two are particularly important. First, *Dei Filius* did not treat the hot-button issue of the First Vatican Council. That honor belonged to *Pastor Aeternus*, the document that defined papal infallibility. While the relationship between faith and reason was a significant concern for Pius, it stood second alongside his desire to be declared infallible by an ecumenical council! Second, the other chapters of the first three schemas, following the model of the Syllabus, were more political than philosophical. Since Pius wanted something done quickly, the fastest way to gain universal acceptance was to trim off any chapters that would hang up for years in deliberations. A heady document of theology and philosophy, especially one that condemned errors already condemned and reinforced doctrines already pronounced, was a far simpler pill to swallow.[23] This is not to say that it was without conflict, but the controversies around *Dei Filius* were minor compared to those surrounding *Pastor Aeternus*.[24]

The four approved chapters of *Dei Filius* are shown in table 4.3. As in the discussion of the Syllabus, our analysis of *Dei Filius* is not historically constrained by those specific heresies mentioned in the document, but instead it aims to understand the text as one of the four major foundational moments upon which a conception of science can be built. To be precise, if the negative guidelines of the Syllabus can be considered the philosophical and theological boundaries within which Catholic scholars can work, the proscriptions of *Dei Filius*, moderating and making positive what the Syllabus declared as negative, should be considered the foundations of Catholic scholarship that is meant to be built within these clearly defined boundaries.[25] While the forthcoming analysis primarily focuses on the fourth chapter, we begin with an examination of the first three chapters so as to frame our discussion of the fourth.

Table 4.3. Final Version of *Dei Filius*, Chapter Headings

---

1. On God as Creator of All Things (De Deo rerum omnium Creatore)
2. On Revelation (De Revelatione)
3. On Faith (De Fide)
4. On Faith and Reason (De Fide et Ratione)

Chapters 1–3: Defining God, Faith, and Reason

The first chapter of *Dei Filius* begins quite close to the first error of the Syllabus:[26]

Dei Filius, Chapter 1	Syllabus
The Holy, Catholic, Apostolic and Roman Church believes and acknowledges that there is one true and living God, creator and lord of heaven and earth, almighty, eternal, immeasurable, incomprehensible, infinite in will, understanding and every perfection. Since he is one, singular, completely simple and unchangeable spiritual substance, he must be declared to be in reality and in essence, distinct from the world, supremely happy in himself and from himself, and inexpressibly loftier than anything besides himself which either exists or can be imagined.[27]	1. There exists no supreme, most wise, and most provident divine being distinct from the universe, and God is none other than nature, and is therefore subject to changes. In truth, God is created in man and in the world, and all things are God, and have the very substance of God. Thus God is one and the same thing as the word, and, in the same manner, spirit is the same as matter, necessity as liberty, true as false, good as evil, and justice as injustice. (§ I)

The rest of the first chapter expands upon this idea, cementing as doctrine the idea of *creatio ex nihilo*, as well as the ubiquity of divine providence.[28] Like the first few errors of the Syllabus, "pantheism and materialism were clearly the targets against which this chapter was directed."[29] Different from the Syllabus, however, was the breadth and strength of the attack: the doctrine of God here, especially the separation of God from the world and the inherent freedom of God, would become the principal argument by which future theologians would condemn all atheistic and pantheistic arguments—for example, Hegelian, Feuerbachian, Marxist, Nietzchean.[30]

The second chapter of *Dei Filius* is the first to address the idea of reason and contains one of the most controversial statements in the short document:

The holy mother church holds and teaches that it is possible that God can be known with certainty from created things by the light of human reason. (*DF*, chap. 2, para. 1)[31]

Bernard Lonergan argues that this sentence is often misunderstood as a declaration of the *actuality* of knowledge of God from reason instead of the potentiality of such knowledge.[32] Leaning explicitly on Pottmeyer's interpretation, Lonergan argues that contrary to popular belief, *Dei Filius* only postulates the possibility that reason can reach true knowledge of God. The council fathers did not intend to make a radical pronunciation but to hold a "traditional stance" between fideism and rationalism:[33]

It is indeed thanks to this divine revelation, that those matters concerning God which are not of themselves beyond the scope of human reason, are possible to be known by everyone expeditiously, even in the present state of the human race, in firm certitude and with no intermingling of error.

Huic divinæ revelationi tribuendum quidem est, ut ea, quæ in rebus divinis humanæ rationi per se impervia non sunt, in præsenti quoque generis humani conditione ab omnibus expedite, firma certitudine et nullo admixto errore cognosci possint.

(*DF*, chap. 2, para. 2)[34]

Lonergan seems correct upon inspection. The document clearly speaks of the *possibility* of knowledge, never mentioning the previous attainment of such knowledge. *Dei Filius* does not read, for example, "many philosophers have gained this certitude in the past, and many will gain it in the future." This potentiality allows for a broad range of interpretations, which, one might argue, was the direct intention of the conciliar authors attempting to allow as broad a range of Catholic philosophy and theology as possible.[35]

Lonergan critiques the definitions of reason laid out in *Dei Filius* by arguing that modern science "is empirical." "In our day," he writes, "the obvious instance of valid knowledge is science. It proceeds from data and it develops by returning again and again to the data. Moreover, it never adds to data any intelligibility, any unity or relationship, that is not verifiable in the data."[36] Since there exists "no data on the divine, God . . . is not a possible object of modern science."[37] Furthermore, there is no verifiable and repeatable principle that would allow us to reach from this world to full knowledge of the divine. In other words, the declaration of the potency of rationality to attain knowledge of the divine is itself a theological declaration with no basis in philosophical or scientific reasoning.[38]

The third chapter of *De Filius* thus defines the nature of faith in contrast to human reason. Faith is defined as "a supernatural virtue," "the conviction of things not seen," something to be "in harmony with reason," a "gift from God," something without which miracles and prophecies are nonsense, and something without which "it is impossible to please God" (*DF*, chap. 3, para. 1–3, 5). The council fathers defined the act of faith both against the "blind leap" arguments popular among Protestants, as well as against the rationalistic arguments of post-Kantian philosophers. Faith is neither a subset of rationality nor a magical property requiring blindness: faith is knowledge of God learned through revelation, inspired through the "illumination" of the Holy Spirit, and confirmed both by the unity of the Catholic Church as well as by the miracles and prophecies of Jesus in the Gospels (*DF*, chap. 3, para. 3, 5–6).

By defining faith in this way, the council fathers walked a line: they did not subsume faith into scientific reason, but they also negated too harsh of a break between the two, something known commonly today by Steven Jay Gould's thesis of nonoverlapping magisteria.[39] By defining faith as something that grows, that learns (from revelation and the Holy Spirit), that leads to more learning, *and* that works in harmony with reason, the council fathers forged a bond between the future of philosophy, the future of modern science, and the future of theology. But what was this harmony, and how could it be carried out in practice?

Chapter 4: A Twofold Order of Knowledge

The perpetual agreement of the Catholic Church has maintained and maintains this too: that there is a twofold order of knowledge, distinct not only as regards its source, but also as regards its object; with regard to the source, we know at the one level by natural reason, at the other level by divine faith; with regard to the object, besides those things to which natural reason can attain, there are proposed for our belief mysteries hidden in God which, unless they are divinely revealed, are incapable of being known. (*DF,* chap. 4, para. 1)[40]

Thus the fourth chapter of *Dei Filius* begins, summing up earlier implicit statements and setting the stage for future delineations. In the view of this author, these five paragraphs are among the most important written in the last few centuries of the Catholic Church. They are sufficiently broad to allow both for the dominance of Neo-Scholasticism in the 1880s and 1890s *as well as* for the transformative philosophies that led to Vatican II. They have been blamed for the pontifical imposition of Neo-Thomism and praised for leaving open the acceptance of historical-critical scholarship and evolutionary theory in the mid-twentieth century.[41]

Conciliar documents, by their nature of being written by committee, are full of political bargaining and theological negotiations: remove one word; add another; remove one phrase; add a paragraph. The final draft of *Dei Filius,* for example, was seen by the drafting bishops as so dense that "every word has had its special discussion, and consequent modification. It is so compact, that each sentence, however short, strikes at one or more errors or heresies, and the uninitiated will require a guide through them."[42]

While such might be true—even in its obvious hyperbole—one can see overarching themes of the document through close examination. To begin with, the fourth chapter opened the door to a much more amenable relationship between theology and modern science:

Not only can faith and reason never be at odds with one another but they mutually support each other, for on the one hand right reason established the foundations of the faith and, illuminated by its light, develops the science of divine things; on the other hand, faith delivers reason from errors and protects it and furnishes it with knowledge of many kinds. (*DF,* chap. 4, para. 5)

It stressed the unquestioning promotion of science by the Church:

Hence, so far is the Church from hindering the development of human arts and studies, that in fact she assists and promotes them in many ways. For she is neither ignorant nor contemptuous of the advantages which derive from this source for human life, rather she acknowledges that those things flow from God, the lord of sciences, and, if they are properly used, lead to God by the help of his grace. (*DF*, chap. 4, para. 5)

Furthermore, it emphasized the necessary independence of the methodologies of every scientific and philosophical inquiry:

Nor does the Church forbid these studies to employ, each within its own area, its own proper principles and method: but while she admits this just freedom, she takes particular care that they do not become infected with errors by conflicting with divine teaching, or, by going beyond their proper limits, intrude upon what belongs to faith and engender confusion. (*DF*, chap. 4, para. 4)

These words were no accident. Pottmeyer notes that several of the council fathers were scientists who specifically entreated the council not to "assess the modern sciences too negatively or unduly limit their freedom."[43] These bishops pleaded with the rest of the council to keep in mind that in the conflict between religion and science, "the cause must not only be sought among scientists."[44] Because of this inherent openness to science and scientific methods, one can see how Pope Pius XII wrote *Humani Generis* in 1950—accepting evolutionary theory as a possibility—within the broad contours set by *Dei Filius*.

But of course, *Humani Generis* did not come until seventy years after *Dei Filius*, and the third paragraph of chapter 4 of *Dei Filius* helps to explain why. This paragraph likely provides the most fuel to the argument that *Dei Filius* also opened the door to a harsh backlash against novel scientific theories—such as natural selection—that seemed to negate theological principles. The paragraph begins with a declaration of independence, inspired by the bull *Apostolici Regiminis* of the Fifth Lateran Council:

Even though faith is above reason, there can never be any real disagreement between faith and reason, since it is the same God who reveals the mysteries and infuses faith, and who has endowed the human mind with the light of reason. God cannot deny himself, nor can truth ever be in opposition to truth. The appearance of this kind of specious contradiction is chiefly due to the fact that either the dogmas of faith are not understood and explained in accordance with the mind of the Church, or unsound views are mistaken for the conclusions of reason. Therefore we define that every assertion contrary to the truth of enlightened faith is totally false. (*DF*, chap. 4, para. 3)

Published on December 8, 1513, *Apostilici Regiminis* confirms the same noncontradictory nature of truth (often called the doctrine of double-truth), while affirming the clear priority given to the dogma of the Church in matters of dispute: "And since truth cannot contradict truth, we define that every [philosophical] statement contrary to the enlightened truth of the faith is totally false and we strictly forbid teaching otherwise to be permitted."[45] Further echoing the sixteenth-century bull, the rest of the paragraph from *Dei Filius* reinforces this priority:

Furthermore the Church which, together with its apostolic office of teaching, has received the charge of preserving the deposit of faith, has by divine appointment the right and duty of condemning what wrongly passes for knowledge, lest anyone be led astray by philosophy and empty deceit. Hence all faithful Christians are forbidden to defend as the legitimate conclusions of science those opinions which are known to be contrary to the doctrine of faith, particularly if they have been condemned by the Church; and furthermore they are absolutely bound to hold them to be errors which wear the deceptive appearance of truth. (*DF*, chap. 4, para. 3)

In the construction of the overarching theological-philosophical framework, one could say that if the Syllabus built boundaries around the limits of proper Catholic thought, *Dei Filius* reinforced these boundaries while laying foundations. Of the many foundations it laid, five seem pertinent to this discussion: the inherent freedom of faith and reason; the priority of faith in disputes with science; the independence and goodness of all scientific methods, as long as theories professed stay within the boundaries of dogma; the necessary and desired harmony of faith and reason; and the simple idea that science, like reason, is a good enterprise in itself. It is a distinct failure of official Catholic teaching in the late nineteenth century that these foundational principles were not properly applied to the growing field of evolutionary biology, causing not only censures but a century of misperceptions concerning the Church and modern science.

The End of the Church's Temporal Power (1870)

The argument thus far in this chapter is that the Syllabus set the boundaries beyond which Catholic doctrine cannot reach, and *Dei Filius* reinforced these boundaries while laying a foundation for a positive understanding of the relationship between faith and reason, and thus faith and science. The chapter continues with the argument that the loss of temporal power—the only moment not attached to a document—created a vacuum that necessitated a stronger doctrinal position from the Holy See. Without this event, which included not only the loss of temporal power but also a premature ending to the Vatican Council, it is difficult to imagine that Pope Leo XIII would have been elected and *Aeterni Patris* published.

This is not to say that the four moments are all causally related. The Italian unification movement began long before the publication of the Syllabus in 1864. Furthermore, the publication of *Dei Filius* would only have been known by a small part of the ecclesial population following its publication in 1870, and thus played no part in the fall of Rome. Neither could one make the argument that the Syllabus caused *Dei Filius*. Pius IX clearly published the Syllabus with the intention of producing a similar document at his future council, but it would be more accurate to say that the Syllabus and *Dei Filius* were two products *of the same intentionality,* both coming from the person of Pius IX. Furthermore, I make clear that neither the Syllabus nor *Dei Filius* caused the publication of *Aeterni Patris*. Of the four moments, the only causal relationship is between the third and fourth: that the fall of Rome in 1870, at least in part, caused the election of Pope Leo XIII and the publication of *Aeterni Patris*. In order to understand this claim, however, one must go back to the reason for the assault: the unification of the Kingdom of Italy was missing a piece.

The Unification of Italy

Four years before the publication of the Syllabus, Pope Pius IX suffered his first major defeat as political head of the Papal States in the Italian peninsula. The unification actions of 1859–60 were politically deft and highly successful. In 1859 Victor Emmanuel II, king of Piedmont-Sardinia in the northwest corner of the peninsula struck an alliance with France and provoked Austria into declaring war on the Italian states. With the help of the troops of Piedmont-Sardinia, the northern part of the Papal States unified with the rest of the northern provinces to defeat the Austrian armies. After the war, most of the other northern states agreed to join the Sardinian goal of creating a unified Kingdom of Italy. France, the pope's only foreign military defender at this point, agreed to cede a large portion of the Papal States to the Kingdom of Sardinia in exchange for the provinces of Nice and Savoy.[46] Thankfully for Pius, the generosity of the French toward Italian unification went only so far, and the French troops guarding the Holy City prevented Emmanuel II from sending General Giuseppe Garibaldi to take the city. When the now-Sardinian army marched back to northern Italy, they reinforced the Papal States that they had already claimed, leaving only Rome and its surrounding region to the French troops protecting Pius. The new Kingdom of Italy was officially proclaimed by Emmanuel II on March 17, 1861, but a Kingdom of Italy that lacked the ancient and holy city of Rome would never be complete.

On July 19, 1870, one day after the document *Pastor Aeternus* was approved by the Vatican Council, and well before the intended work of the council was completed, France declared war on Prussia. Because of the political upheaval, bishops and cardinals began to flee

Rome to their respective states, and the council was left with "something under 150 members."[47] Less than a month later, on August 7, Napoleon called French troops back from Rome to aid the war effort. In response, Pius called on his own troops to assemble and fight now that the French were in retreat, but his efforts were in vain as he did not have enough skilled soldiers locally.

On September 6, 1870, the Italian army crossed the boundaries of the Papal States. On September 11, Pius officially refused an offer of security while annexation of the Papal States took place. Because of this, the Italian forces bombarded the walls of Rome for five hours on the morning of September 19, breaching one section of the wall and forcing Pius to order a full surrender. On October 9, King Victor Emmanuel II declared Rome and its provinces as part of the Kingdom of Italy. In famous words to his advisors, the pope resigned himself to remain at the Vatican, whatever happened: "I surrender to violence. From this moment I am the prisoner of King Victor Emmanuel."[48] On October 20, with no other options, Pius officially adjourned the Vatican Council.

Death and Election

Pius lived in captivity and in freedom for eight years following the overthrow of Rome.[49] He was steadfast in his approach to the world: the modern reforms of politics and economics were "a snare devised to divide the faithful."[50] He despised the progress of modernity and judged that "the triumph of liberalism and nationalism [was] attained at the expense of the faith and the enslavement of the Church."[51] To the end, it was Pius against the world, Pius against progress, Pius against liberalism. "It is true," he would note in 1873,

> that those who are imbued with these principles [of Liberal Catholicism] make a profession of love and respect for the Church, and seem to consecrate to her defence their talents and their works; but they labour nevertheless to pervert her doctrine and her spirit and, each of them according to the diversity of his taste and temperament, is disposed to place himself at the service, either of Caesar, or of those who claim rights in favour of a false

liberty. They fancy that it is absolutely necessary to follow this course, in order to remove the cause of dissensions, to reconcile human progress with the Gospel, to re-establish order and tranquillity; as if light could co-exist with darkness, and as if truth did not cease to be truth when it is violently turned from its true signification, and when it is divested of the fixity inherent in its nature.[52]

Pius reigned until 1878, strengthening his grip on the doctrines of the Catholic Church as his political power was all but extinguished. "A big part of the rise in the Pope's authority as a churchman," Chadwick writes, "was connected with the collapse of his authority as a politician."[53] The older Pius grew, the more staunchly he defended his political and religious antiliberal contrarianism.

The death of Pius IX brought many tears around the world for the pope who defended the Church, but it also brought hope. There was little doubt the cardinals wished for something of a change after thirty-two years of contrarian practices and policies. From the beginning, the name of Vincenzo Gioacchino Pecci, cardinal archbishop of Perugia, rose among the sixty-one cardinals at the papal conclave.[54] Since he was an Italian perceived as being "outside the curia," he gained popularity quickly among the conclave and was elected during the third session of votes.[55] Pecci was a scholar of the medieval church, a lover of literature, and a ruler with the air of a monarch.[56] With Pecci, the cardinals hoped, they would see the principles of Pius continue, but perhaps without the contrarianism that marked so much of Pius's pontificate.[57]

Defining the Moment

The loss of temporal power began a new age in the Catholic Church. No longer would the curia be chosen for their knowledge of provincial administration. No longer would the pope be assumed to be a political monarch, balancing the governance of commoners as well as spiritual followers. He would not have to choose a political economy or haggle with democracy in his own territory. The pope, in many ways, would be free to rule simply in Spirit, with the authority of the Chair of St. Peter, as he already had for so many Catholics prior to

1870. Pius could never see this opportunity, of course, since he sat upon the throne as the last vestiges of political power were taken forcibly from the Vatican's hand. To him the end of the Vatican's political holdings was a tragedy of the modern age and a representation of all that was antithetical to the Christian message.

When Pius died in 1878, the Church did not just need another leader who would fight against the world. It needed a way *to be* a Catholic Church in a world that was already progressive in so many of the ways that Pius deplored. The Church needed a moral and spiritual leader who accepted the Holy Roman monarchy as something of the past. It was into this need—in this vacuum—that Cardinal Pecci was elected. Continuing the metaphor of this chapter, if the Syllabus built the walls around Catholic doctrine and *Dei Filius* fortified the walls and built foundations for positive statements, one can argue that the loss of temporal power created a political instability in which only a strong and nuanced theological and philosophical stance could prevail. The Church did not need another Syllabus; it needed an example of Catholic thought and Catholic practice upon which a new age of spiritual power would rest. To this need the College of Cardinals delivered Pope Leo XIII, and to this need Leo delivered Thomas Aquinas.

Aeterni Patris (1879)

The fourth and final moment of the intellectual framework that defined the relationship between faith and reason in the late nineteenth century is, unquestionably, the writing and publication of Leo XII's encyclical *Aeterni Patris*. Schools were built because of its publication. Faculty were fired; others were hired. Entire courses of priestly formation were transformed out of a new respect for and adulation of the writings of Thomas Aquinas. *Aeterni Patris* stands alone, perhaps unique even among encyclicals, in its political impact in the world. This is not to say, of course, that everyone saw the document in the same light but that *Aeterni Patris* set a standard for how one considered the relationship between faith and reason, and thus faith and science, during Leo's pontificate (1878–1903).

The encyclical itself was a document of improbable beginnings, whose inspiration first came in the Jesuit seminaries of the 1830s. It was there that the future pope would learn of the importance of Aquinas, and there that he would join with several others on a half-century quest to revive the philosophical importance of the Angelic Doctor in Catholic thought. Modeled after the sixteenth-century movement by the same name, they called themselves "Scholastics," a moniker that transformed into "Neo-Scholastics" and "Neo-Thomists" as the movement grew in popularity and found more than its fair share of critics.[58] This movement to revive Aquinas shadowed much of the nineteenth century and affected more than just *Aeterni Patris,* as a brief history of its origins will show.

Defining Neo-Scholasticism

The history of Neo-Scholasticism is one small part of a nine-hundred-year history of interpretations of Thomas Aquinas. It has been told many times, in many different ways, in countless books, articles, and lectures. Instead of attempting a novel history of Neo-Scholasticism, this section will view the movement as a historical way to understand the influential encyclical of 1879, *Aeterni Patris* (see table 4.4). In this light, the vision of Neo-Scholasticism here begins and ends with the person of Gioacchino Pecci, the future Pope Leo XIII, who was born in 1810.

In 1818, at eight years old, Gioacchino Pecci left home with his older brother Guiseppe to study to become a priest. In 1824 he and his brother were transferred to the Roman College, recently entrusted to the Jesuits, to be closer to their family. When Pope Pius VII reinstated the Jesuit order, one of the first new novices was a scholar named Serafino Sordi, whose admiration and love of Aquinas would become contagious, influencing his fellow Jesuit novice Luigi Taparelli d'Azeglio. Several years later, in 1824, Taparelli was appointed rector of the Roman College in the same year that Pecci and his brother began studying there. Taparelli introduced the Pecci brothers to the Angelic Doctor and set them on a course to change the face of Catholicism. A year before Taparelli was transferred, the future Pope Leo XIII would choose to become a diocesan priest, while his older brother would continue the scholarly route and become a Jesuit.

Table 4.4. A Long History of *Aeterni Patris*: Neo-Scholasticism, 1814–79

1814	Jesuit order reinstated by Pius VII.
1806–24	Vincenzo Buzzetti teaches Thomistic theology and philosophy at episcopal seminary in Piacenza, Italy. Two of his students are Jesuits, the brothers Serafino and Domenico Sordi.
1814–20	Serafino Sordi is transferred to Rome, where he befriends and influences his fellow Jesuit Luigi Taparelli d'Azeglio, who quickly becomes a full-hearted Thomist.
1824	Taparelli is appointed first rector of the newly Jesuit-run Roman College. Tries to push Aquinas as model of Jesuit philosophical studies but fails.
	Giuseppe Pecci and his younger brother Vincenzo Gioacchino Pecci (future Leo XII) are transferred to Roman College to be closer to their family. Taparelli introduces the brothers to the virtues of Aquinas. Taparelli also makes convert of the Jesuit Carlo Curci, future cofounder of *Civiltà Cattolica*.
1829	Because of his open Neo-Scholastic views, Taparelli is transferred to Massimo College at Naples. Giuseppe Pecci begins to teach Aquinas-based philosophy at Roman College.
1830s	Taparelli establishes center of Thomist thought at Massimo College, bringing a former mentor, Domenico Sordi, and others to teach and to discuss, in secret, the revival of Scholasticism.
1840s	In Naples, Gaetano Sanseverino publishes Thomist journal, *La Scienza e la Fede* (1840), and founds the Academy of Thomistic Philosophy (1846). Also in Naples, Virgilii Press begins to reprint complete works of Aquinas (1846).
1846	Joseph Kleutgen publishes first book, *Über die alten und die neuen Schulen*, condemning Enlightenment and lifting Aquinas as model.
1850	In Naples, Carlo Curci founds *Civiltà Cattolica* with the help of Taparelli and Matteo Liberatore, who will become convinced of the Thomist system several years later.
	Gioacchino Pecci is appointed archbishop of Perugia by Pius IX. He is joined by his brother, Giuseppe, and the two brothers transform the small diocesan seminary into a center of Neo-Scholasticism.
	Joseph Kleutgen, Jesuit, friend of the *Civiltà Cattolica* crowd, is appointed consultor to the Congregation of the Index. He will influence dozens of cases before he leaves in 1870.
1853	Curci, Taparelli, and Liberatore write a series of essays explicitly arguing for a return to Aquinas in the Catholic Church, assuming the support of Pius IX. Serafino Sordi is appointed provincial of Rome. Giacchino Pecci is elevated to the College of Cardinals.

Table 4.4. (continued)

1853–63	Besides his work with the Congregation of the Index, Kleutgen publishes two major volumes, *Die Theologie der Vorzeit; Die Philosophie der Vorzeit*, both anti-Enlightenment and pro-Aquinas. Kleutgen will continue to publish books until his death in 1883.
1858	Liberatore, Taparelli, Sordi, Curci, and Kleutgen prepare a new *Ordinatio Studiorum* for the Society of Jesus, incorporating the Neo-Scholastic approach, and make it mandatory for all Jesuits by the superior general of the order.
1860s–70s	Liberatore publishes *Del composto umano* (1862), *Istituzioni di Etica e Diretto naturale* (1865), *Dell'uomo* (1874), *Dell'anima umana* (1876).
1868–69	Kleutgen helps to draft *Dei Filius*.
1878	Gioacchino Pecci is elected Pope Leo XIII.
1879	Leo appoints Kleutgen prefect of studies at the Gregorian University in Rome and names his brother, Giuseppe, and a Dominican Neo-Scholastic, Tommaso Zigliara, as cardinals. He begins a series of Thomistic training seminars at Gregorian and replaces non-Thomist faculty with faithful Thomists.
4 August	*Aeterni Patris* published, based upon draft written by Kleutgen.
15 October	Pontifical Academy of St. Thomas Aquinas, still thriving today, created by Leo XIII as a practical exemplar of the desires of *Aeterni Patris*.
1880s–90s	Leo urges and often commands the study of Aquinas at Catholic academies and seminaries around the world.

Sources: Boyle, "A Remembrance of Pope Leo XIII," 7–22; Inglis, *Spheres*, 57–104; McCool, *Nineteenth-Century Scholasticism*, 59–87, 129–44, 216–40; Weisheipl, "The Revival of Thomism"; and Wolf, *Römische Inquisition und Indexkongregation. Grundlagenforschung: 1814–1917*, 3:806–17.

The Neo-Scholastic movement did not catch on quickly or easily. Taparelli was transferred to Naples, where he labored for twenty years to build a devotion to Aquinas, and only after such labor—and many students—did his work begin to show dividends. A devoted Neo-Scholastic and former student of Taparelli named Gaetano Sanseverino published an explicitly Thomist journal, *La Scienza e la Fede*, in 1840, and founded the Academy of Thomistic Philosophy in

1846. In the same year, a young but highly skilled Jesuit named Joseph Kleutgen would publish his first book, *Über die alten und die neuen Schulen,* condemning the Enlightenment and lifting up Aquinas as a model for modern philosophy. Kleutgen was educated under the Jesuit Giovanni Perrone at the Roman College, an appreciator of Aquinas in his own right.

The election of Pope Pius IX, combined with the revolution of 1848, however, would shift the tides decisively toward Neo-Scholasticism. First, in 1850, Pius appointed Pecci as archbishop of Perugia. Pecci asked his brother to join him, and together they transformed the small diocesan seminary of Perugia into a thriving seminary of Neo-Scholasticism. Second, in the same year, Taparelli and two burgeoning Jesuit scholars named Carlo Curci and Matteo Liberatore founded the influential *Civiltà Cattolica* at Pius IX's request. This journal quickly became not only a strong voice for the movement but also an explicit philosophical and theological voice for Pope Pius IX, with the assumed backing of the Holy Father himself. Third, on July 11, 1850, Kleutgen was appointed consultor to the Congregation of the Index by Pius and played a key role in condemning the works of Anton Günther, Jakob Froschammer, Johann Hirscher, and many others.[59] Kleutgen would rise in estimation throughout the next two decades, writing dozens of reports for the congregation as well as publishing two major volumes detailing a novel systematic approach to theology and philosophy, *Die Theologie der Vorzeit* and *Die Philosophie der Vorzeit,* both anti-Enlightenment and both pro-Aquinas.

After these events in the 1850s, things began to coalesce for the Neo-Scholastic movement. Kleutgen was enlisted as a drafter of *Dei Filius* during the First Vatican Council, which Pecci also attended. Directly before his death, Pius appointed Pecci as camerlengo of the Church, an administrative post that made him a resident of the Holy City.[60] The voice of *Civiltà Cattolica* was rarely stronger than when Pecci was elected pope, and Kleutgen's philosophical views were close at hand to the new pontiff. But these few scholars and priests were not alone in reviving a love of Aquinas.

In the 1850s and 1860s, the movement grew in various ways. Neo-Scholastics could be found in teaching posts not only in Italy but in France and Germany as well.[61] Furthermore, while Jesuits clearly began the movement, priests and theologians of many stripes and shades took up this particular method of interpreting the works of Aquinas in a philosophical battle against the Enlightenment.[62] Due to the movement's growing popularity, a predictable side effect also occurs around this time: it becomes difficult to separate the specific form of philosophical argument under Neo-Scholasticism from the general appreciation for studies of Aquinas.[63]

It is helpful to remember that ever since his canonization in the early fourteenth century, and especially since the blossoming of Thomistic interpretations in the sixteenth century, Aquinas had always been a revered figure in Catholicism, and Thomism had nearly always been a part of the Catholic educational experience.[64] One must be careful to differentiate between the general sense of appreciation for Aquinas's delineation between faith and reason and the specific arguments made about the application of such delineation by the Neo-Scholastics, however. What marked Taparelli, Sordi, Pecci, Liberatore, Kleutgen, and others as significantly different was not that they appreciated Aquinas when others did not. For example, *Dei Filius* was approved readily by hundreds of council fathers, and it unquestionably affirms the largely Thomistic notion that Christian faith and human reason are separate but interdependent faculties of the human mind and that they cannot contradict one another.[65]

The differences between a general appreciation for Aquinas and the movement of Neo-Scholasticism could be summarized by the following four precepts, although delineations of this sort are necessarily debatable.[66] First, the leaders of the Neo-Scholastic movement insisted on a singular philosophical structure for all Catholic scholarship that was both objective and universal, for doctrine could not exist in a world where the roots of philosophy were being forever debated.[67] Second, the Scholastic interpretation of the philosophy of Aquinas was to be revered as the model of this universal structure, over against any philosophical systems based on Descartes, Kant, Locke, or anyone else in the modern world, *as well as* over against the theological interpretations of any other theologian, such as Augustine, Bonaventure, or Scotus. Third, Neo-Scholastics argued that by relying on Aquinas and other medieval philosophers, contemporary Catholic philosophy could be constructed as a single objective whole. Fourth and finally,

Neo-Scholastics resisted anything resembling a historical approach to philosophical or theological development, for if doctrine could be changed over time, it would be impossible to test its veracity.[68] One could add to these four precepts certain views of epistemological realism, adherence to an Aristotelian vision of the sciences, and many other positions, but these four limit the field substantially.[69]

Based on the timeline and arguments above, it should be clear that the Neo-Scholastic movement was heavily influential in the writing of *Aeterni Patris*. However, the degree to which these four precepts of Neo-Scholasticism can be concluded from the encyclical is another question. The remainder of this chapter will investigate precisely this question by, first, conducting a close analysis of the text of the encyclical and, second, studying the influence on and reception of the encyclical by a leading member of the Neo-Scholastic movement, Joseph Kleutgen.

Aeterni Patris: A Dogmatic Foothold

Aeterni Patris was published on August 4, 1879. Following the tradition of encyclicals in the nineteenth century, it is not a particularly long document, consisting of around six thousand words in Latin (eight thousand in English).[70] The encyclical is not divided, except into paragraphs, but could be outlined as shown in table 4.5. The first section (para. 1–9) begins in praise of philosophy and philosophical work as a necessary foundation for sacred theology to "assume the nature, form and genius of a true science [i.e., a true pursuit of knowledge]."[71] Following closely the design of *Dei Filius*, Leo notes the historical relationship between theology and philosophy, quoting the same lines as *Dei Filius* did from the Fifth Lateran Council:

Table 4.5. The Five Sections of *Aeterni Patris*

---

1. Importance of Philosophy in Relation to Sacred Theology (para. 1–9)
2. History of Philosophy Leading to Aquinas (para. 10–16)
3. The Greatness of the Angelic Doctor (para. 17–18)
4. The Reception of Aquinas by the Church (para. 19–23)
5. The Importance of Aquinas Now (para. 24–33)

Moreover, the Church herself not only urges, but even commands, Christian teachers to seek help from philosophy. For, the fifth Lateran Council, after it had decided that "every assertion contrary to the truth of revealed faith is altogether false, for the reason that it contradicts, however slightly, the truth," advises teachers of philosophy to pay close attention to the exposition of fallacious arguments. (*AP*, para. 7)[72]

He finishes the first section by reminding the faithful of what *Dei Filius* proclaimed: that the ideal of philosophy is the unity of philosophical work and Christian obedience:

Those, therefore, who to the study of philosophy unite obedience to the Christian faith, are philosophizing in the best possible way; for the splendor of the divine truths, received into the mind, helps the understanding, and not only detracts in nowise from its dignity, but adds greatly to its nobility, keenness, and stability. (*AP*, para. 9)

The second section (para. 10–16) begins with an argument for the importance of a standard relationship of philosophy and theology from the Greeks until the Medieval Age:

If, venerable brethren, you open the history of philosophy, you will find all we have just said proved by experience. The philosophers of old who lacked the gift of faith, yet were esteemed so wise, fell into many appalling errors. . . . But the learned men whom we call apologists speedily encountered these teachers of foolish doctrine and, under the guidance of faith, found arguments in human wisdom also to prove that one God, who stands pre-eminent in every kind of perfection, is to be worshiped; that all things were created from nothing by His omnipotent power; that by His wisdom they flourish and serve each their own special purposes. (*AP*, para. 10–11)

By the end of this section, Leo has traversed over one thousand years of Christian philosophy and entered into praises of the unique moment of the Scholastics:

For, the noble endowments which make the Scholastic theology so formidable to the enemies of truth . . . are only to be found in a right use of that philosophy which the Scholastic teachers have been accustomed carefully and prudently to make use of even in theological disputations. Moreover, since it is the proper and special office of the Scholastic theologians to bind together by the fastest chain human and divine science, surely the theology in which they excelled would not have gained such honor and commendation among men if they had made use of a lame and imperfect or vain philosophy. (*AP*, para. 16)

While the section begins with a historical argument for the right relationship between philosophy and theology, it ends with this assumed high moment of philosophy in the persons of the Scholastics.

The third section (para. 17–18) narrows the praises of the Scholastics to the person of Aquinas. Leo spares no superlatives in his description of the Angelic Doctor,

With his spirit at once humble and swift, his memory ready and tenacious, his life spotless throughout, a lover of truth for its own sake, richly endowed with human and divine science, like the sun he heated the world with the warmth of his virtues and filled it with the splendor of his teaching. (*AP*, para. 17)

Furthermore,

Philosophy has no part which he did not touch finely at once and thoroughly; on the laws of reasoning, on God and incorporeal substances, on man and other sensible things, on human actions and their principles, he reasoned in such a manner that in him there is wanting neither a full array of questions, nor an apt disposal of the various parts, nor the best method of proceeding, nor soundness of principles or strength of argument, nor clearness and elegance of style, nor a facility for explaining what is abstruse. (*AP*, para. 17)

While Leo leans toward the four precepts of Neo-Scholasticism discussed above, the encyclical is better understood as a piece of rhetoric, an *apologia* for Aquinas perhaps, rather than a dogmatic treatise:

Clearly distinguishing, as is fitting, reason from faith, while happily associating the one with the other, [Thomas] both preserved the rights and had regard for the dignity of each; so much so, indeed, that reason, borne on the wings of Thomas to its human height, can scarcely rise higher, while faith could scarcely expect more or stronger aids from reason than those which she has already obtained through Thomas. (*AP*, para. 18)

One would be hard pressed to employ higher praises for a Christian scholar!

The fourth section (para. 19–23) turns to the reception of Aquinas for further proof of his importance in the Church by cataloging his impact on religious orders, universities, the papacy, the ecumenical councils, and even the enemies of the Church. For Leo, the section completes the historical argument for Aquinas's stature. Early Christian philosophy was coordinated and assembled perfectly in Aquinas, and all (or at least many important) Christians since have recognized his greatness.

The fifth and final section (para. 24–33) is Leo's attempt to apply Aquinas's philosophy to the present day. He describes four reasons why Aquinas must be sought for a true dogmatic foundation: philosophical subjectivity, rationalism, civil unrest, and advancement of all scholarship. First, he argues that Aquinas could cure the central error of modern philosophy, that terrible idea known as subjectivity. For those who accept this error, the search for philosophical truths, he writes, "depends on the authority and choice of any professor, has a foundation open to change, and consequently gives us a philosophy not firm, stable, and robust like that of old, but tottering and feeble" (*AP*, para. 24).

Second, for all those who "have reason as their sole mistress and guide,"

nothing is better calculated to heal those minds and to bring them into favor with the Catholic faith than the solid doctrine of the Fathers and the Scholastics, who so clearly and forcibly demonstrate the firm foundations of the faith, its divine origin, its certain truth, the arguments that sustain it, the benefits it has conferred on the human race, and its perfect accord with reason, in a manner to satisfy completely minds open to persuasion, however unwilling and repugnant. (*AP*, para. 27)

Third, "domestic and civil society . . . would certainly enjoy a far more peaceful and secure existence if a more wholesome doctrine were taught in the universities and high schools—one more in conformity with the teaching of the Church, such as is contained in the works of Thomas Aquinas" (*AP*, para. 28).

Fourth and finally, because of Aquinas's vast command of human knowledge, "all studies ought to find hope of advancement and promise of assistance in this restoration of philosophic discipline which we have proposed" (*AP*, para. 29). In particular, he argues, one must investigate natural occurrences and conceptions of natural laws:

For, the investigation of facts and the contemplation of nature is not alone sufficient for their profitable exercise and advance; but, when facts have been established, it is necessary to rise and apply ourselves to the study of the nature of corporeal things, to inquire into the laws which govern them and the principles whence their order and varied unity and mutual attraction in diversity arise. (*AP*, para. 29)

Leo continues, explicitly promoting the natural sciences:

And here it is well to note that our philosophy can only by the grossest injustice be accused of being opposed to the advance and development of natural science. For, when the Scholastics, following the opinion of the holy Fathers, always held in anthropology that the human intelligence is only led to the knowledge of things without body and matter by things sensible, they well understood that nothing was of greater use to the philosopher than diligently to search into the mysteries of nature and to be earnest and constant in the study of physical things. And this they confirmed by their own example; for St. Thomas, Blessed Albertus Magnus, and other leaders of the Scholastics were never so wholly rapt in the study of philosophy as not to give large attention to the knowledge of natural things; and, indeed, the number of their sayings and writings on these subjects, which recent professors approve of and admit to harmonize with truth, is by no means small. Moreover, in this very age many illustrious professors of the physical sciences openly testify that between certain and accepted conclusions of modern physics and the philosophic principles of the schools there is no conflict worthy of the name. (*AP*, para. 30)

This paragraph, tracing the studies of the natural world from Aquinas to the late nineteenth century, is an example of the ideal, rightly ordered science that *Dei Filius* implicitly mentioned and that Leo explicitly references early in the encyclical. It is also, however, misleading in its positive outlook.

The final sentence of the paragraph, taken from the official translation above, offers a helpful insight into the orientation of theology, philosophy, and the sciences. First, the sentence speaks of modern physics instead of the highly controversial realm of biology in 1879. Second, the phrase "certain and accepted conclusions" is clearer in the English than in the Latin, "certas ratasque conclusiones." The phrase could just as easily be translated "fixed and established conclusions." With this phrase Leo points to a degree of certainty in the scientific community, and perhaps among scholars as a whole, but particularly among scholars operating on correct philosophical foundations. Who else can properly struggle for and believe a scientific theory? What makes a scientific theory believable in the first place?

Unfortunately, Leo does not address the obvious question at the end of the paragraph: what if a scientific conclusion is *certas ratasque* and yet in conflict with a philosophical argument held by the Church? Given the focus of this book, this omission seems a missed opportunity that could have given much clarity to the evolution debates. How does one judge the certainty of a scientific theory in terms of theological truth? Where does theology end and scientific truth begin? Are some beliefs—the age of the world, the immediate creation of Adam and Eve—more malleable than others—the Trinity, the divinity of Christ? By leaving the question open, Leo unintentionally opens the door for the problems of many, including John Zahm.

The encyclical concludes with a general precept for future studies of Aquinas around the world:

> Let carefully selected teachers endeavor to implant the doctrine of Thomas Aquinas in the minds of students, and set forth clearly his solidity and excellence over others. Let the universities already founded or to be founded by you illustrate and defend this doctrine, and use it for the refutation of prevailing errors. But, lest the false for the true or the corrupt for the pure be drunk in, be ye watchful that the doctrine of Thomas be drawn from his own fountains, or at least from those rivulets which, derived from the very fount, have thus far flowed, according to the established agreement of learned men, pure and clear; be careful to guard the minds of youth from those which are said to flow thence, but in reality are gathered from strange and unwholesome streams. (*AP*, para. 31)

In one light, this paragraph reads as a clear proclamation to employ only Neo-Scholastic theologians and philosophers to teach Aquinas. Read from the point of view of bishops who knew little of the Neo-Scholastic controversies, it cautions future generations to stay as close to the writings of the Angelic Doctor as possible, lest they fall from correct philosophy.

————

The Syllabus set the boundaries of right doctrine in 1864. Six years later, *Dei Filius* reinforced those boundaries and built foundations for future work. In the same year, the fall of temporal power began a vacuum in the propagation of these foundations so much so that a new face with fresh energy, Pope Leo XIII, was elected to replace Pius IX. One of Leo's first acts upon election was to fill the lacuna in Catholic doctrine with a document like *Aeterni Patris*, written, it seems clear, to finish what *Dei Filius* began. *Aeterni Patris* not only reaffirmed the necessity of Catholic doctrine in a disordered and violent world but also posited Aquinas as the perfect exemplar of the relationship between the Church and the three secular powers of the world:

philosophy, science, and politics. Aquinas not only solved the problems of philosophy but also was the answer to every Catholic problem in the late nineteenth century.

The above interpretation of *Aeterni Patris* largely represents an attempt to see the document through the lens of those unfamiliar with the details of Neo-Scholasticism (a common occurrence in a place like the United States or among nonscholars) in the nineteenth century. Of course, many *were* familiar with both the details and controversies of the movement and knew well the role Pope Leo had played in its origins. To them, as well as to some modern scholars, the above reading of the encyclical would appear overly simplified. For example, the four precepts of Neo-Scholasticism listed above could easily be found in *Aeterni Patris* if one was watching for them: universalism (para. 9), the unique importance of Aquinas (para. 17–23), universalism in Aquinas (para. 17–18), antihistorical development (para. 17, 19–23, 24–30. In this light, the following section attempts to understand such a reading of the encyclical, and its effects, by examining a philosopher who would be eulogized by Leo in 1833 as "the prince of the philosophers," Joseph Kleutgen.[73] Not only does an analysis of Kleutgen's philosophy provide an example of a dominant form of Neo-Scholasticism, but it also gives us a broader frame of reference to *Aeterni Patris* and its part in the theological-philosophical framework that defined the relationship between faith and science in the nineteenth century.

The Influence and Philosophy of Joseph Kleutgen

Joseph Kleutgen, writes McCool, "was the most profound and original thinker among the Jesuit neo-Thomists. He was also the most influential."[74] McCool notes Kleutgen's appointment to the Congregation of the Index in 1850, his influence during Günther's condemnation, his well-received commentary on the Holy See's condemnation of ontologism, and his role in helping to draft *Dei Filius*.[75] What is not clear in his biography of Kleutgen, however, is the philosopher's role in the authorship of *Aeterni Patris*. Thankfully for the purposes of this study, historian and philosopher John Inglis has researched this precise question, the answer to which has been argued as a definite yes or no, depending on the author and work of scholarship.[76]

Inglis posits four arguments in favor of Kleutgen having a significant role in drafting the encyclical. First, Inglis argues that Leo shows a clear preference for Kleutgen's scholarship: he called Kleutgen to teach in Rome in 1878, and, as stated above, when Kleutgen died five years later, Leo eulogized Kleutgen as "the prince of the philosophers."[77] Second, ever since *Aeterni Patris* was published, a strong but unverified tradition has existed in the Jesuit order that Kleutgen "was a co-author of the encyclical and prepared a draft."[78] Third, Kleutgen's *Philosophie der Vorzeit* was translated into Italian in the 1870s by two influential members in the curia and was published by the Vatican Propaganda of the Faith Press.[79]

Fourth and perhaps most persuasively, Inglis argues, Kleutgen reminisces about talking with Leo about the encyclical in an 1879 letter to his former teacher:

In *Aeterni Patris*, the tendency and principle of all my writings have received a confirmation through the words of the representative of Jesus Christ on earth that I could not have hoped for. I had been in Rome for hardly a few weeks when the Holy Father had me called and elaborated for almost an hour about the encyclical, which he intended to issue. For me it seemed like a miracle to hear my own thoughts from such a source.[80]

Kleutgen could and would never have admitted that he had been asked to write a draft, of course, but this letter proves that "whether or not Kleutgen did write a draft . . . he thought he was receiving from Leo the highest level of confirmation for his life-long project."[81] While there may be no way to prove the case, it seems highly likely that Kleutgen did indeed author a draft of *Aeterni Patris*.

With this established, one also must discern why an analysis of Kleutgen's epistemology is necessary beyond the confines of the encyclical. Many, McCool included, take the encyclical to be the epitome of Neo-Scholastic ideas, as it includes the independence of philosophy from history, the focus on a metaphysical system, and confidence that the arguments of Kleutgen and others could produce a Catholic dogmatic philosophical theology that could attain objective universality.[82] But the encyclical did not do any of this specifically. As noted above, the encyclical stressed the importance of Aquinas above all others, the necessity of a single goal for all human sciences, the independence and potentiality of rightly ordered natural sciences, and the requirement that all future priestly training include education in the works of Aquinas. Not only did the encyclical fail to mention Kleutgen but also concepts such as the negation of history and the possibility of objective universality can *only* be gleamed from the document *with the foreknowledge* of more specific philosophical systems.[83] In other words, only those conversant with Neo-Scholasticism before the publication of *Aeterni Patris* would have seen the direct comparison to the Neo-Scholastic movement.

Although it is impossible to prove, it seems reasonable to assume that most if not all the members of the Congregation of the Index in the 1890s were conversant, if not fluent, in the philosophical project of Pope Leo's favorite Neo-Scholastic philosopher and an author of *Aeterni Patris*, Joseph Kleutgen. As such, the remainder of this chapter more closely analyzes Kleutgen's epistemology, especially with regard to the natural sciences. If Leo, through *Aeterni Patris*, standardized Kleutgen's wider work for the Catholic intellectual elite, what would they consider to be Kleutgen's approach to the sciences?

Generally following Inglis, I answer this question by contrasting Kleutgen's philosophical epistemology of realism with the dominant systems of Kant, Locke, and Bacon in the nineteenth century. I look at Kleutgen's massive corpus through the closest lens to natural science possible, especially in Kleutgen's understanding of the connection of subject to object and the necessity of objectivity in observation. The goal of Kleutgen's epistemological project in this regard was to "safeguard perceptual and intellectual knowledge against the dangers of skepticism and subjectivism, which lead to revolution."[84] To achieve this goal, Kleutgen's massive *Philosophie der Vorzeit* goes well beyond the ecclesial foundations provided in *Dei Filius* and *Aeterni Patris* on the relationship of faith and reason.

The problem to be fixed in contemporary philosophy, Kleutgen argues, is a Kantian and Cartesian declaration of the lack of certain knowledge. Without a rational basis in certain, or objective, knowledge, there cannot possibly exist a theological argument for the *potentiality* of reason to achieve certain knowledge of God without faith, as was proclaimed in *Dei Filius*. Without such a *potentiality*, the entire philosophical edifice of Catholic theology would fall away in favor of one of the modern systems of philosophical epistemology. Kleutgen contends that if he can disprove Kant on this question of subjective epistemology, he can simultaneously discredit Descartes, Locke, Fichte, Schelling, Hegel, and any Catholics—like Hermes and Günther—who have imitated them.[85]

Kleutgen's argument is not a simple one, but it is important to try to understand. To begin, Kleutgen argues that Kant's subjectivism is closely related to the philosophical project of empiricism (i.e., Francis Bacon), in that nothing we sense is the *thing in itself,* but only *the appearance* of such a thing. Our knowledge, then, is devoid of "real objects in the ordinary sense" because such knowledge depends upon certainties of *a priori* structures such as space and time.[86] Since these certainties, these structures, cannot themselves be verified by sense experiences, one must limit knowledge due to a lack of objectivity. Kleutgen first rebuts Kant's dependence upon the *a priori* knowledge of space and time, by arguing that such a dependence forces Kant to "construct two spheres that do not intersect": the experiential world and the *a priori* world. This construction not only limits Kant's epistemology but also negates the simple fact that human experience itself is bounded in space and time.[87]

"Kant came to his subjectivism," Kleutgen wrote, "because he . . . referred to the original ideas of space and time to something *external*, and did not recognize that we know ourselves as spatial-temporal beings rather than knowing space and time outside ourselves."[88] Kleutgen repairs the subjective-empirical lens of Kant by removing this distance from subject to object and declaring that an epistemological foundation rests in the experience of *actual things* in one's scientific knowledge of the world. Inglis argues that it was this epistemological shift that not only offered Kleutgen his strongest argument against Kant but also allowed him to return to pre-Enlightenment philosophy to fill out the rest of the epistemological picture.[89]

After dispatching the foundations of modern skepticism through this argument, Kleutgen posits an argument for epistemological objectivity based on three principles, which he characterizes as a "common theory . . . among a number of significant pre-modern thinkers including Augustine, Anselm, Aquinas, Suarez and Maurus."[90] The first principle is Kleutgen's attempt at removing the distinction between subject and object: "knowledge arises through an image of the known's being produced in the knower by the knower and the known."[91] This union of the subject and the object allows for an objectivity unmatched in post-Kantian philosophical theories.

The second principle continues the departure from Kantian philosophy: the manner in which each knower knows is not subjective experience but can be quantified and understood as a general methodological principle. Humans know objects in a certain manner, but this *manner does not change* based on an individual's experiences. The third principle completes the argument: "knowledge is all the more perfect the further the knowing principle is removed in its being from materiality."[92] While one's senses perceive an object in part, the true knowledge of that object attains higher degrees of perfection the further it can be removed from sense perception and the more it can be founded in "intellectual knowledge."[93]

Kleutgen distinguishes himself from the empiricists and subjectivists of the nineteenth century with these three principles, but a question still remains: how can the knower create intellectual knowledge with only the benefit of sense perception to understand the known? To solve this, Kleutgen turns to a concept widely employed in the thirteenth through sixteenth centuries known as *abstraction*. He argues that each human possesses an ability to abstract "the general, the necessary, and the essential" from sense perceptions.[94] For example, having seen an apple, even once, a human can begin to abstract various qualities of the apple completely unrelated to the sense data received. Apples are a fruit, they grow on trees, they are a substantial source of food, they are related to other foods, they can be fed to other animals, etc. Kleutgen's utilization of the Scholastic notion of abstraction allows him to keep a priority on sense perception (paramount during the age of scientific novelty) while supporting "the elusive *thing-in-itself* as one of the grounds of human knowledge, something Locke hoped to do, but Hume and Kant agreed could not be done."[95] And, as one would suspect, who epitomized the conception of abstraction in the Middle Ages? Thomas Aquinas.

To those who generally understood Kleutgen's arguments against the dominant philosophies of the nineteenth century, *Aeterni Patris* was a papal stamp of approval on the philosopher's entire corpus of work, and a philosophical placement of the natural sciences quite different from the one that came out of the Baconian vision of progress and liberty and thus quite different from the vision of John Zahm. While Kleutgen himself did not discuss the natural sciences specifically, one can extract some general precepts from his aforementioned principles and arguments for epistemological objectivity. First, natural science, as construed empirically, can never bring progress because scientific knowledge correctly understood is always based on *a priori* structures that are not conditioned by sense experiences. In other words, for Kleutgen, true science must begin with a rejection of any philosophy of "strict empiricism." Second, science does not discover new objects from the outside alone, but discovers traits based on a specific cognitive structure that unifies and is shared by both subject and object. In practical terms, this argument, extracted from the second principle of realism combined with the notion of abstraction, supports a general method of knowledge production that could otherwise be known as a "scientific method," as long as said method acknowledges the *a priori* existence of the method in the essence of the knower and the known. The method does not arise from philosophical argumentation, but from existence itself.

Third and finally, the natural sciences are incomplete, even in their own sphere, to the philosophical and theological sciences, since, based on the third principle above, true knowledge of an object becomes more perfect the further one is removed from sense perception. In other words, the natural sciences may be able to explain weather patterns and the temperature of the ocean, but they can never obtain true knowledge of the ocean. What is true knowledge? For example, Kleutgen's answer to the question, What is the ocean? would not have been immediately technical. The ocean would not be inherently defined by sense experience: size, color, sound, temperature, or smell. The ocean would be inherently defined and *truly known* only through understanding its wider place in the world, its immediate function, and its final purpose. The more we rely on sense perception,

Kleutgen would argue, the less we are able to understand the true essence of the ocean.

Two Visions of Science

This short exploration of Kleutgen's rebuttal of Kantian philosophy illuminates the two different ways that late nineteenth-century Catholic theologians and philosophers would have understood *Aeterni Patris*, and, by extension, science. First, like Zahm himself, they would have seen the encyclical rather separate from Neo-Scholasticism and Kleutgen, as a document professing the need for a return to Aquinas generally. In an 1896 article, Zahm argues that the central point of the encyclical is both to "urge the study of the philosophy of St. Thomas Aquinas" and to show "the necessity of philosophy as a guide in the study of nature."[96] Given the lack of any argument resembling Neo-Scholasticism in Zahm's own corpus, it seems clear that he saw the encyclical as independent from the Neo-Scholastic movement, and thus apart from Kleutgen's philosophy. This view of the encyclical on Zahm's part is evidence for the difference between his understanding of science and Kleutgen's.

The second perspective, held by figures such as Kleutgen, Pope Leo XIII, and other members of the Catholic intellectual elite, would have seen *Aeterni Patris* as a direct inheritance of over forty years of efforts to reintroduce an ahistorical, objective universal approach to contemporary dogmatic theology by means of a particular philosophical retrieval of Thomas Aquinas. Following Kleutgen, this retrieval rejected a strict empiricism of the natural sciences, understood objective methods as existing prior to, and thus being superior to, the subjectivity of sense perception, and saw the sciences as inherently incapable of providing true knowledge of the world on their own. While truth cannot contradict truth, the truths of biological sciences, for example, ranked well below the truths of faith and metaphysics for such followers of Kleutgen, and always needed to be complemented by those "higher" truths.

But Kleutgen's full system was only understood by some, albeit those who had great ecclesiastical power, especially in the Congregation of the Index. Most modern scientists such as Zahm had little understanding of the intricacies of Kleutgen's philosophical system. For them, science was progress, knowledge, and enlightenment. Science could stand alongside faith because the two stood side by side in their search for truth, as they understood both *Dei Filius* and *Aeterni Patris* to declare. As we will see in the following chapter, it was this precise misunderstanding that led to the inevitable conflicts between Catholic scientists in the late nineteenth century and the ruling Neo-Scholastic philosophies of the 1880s and 1890s, exemplified by the trial and censure of John Zahm.

CHAPTER 5

Trials and Tribulations

It should be clear at this point that while none of the previous scholars on John Zahm were necessarily *incorrect* in their assessment of the impact that Zahm's scientific and political views had on the outcome of his case, neither did they offer a complete story. One cannot understand the rise of Neo-Scholastic approaches to science and reason in the 1890s without a conceptual framework for understanding the rest of the Vatican in the nineteenth century. Similarly, one cannot fully understand the works of Zahm without understanding his own determined effort to herald the possibilities and hopes of modern science during the second half of the nineteenth century.

This chapter completes this story of Zahm by looking at the documents of the trial behind the scenes at the Sacred Congregation of the Index of Prohibited Books with an ear to the theological and philosophical conceptions of modern science and evolution that informed the congregation's decisions. It explains how two divergent philosophies of science—one from Zahm and one from the Vatican—collided in the congregation's hearings on Zahm's *Evolution and Dogma* in 1898. As such, we begin with a brief recap of the events of the trial, along with an explanation of the inner workings and purpose of the congregation.

We then look at the most important arguments against Zahm, which turned the Congregation of the Index against *Evolution and*

Dogma, not the least of which was the official accusation by Archbishop Otto Zardetti that opened the case. We consider the many reasons why Zardetti accused Zahm in the first place, including Zardetti's connections with anti-Americanist movements in the United States as well as Zardetti's own ideas of science. We also consider the two documents that Zardetti included with his accusation: a printed retraction by another Catholic evolutionist, Marie-Dalmace Leroy, and a negative review of Zahm's book in *Civiltà Cattolica*.

After Zardetti, the most influential voice in Zahm's trial was that of Fr. Enrico Buonpensiere, the Dominican who was commissioned to write the report on *Evolution and Dogma* for the Congregation of the Index. In order to understand Buonpensiere's anti-evolutionary arguments one must first look to his teacher and mentor, Cardinal Tommaso Zigliara, who explicitly argued for a Neo-Scholastic anti-evolutionary stance in one of the most-read volumes on Aquinas in the late nineteenth century. We then examine Buonpensiere's report on Zahm in this light, focusing not on the scientific details but on the manner in which the Italian Dominican's arguments were predictable, eloquent, and entirely dismissive of Zahm's claims to the scientific probability of evolutionary theories.

Zahm and the Congregation of the Index

The Sacred Congregation of the Index of Prohibited Books is best understood as a premodern work of theological censorship. From a modern perspective it is easy to think the entity barbaric. Book censorship is a feared concept, and public libraries often post histories of "banned books" that include a wide range of literature deemed unreadable by various organizations. But censoring people in one's care from harmful material is a natural human tendency. Elementary and secondary schools, for example, allow some books in their library but reject others. Parents allow children to watch some television shows but not others. Censorship will always be a part of life, whether on the internet or in the bookstore. Indeed, before the creation of the Congregation of the Index in 1571 by Pope Pius V and before indices were published across Europe in the mid-sixteenth century, bishops and groups of bishops had been publishing lists of prohibited books for over a thousand years.[1]

With the advent of the printing press and the political and theological effects of the Reformation, the Council of Trent mandated a centralized index for prohibited books to be kept in Rome, beginning with a copy of the first published index from the Faculty of Theology at the University of Paris in 1544.[2] Within twenty years, nearly a dozen more indices were published by authorities from Venice, Milan, Anvers, Louvain, Portugal, and Rome.[3] Realizing the need for constant updating of the growing list of indices, Pope Pius V created the Sacred Congregation of the Index of Prohibited Books in 1571, which would not only collect other indices but also publish its own within a few years.[4] Nearly four hundred years later, the congregation was formally abolished by Pope Paul VI in 1966, eighteen years after the publication of the last index in 1948.[5]

While the actions of Congregation of the Index may seem bizarre and cruel to us today, and did indeed inflict harm upon those whose published books were condemned, the actions themselves were done by men whose aims were virtuous by their own lights. They desired the Church to remain holy, to protect believers from heresy, to bring people salvation, and to protect the Church from the evils of the modern world. In the late nineteenth century, as the previous chapter showed, such desires were understandable. By and large, Zahm's accusers wanted nothing less than to keep the Catholic Church from falling into theological, moral, and political peril. Their decision was a product of a vast institution that had lasted many centuries, and one that felt it had to rely on banning books to keep the faithful in line.

Archbishop Otto Zardetti

As table 5.1 shows, when Otto Zardetti first brought *Evolution and Dogma* to the attention of the Congregation of the Index in late 1897, the wheels were already in motion. Reviews and critiques of the book blanketed the Catholic world from Italy to France to Ireland to the United States.[6] Some praised its eloquence and courage while others maligned its overreaching evolutionary ideas. It is difficult to say how

Table 5.1. Timeline of Trial and Censure of John Zahm

5 November 1897	Archbishop Otto Zardetti sends letter to the Congregation of the Index asking for an investigation of Zahm's *Evolution and Dogma*.
1898	
15 April	Enrico Buonpensiere completes commissioned report for the Congregation of the Index.
10 June	Bernhard Doebbing completes report on accuracy of Italian translation.
5 August	Preparatory Congregation meets and votes on reports, with records in the ACDF.
1 September	Meeting of General Congregation, no records in ACDF of meeting.
3 September	Decision brought before Pope Leo XIII, censuring Zahm's book but not publishing index until submission received.
5 September	Index of prohibited books published, excludes *Evolution and Dogma*.
9 September	Gilbert Français, superior general of the Congregation of Holy Cross, informed by the Congregation of the Index about Zahm's predicament and immediately (10 September) sends letter to Zahm.
25–28 September	Français's letter asking for submission received by Zahm; Zahm responds in early October.
28 October	Zahm's submission letter received by Français, who immediately travels to Rome.
4 November	Français delivers two letters to the Congregation of the Index. The first informs the congregation of Zahm's submission; the second begs them not to publish the decree.
September– December	Français sends additional letters to prefect of the Congregation of the Index and Pope Leo XIII on Zahm's behalf. In-person meetings held by Français, O'Connell, Ireland, and Keane.
1899	
22 January	Pope Leo XIII publishes "anti-Americanism" encyclical, *Testum Benevolentiae*.
3 February	Pope instructs Congregation of the Index to indefinitely suspend publication of Zahm's censure until Zahm can come to Rome to defend himself. Zahm never travels to Rome and the condemnation is never published.

Sources: Index, Protocolli, 1897–99, fols. 179–95, ACDF; Diari, vol. 22, fols. 38r–v, 39r–v, 42r, 48r, ACDF; and "Evolution and Dogma Correspondence," box 1, folder 12, JZA, UNDA.

much these reviews affected the outcome of Zahm's case, but it is clear that at least one deeply affected Zahm's accuser. The brief condemnation letter by Zardetti included two documents: first, a statement of retraction on the doctrine of human evolution by Marie-Dalmace Leroy, published February 26, 1895; second, an extremely negative review of *Evolution and Dogma* by Francesco Salis-Seewis in *Civiltà Cattolica*, published January 16, 1897.[7] Zardetti's letter condemned Zahm's book first by arguing that Zahm fully supported human evolution and ridiculed the Church's doctrine of special (immediate) creation. Second, Zardetti showed how Salis-Seewis, a trusted theologian and philosopher, could be drawn on to support Zardetti's condemnation. Third and finally, Zardetti presents Leroy's retraction letter in order to remind the members of the congregation that it had condemned human evolution in the past. Zardetti's letter and accompanying documentation proved remarkably effective and laid the basis for all of Buonpensiere's arguments in his official report on Zahm's book.

In the following sections we briefly examine Zardetti's life and works, showing his clear political and intellectual allegiance to both American and Vatican conservativisms. We then look at the content and importance of the two attachments to Zardetti's letter as well as Zardetti's own condemnation of Zahm's book. Included as appendix B is the first full English translation of Zardetti's letter, with his citations from the Italian version of *Evolution and Dogma*, cross-referenced and quoted from the English version.

Otto Zardetti: Conservative, Intelligent, and Forceful

John Joseph Frederick Otto Zardetti was born on January 24, 1847, in Rorschach, Switzerland, just four years prior to Zahm. After earning high marks throughout his studies at the University of Innsbruck, he was ordained a priest in 1870. Similar to Zahm, he was appointed professor of rhetoric at the Seminary of St. Gall in 1871, and, similar to Zahm, began to yearn for greater things soon afterward. In mid-century Europe, the great Catholic mission field was undeniably the United States. Bustling with immigrants and rapidly expanding westward—to the great detriment of the tribal populations—the

United States was driving many prelates to travel across the ocean and seek new adventures.[8] But Zardetti's local bishop acted boldly "to prevent the wanderlust from afflicting his young priest," so, like Zahm, Zardetti rose quickly in administrative duties.[9] In 1873 Zardetti was appointed librarian of St. Gall's famous monastic library, and in 1876 he became the youngest priest to be appointed canon of the Cathedral of St. Gall. But in 1881, despite growing in popularity in his homeland, Zardetti accepted an invitation to teach dogmatic theology and homiletics at St. Francis Seminary in Wisconsin, leaving behind a promising career in St. Gall.

Between 1881 and 1889, Zardetti both fell in love with the United States and became decidedly close to the anti-Americanists. He taught at St. Francis Seminary in Milwaukee from 1881 to 1887, after which he was appointed vicar general of Yankton, South Dakota. In 1888 he wrote a small book called *Special Devotion to the Holy Ghost*, designed largely for seminarians, which was a "testament to the transformation of the devotion."[10] A year later, in 1889, he was moved to St. Cloud, Minnesota, where he reveled in his new position as the diocese's first bishop. "Long before I saw my adopted country," he wrote in his first pastoral letter as bishop, "I loved it; when I first beheld it, its surpassing loveliness conquered me, and so fully that, retaining all my old and tender remembrance of my native land, I gladly sought the embrace and avowed myself a devoted citizen of the glorious American republic."[11]

But 1889–94 were contentious years in American Catholicism, and Zardetti placed himself in the middle of the fight. Zardetti aligned himself closely with Archbishop Corrigan of New York, the leader of the "conservative wing of American bishops," and argued strenuously for an end to the perceived influence of the Americanist wing, led by Bishop Ireland.[12] For Zardetti, the argument was first and foremost about public versus private education. "The state," he wrote, "does not have the right to interfere with the judgment of the parents. . . . It is not the right of the state to prescribe what must be taught, what language must be used, and to give free textbooks."[13] Ireland was a champion of taxpayer-funded universal public education, but Zardetti strenuously objected, and even traveled to Rome in May 1892 to argue his case before the pope.

With his trip to Rome, Zardetti saw his importance grow in the cause against the Americanist bishops, encouraging Corrigan to continue to act strongly against Ireland and his agenda.[14] In late 1892, he wrote:

I am glad that Archbishop C[orrigan] comes out a little more strongly. We must be bold, strong, impulsive, also in our dealings with Rome. That is the way I[reland] carried his point. This is the only way we can obtain something. I was in Rome and . . . was disgusted. I[reland] had carried with him [Pope] Leo . . . and the other Card[inal]s not daring to antagonize him. I[reland]'s principal agent is Msgr. O'Connell and I am sorry, as, when with him in Europe 3 years ago, he seemed to me a friend. But he does all he can for I[reland] and against C[orrigan].[15]

One should recall at this point, that outside of his superior, Français, Zahm's chief interlocutors postcensure were Archbishops Ireland, Keane, and O'Connell. Zardetti's frustration often bubbled to the surface of his ecclesiastical life, as he was engaged in several disputes with members of his diocese in St. Cloud in the last two years of his tenure, disputes that undoubtedly contributed to his being appointed archbishop of Bucharest in January 1894.[16] Zardetti attempted to turn down the appointment, but on April 9, 1894, he received the official papal pronouncement naming him archbishop-elect of Bucharest, Romania. After many heartfelt letters and apologies, Zardetti left the land he loved for the last time.

The final years of Zardetti's life were ones of travel, sickness, and frustration. He resigned from the archbishopric of Bucharest after only nine months of service, to the great surprise of many. "When I finally resolved to resign, the real motives," Zardetti wrote, "were only the complete insufficiency of means to carry out my mission in saving the souls especially of the children without schools. . . . The people there cannot be brought to pay for such purposes and all must be done by outside subsidies. My resignation there was in my view a kind of a *coup d'état* to force Rome and government to do something more."[17]

"There can be little doubt," Zardetti's biographer writes, "that Zardetti was a sick man when he left Bucharest."[18] After a year of rest and recovery in Switzerland, Zardetti traveled to Rome and continued his previous lobbying work against the perceived threat of the Americanist bishops, having been appointed to an honorary position of titular archbishop of Mocissus and a canon of the Basilica of St. Mary Major. He lived with the Holy Cross community, where he had his own apartment but would eat with the brothers, including, undoubtedly, priests from Notre Dame who knew Zahm and Zahm's work.[19]

Zardetti "could not remain a non-entity in Rome very long."[20] In 1898 Pope Leo XIII appointed him a consultant both for the office of Extraordinary Affairs in the Secretariat of State and for the office of the Governance of Bishops and Religious. Less than a year later Zardetti was also named "Assistant to the Pontifical Throne." This last title was given to him on February 14, 1899, less than a month after Leo issued *Testem Benevolentiae* against Americanism and modernism. His biographer writes,

> It is not known what Zardetti did during these years in Rome concerning the condemnation of Americanism but we do know where his sympathies were. His first biographer makes this claim for Zardetti: "He knew the new world. We also know from reliable sources he had done much for the condemnation of the misguided religious movement called 'Americanism,' which compromised Christian truth in order to win over non-Christians and Protestants.'". . . It would seem, given the positions he held, that Zardetti had some influence in bringing about the ultimate condemnation of Americanism and its subsequent effect on the Church in the United States.[21]

Unfortunately, there is simply too much we do not know about Zardetti's reasons for condemning Zahm. We *do* know that Zardetti's letter was the original impetus for the condemnation hearing by the Congregation of the Index. We also know that the Jesuit Salvador Brandi, the editor of *Civiltà Cattolica* who authorized the writing of the condemnatory review of Zahm's book, was another "agent" for Corrigan in Rome in the late 1890s.[22] We know that Satolli—whom

Zardetti quotes against Zahm—lived in Rome in the late 1890s, was an active member of the anti-Americanist movement, and owned an English copy of Zahm's book that he later supplied to the congregation to aid in their report.[23] The authors of *Negotiating Darwin* even admit that "one cannot dismiss the notion that Zardetti's denunciation may have been not his own" but "part of a plan in which others also participated."[24]

Of Corrigan and his vast influence, historian Michael Emmett Curran writes: "What is uncertain [and remains so] is how actively and in what ways Corrigan was using his own network of influence in Rome to counteract the strategy of the Americanists. Very little evidence survives to indicate his exact role during this crucial period."[25] Indeed, Curran notes in a footnote, "one of the puzzling aspects of the Americanist crisis is the surprisingly sparse correspondence on the subject among the American conservative prelates. What there is of it is consistently in a low-key, a stark contrast to the strident military language of the Americanists."[26] Nevertheless, in addition to Brandi and Zardetti, it is clear that "Corrigan had now [from 1897 to 1899] more effective voices at the Vatican against the Americanists than he had ever had: three powerful religious orders (Jesuits, Dominicans, Redemptorists) and several Cardinals including Ledochowski, Mazzella, Satolli, and Parocchi."[27] Zardetti's letter was written from Rome in the midst of a clear political movement against Archbishop Ireland and the Americanist Catholics. Given Zardetti's lack of previous work in science, his lack of writing any *other* condemnatory letter to the congregation,[28] and his many political connections and desires, it seems highly likely that Zardetti did not conceive of or compose the letter on his own.

The impact of the anti-Americanist movement in Rome was immediate and decisive. Leo promulgated the anti-Americanist encyclical *Testem Benevolentiae* in February 1899, and Corrigan, in the United States, heralded the publication as a great victory for the cause.[29] Despite the victories and his favor with the pope, Zardetti's time was nearly done in Rome. His health worsened considerably between 1899 and 1902, and Zardetti died on May 10, 1902, just a year before the death of Pope Leo XIII. Had he lived, Zardetti may have held a high place in the new pontificate, since one of his last close friends was a certain Monsignor Rafael Merry del Val, who would become a strong advocate against modernism as papal secretary of state for Pius X's entire pontificate (1903–14).[30]

Zardetti's Corpus of Modernist Writings

As with all of the historical characters in this study, Zardetti's political leanings were grounded in a wider intellectual approach to the modern world in the nineteenth century. While he wrote numerous books and articles, three books are worthy of examination here as they address larger notions of science, modernity, and philosophy. The first, published by Zardetti in 1879, is a reverential reflection on the recently deceased Pope Pius IX, titled *Pius der Große: Immortellenkränze auf den Sarkophag Papst Pius' IX* (Pius the Great: Immortal Wreaths on the Sarcophagus of Pope Pius IX). Zardetti holds little back in his praise and admiration for the late pope. Pius, for example, "saw how the Reformation, the grandmother, had born a daughter, philosophy, who in turn had grown twins, rationalism and revolution. [Pius] saw the great indescribable confusion on the earth, so much so that hardly anyone understood the language of the underworld coming through."[31]

Zardetti's Pius was a man who brought light to a troubled world, who gave the world its last hope. Much of the book employs similar language and sentiment to that above, using flowery metaphors to describe the grandeur and holiness of the late pontiff. Emblematic of Pius's governance, on Zardetti's reading, was the promulgation of Vatican I's *Pastor Aeternus*, the document that declared papal infallibility. "The divine idea flashed on July 18, 1870, from the divine right of the Papacy, and this flash of lightning blinded the eyes of the world," Zardetti writes, "and inspired the faithful."[32] Pius's role was akin to Moses's, leading the faithful through the desert of modernity to the boundaries of the Promised Land, although, like Moses, never to enter. "Who knows in which successor of Peter Joshua will enter, and who knows who will see the walls of Jericho fall!"[33] Zardetti's enthusiasm is tangible throughout the text, as is his undying love for the infallible papacy and the war against modern thought.

A second important work, the only book-length publication Zardetti wrote in English, is the previously mentioned *Special Devo-*

tion to the Holy Ghost. It was published in 1888 during his time at St. Francis Seminary in Wisconsin and was written as a manual of instruction on the theology of the Holy Spirit. In this text, a more theologically mature Zardetti presents a pneumatological vision of Catholicism that supported and bolstered the antimodernist monarchical approach of Pope Pius IX:

> The age is materialistic; it needs the gift of Intelligence, by the light of which the intellect penetrates into the essence of things. The age is captivated by a false and one-sided science; it needs the gift of Science by the light of which is seen each order of truth in its true relations to other orders and in a divine unity. The age is in disorder, and is ignorant of the way to true progress; it needs the gift of Counsel, which teaches how to choose the proper means to attain an object. . . . The age is sensual and effeminate; it needs the gift of Fortitude, which imparts to the will the strength to endure the greatest burdens, and to prosecute the greatest enterprises with ease and heroism.[34]

In addition to using the language of antimodernism and antiscience, Zardetti defends the devotion to the Holy Spirit while "uniting it to the institutional values closely associated with the Sacred Heart."[35] This effort to "relate the devotion . . . to a more hierarchical understanding of the Church" flows through Zardetti's description of the infallible papacy, the role of the priesthood, and the necessity of ecclesial authority.[36] "The first and decidedly the most important [criteria for recognizing the Holy Ghost]," notes Zardetti, "is a *loving filial submission* to our Holy Mother the church in all that she teaches, purposes, commands or even advises us to think and believe."[37] Such language not only allows us to understand Zardetti's approach to ecclesial politics but also illustrates the dangers of such restrictive theological arguments. Joseph Chinnici writes:

> Paradoxically, the very success of this more institutional approach would at the same time lessen the importance of the devotion to the Holy Ghost. Once structures and boundaries were clearly defined and pious practices popularized, the need to emphasize an

interior vivifying force which continually renewed and reformed Catholic identity in Church and society was no longer a pressing concern. In such an atmosphere, it was not surprising that devotion to the Holy Ghost as a major symbol of Catholic experience declined.[38]

The third relevant book by Zardetti, *Westlich! oder Durch den fernen Westen Nord-Amerikas* (*Westward! or, Through the Far West of North America*), was written and published after he had moved back to Europe in the late 1890s, and was his final extended work.[39] Zardetti uses its many pages to reflect on multiple aspects of the new country he loved, and only briefly touches upon the evils of modernity and science, with its "most critical and unbelieving tendencies."[40] Apparently, for Zardetti, science was another name for an unbelieving world and a path to unbelief and apostasy. It represented a "modern heathenism" for America and could only be counteracted "by means of Providence" against which "no science or criticism ever dared to doubt in its clarity."[41]

As one can see, Zardetti did not write much on evolution or science in general. In fact, as far as I can tell, he did not mention evolution even a single time, in any writing, before Zahm's condemnation. Zardetti was not, nor did he ever claim to be, a scientist. And yet, this notwithstanding, his condemnation dethroned one of the most prominent Catholic scientists in late nineteenth-century America.

Leroy's Retraction

Before examining Zardetti's specific arguments against Zahm, it is helpful to inspect the two documents attached to his letter, as they provide the philosophical and theological weight behind Zardetti's condemnation. The first document is the letter of retraction written by Dominican priest Fr. Marie-Dalmace Leroy after receiving word from the Congregation of the Index in early 1895. In the 1890s Leroy was in much the same difficulty as Zahm: he had written several books on theories of evolution, and his books had obtained a certain level of popularity. He was not as popular a figure as Zahm, but many, including Zahm, were already citing him regularly for defense of certain aspects of Darwinian evolutionary theory. On January 26, 1895, the congregation decided to condemn Leroy's book but, as in Zahm's case, not to publish the decree. Orders to pull the book from the shelves and recant were sent to Leroy, and his reaction was immediate. In contrast to Zahm, perhaps because of orders of his superior, Leroy decided to publicly recant in a letter to the popular daily paper, *Le Monde. Negotiating Darwin* includes a full translation of the letter, which I cite in part:

> To the Editor:
> When Darwinism began to cause a stir, I thought it my duty to study that doctrine from which our enemies hoped to be able to derive a great advantage against the teachings of the faith. When I studied it in depth, it seemed to me that not everything in it was reprehensible. . . . I believed that what should be done was to separate the chaff from the wheat, with the objective of making what was plausible in the system of evolution serve in the defense of revealed truth. . . .
> Now I learned that my thesis, examined here in Rome by the competent authority, has been judged untenable, above all for that which refers to the human body, which is incompatible both with scriptural texts and with the principles of sound philosophy. . . .
> I declare that I disallow, retract, and repudiate all that I have said, written, and published in favor of this theory.[42]

Soon after Zahm's ordeal, it was clear to everyone involved— including Zahm himself—that not seeing Leroy's retraction letter was a tremendous oversight in making the decision to publish *Evolution and Dogma*. In Zahm's defense, as the theological portions of the book were all but identical to the lectures of 1893, even if he *had* seen the retraction, there was little he could do without fully rewriting the text. Zahm's book attempted to do, quite explicitly, what Leroy specifically retracted—to "separate the chaff from the wheat, with the objective of making what was plausible in the system of evolution serve in the defense of revealed truth." Zahm's citations of Leroy were secondary to his defense of evolutionary theories, which he had already defended in separate publications of the lectures in 1894 and 1895. Zardetti, of course, neither mentions Zahm's previous work nor the fact that, since Leroy's book was never officially placed on the index, Zahm could not have been expected to know that evolution had been found incompatible with the faith.

Salis-Seewis's Review

The second and final attachment to Zardetti's letter is a negative review of *Evolution and Dogma* by the Jesuit Francesco Salis-Seewis in *Civiltà Cattolica* on January 16, 1897.[43] Salis-Seewis's review, atypically in comparison to other treatments, focuses on the scientific defense of evolutionary theory given by Zahm. He does not, however, cite a single page from Zahm's book in his critique of Zahm's arguments. "As if the primary and real impediment to the acceptance of evolution," Salis-Seewis writes, "is the fear of going against the Bible! Not at all!" The defects "come from the scientific defects of that beautiful system."[44] Salis-Seewis's sarcastic and sardonic tone runs throughout the review. Salis-Seewis not only fails to cite a single page of Zahm's book, but he also neglects to mention any specific piece of evidence against theories of evolution, despite the many examples of scientific flaws that Zahm himself adduced in his book. One looks in vain for some virtue in Salis-Seewis's review, but can only conclude that it is not really a review at all but rather a piece of rhetoric that casts Zahm's work as something that bears no resemblance to the actual book: a theological work telling people that evolution is acceptable because it does not contradict the Bible. Salis-Seewis's use of Gladstone—twice, in fact—seems proof enough that Salis-Seewis neither read nor cared to read Zahm's book closely. At least Zardetti and Buonpensiere did Zahm the honor of reading and citing closely from the text, *even if* both men ignored the entire first half of the book!

But, of course, much of this was expected from Salis-Seewis. He was, as Joseph Perrier wrote in 1909, "among the recent defenders of Neo-Scholasticism in Italy" and was known for an 1881 work on incorporating the psychological and physiological sciences into the wider Kleutgen-inspired work on epistemological objectivity.[45] What Zahm felt to be empirically accurate, as was shown in chapter 2, was not empirically accurate to the Neo-Scholastic theologian, as was shown in the previous chapter. Salis-Seewis may have gone a bit over the top, but one can safely assume that in his mind the entire book was founded on a false sense of empirical evidence and modern science.

Zardetti's Condemnation

"Having made a careful examination," Zardetti writes in his cover page, "I declare this book worthy of denunciation and censure . . . as a consequence of certain points contained in chapters 6, 7, and 8 of the second part." These three chapters are the final chapters of Zahm's book and compose less than one-fourth of the overall text. They are significant in that they encompass the conclusion of the book, not the scientific arguments that serve as the foundation for those conclusions. On its own, this fact might not strike one as significant. However, in the context of Zardetti's condemnations, wherein Zahm is condemned for arguments he made after careful scientific analysis over hundreds of pages, the absence of focus on any aspect in the first half of the book is striking.

As can be seen clearly in the translation, Zardetti's first four points critique Zahm's discussion of evolution by assuming a dogmatic rejection of human evolution by the Congregation of the Index, to which Zardetti writes (see appendix B). Note that Zardetti does not show *how* Zahm comes to claim, for example, that Catholics "are at liberty to accept the theory of Evolution" (point 3).[46] He confines himself to stating that Zahm claims that, first, we are at such liberty; second, the theory of evolution is nobler than the theory of special creation; and third, the theory of evolution can be applied to humans. Zardetti's clear underlying assumption is that such declarations alone are punishable.

Points 5–7 move into similar discussions about evolution. Zardetti's fifth point places Zahm with Mivart, who was forced to recant a doctrinal point about the theological nature of hell in 1893. The sixth point argues that Zahm's incorporation of Aquinas and Augustine has been effectively dismissed by Salis-Seewis's *Civiltà Cattolica* review— which, recall, cites no specific text of Zahm's book itself—and the seventh argues that, if these were not enough, Zahm's inclusion of Leroy shows that Zahm has "ignored the judgment of the competent authority" on the matter of human evolution.[47]

The eighth, ninth, and tenth points complete Zardetti's litany. Zardetti's eighth point restates his objections both to Zahm's incorporation of church fathers as well as to Zahm's preference for evolution over special creation. His ninth point seems intended to shock the audience, as it not only averts to Zahm's promotion of evolution but also to his claim that evolution is a theory that actually ennobles the ape and heightens humanity's place before God. Finally, his tenth point restates the problematic reliance upon Leroy and Mivart and directs the congregation to anti-evolution treatises written by Cardinals Mazella and Satolli.

In short, Zardetti's argument, while more substantial than Salis-Seewis's, is not a thorough review of Zahm's text and ideas. First, Zardetti fails to address *why* Zahm supports and uplifts the ideas of human evolution over special creation. Second, Zardetti fails to address Zahm's arguments for the probability of human evolution as well as plant and animal evolution. Third, Zardetti fails to acknowledge that while Zahm employs Leroy's and Mivart's work, their statements are only tangential to his central theological and scientific arguments. Fourth and finally, Zardetti ignores Zahm's review of the evidence for and objections against evolution that lead Zahm to his judgment about the probability that evolution is correct.

Zardetti does, however, point out several of Zahm's mistakes. For example, Zahm clearly did not know about the process unfolding against Leroy in the Congregation and thus did not anticipate that any application of evolution to human origins would be ruled off limits. Furthermore, Zahm's bravado often turned a straightforward statement into a matter-of-fact discussion: for example, for Zahm, it was not a *possibility* that Aquinas and Augustine supported evolution; it was *definite*. It was not a possibility that evolution could be nobler than special creation; it was absolutely nobler![48]

This analysis reveals that Zardetti's motives were formed by the same Neo-Scholastic philosophy as discussed in the previous chapter inasmuch as both Leroy's retraction *and* Salis-Seewis's review were deeply influenced by Neo-Scholasticism. While Zardetti himself seems to have been more influenced by American political motives, Neo-Scholasticism provided him—or any other who contributed to the letter—with the theological and philosophical tools to argue persuasively that Zahm had erred.

The Neo-Scholastic Anti-evolutionism of Enrico Buonpensiere

If Zardetti lit the fire that would burn *Evolution and Dogma,* Buonpensiere poured on the oil. Enrico Buonpensiere was not the dynamic world traveler of a Zahm or Zardetti. He did not seek the perils and thrills of ocean voyages nor did he share their commitment to the adventure that was America. No, Enrico Buonpensiere was born, lived, and died in Italy, serving and working largely within the Vatican world of Italian brothers, priests, and bishops. This section will first examine his life, highlighting his association with Tommaso Zigliara and how this association led to Buonpensiere's concept of Neo-Scholasticism. We then turn to Zigliara's own anti-evolutionary Neo-Scholasticism and its effects on Buonpensiere's approach. Finally, we examine Buonpensiere's writings, including his discussion of Zahm's *Evolution and Dogma,* which represent one of the clearest cases of the connection between a Neo-Scholastic "philosophy of science" and the condemnation of Zahm.

A Life Devoted to Thomism: Buonpensiere and Zigliara

Enrico Buonpensiere was born in Terlizzi, Italy, on October 26, 1853.[49] He completed university studies in Naples and became a Dominican friar in Viterbo, just north of Rome, at the age of seventeen, in the midst of the First Vatican Council and the collapse of the Vatican's political holdings. From Viterbo he traveled south to Rome where he completed philosophical and theological studies under the tutelage of Tommaso Maria Zigliara, a devoted friend of the future Pope Leo XIII and ardent Neo-Scholastic theologian.

Buonpensiere traveled with Zigliara from Viterbo to Rome in 1869. In 1873 Zigliara was appointed rector of the Dominican College of St. Thomas, which just that year had been banished from its historical home at the Basilica of Santa Maria sopra Minerva by the Minervan government. He remained rector of this transitory college until Leo's election to the papacy in 1879, whereupon Leo named him cardinal and co-president, with Leo's brother, of the newly formed Pontifical Academy of St. Thomas Aquinas, which still thrives today.[50] Buonpensiere, in the same year, was appointed professor of philosophy, mathematics, morality, and physics at the transitory College of St. Thomas mentioned above.

Cardinal Zigliara wrote, taught, and preached tirelessly during the 1880s and early 1890s until his untimely death in 1893, and Buonpensiere, undoubtedly, continued to learn from him. At the time of Zigliara's death, aside from being president of the Pontifical Academy, the cardinal was also a member of seven Roman congregations, including the Congregation of the Index; he was also the cardinal prefect of the Congregation of Studies.[51] As a sign of his influence, *The Catholic Encyclopedia* of 1912 accorded the highest praises to the late cardinal: "by his teaching and through his writings, [Zigliara] was one of the chief instruments, under Leo XIII, of reviving and propagating Thomistic philosophy throughout the entire Church."[52]

After Zigliara's death, Buonpensiere followed in his teacher's footsteps, becoming one of the youngest consultors to both the Congregation of the Index (June 20, 1894) and the Congregation of the Propagation of the Faith (December 28, 1895). Buonpensiere was soon named a theologian of the apostolic datary and appointed a consultor of the Congregation of Studies.[53] On April 9, 1897, Buonpensiere was promoted to professor and regent of the aforementioned College of St. Thomas, now known as *de Urbe* instead of *de Minerva* due to its new location in Rome. As regent, Buonpensiere was the central orchestrator behind its promotion to a pontifical college in 1906.[54] From then on it became known as the Pontifical College (later university) of St. Thomas Aquinas or, as it is known today, the Angelicum.

Buonpensiere remained a professor at this bastion of Neo-Scholastic thought until 1910, when he was named professor at the Lateran Seminary in Rome, a position he held until 1925. At that point Buonpensiere retired from teaching due to failing eyesight, and in January of 1929 he passed away.[55] Toward the end of his life he completed the second of two major works on Thomas Aquinas. The first, completed in 1902, was a 976-page treatment of questions 1–23 of the *Summa Theologiae*; the second, published posthumously in 1930, covered questions 27–43.[56] Buonpensiere may not have gained the fame of his teacher, Zigliara, or his student, Reginald Garrigou-Lagrange, but he was well known in Neo-Scholastic circles in the first few decades of the twentieth century.[57] Shortly before his death, he was lauded by a leading Dominican journal as "one of the greatest theologians in the Order."[58]

There should be no doubt as to the extent of Buonpensiere's connection with the Neo-Scholasticism introduced in chapter 4 of this volume. If any still existed, however, one need only point to the best known work of the most famous Neo-Scholastic of the early twentieth century, Reginald Garrigou-Lagrange, who taught at Buonpensiere's Angelicum from 1909 until 1960. In his *La Synthèse Thomiste*, known in English as *Synthesis*, Garrigou-Lagrange writes: "Among those who contributed to the resurgence of Thomistic study, before and after Leo XIII, we must mention eight names: Sanseverino, *Kleutgen*, S. J.: Cornoldi, S. J.: *Cardinal Zigliara*, O. P.: *Buonpensiere*, O. P.: L. Billot, S. J.: G. Mattiussi, S. J.: and Cardinal Mercier."[59] Note how Buonpensiere is mentioned in the same sentence as not only his teacher, Zigliara, but also the originators of Neo-Scholasticism, Kleutgen and Sanseverino. Before a single line of Buonpensiere's reports are examined, it is vital to understand that the man who would negotiate Zahm's censure was widely known as a central member of the rising Neo-Scholastic movement during the 1890s. But was this movement against evolution? The answer is, unequivocally, yes.

A Neo-Scholastic Anti-evolutionist Argument

The end of chapter 4 offered an analysis of the essential features of Neo-Scholasticism's approach to science in general, focusing on Kleutgen's philosophical epistemology. As this chapter focuses on Zahm's case in particular, we must take a moment to look at specific critiques of evolution by Zigliara, which illuminate our reading of Buonpensiere. Indeed, Tommaso Zigliara, Buonpensiere's longtime teacher and colleague, wrote in 1876 that the general doctrine of evolutionary transformism (that is, the idea that one species can transform into another species) is simply a new form of ancient Greek materialism.[60] He applied this critique as much to the French naturalist Jean-Baptist Lamarck's evolutionary hypotheses as to Darwin's natural selection. Zigliara wrote that while Darwin "amplified and explained" Lamarck's theories, to the point where he posited the evolutionary development of humanity, both human evolution and general evolution have been "principally and fundamentally" disproved by Aristotle.[61]

This refutation, as one might expect given the arguments laid out in chapter 4 of this book, is based not on the status of the scientific demonstrations themselves but on metaphysical arguments. For example:

> Let us hear Saint Thomas describe and refute a similar opinion to the recent evolutionary theories: "And so others have replied that the very same soul which at first was merely vegetative is afterwards, through the action of the power that exists in the semen, brought to the point of becoming sentient, and, finally, is brought to the point that the very same soul becomes intellective . . . . But this position cannot stand. First of all, no *substantial* form admits of more and less; instead, the addition of greater perfection makes for a different species, in the way that the addition of a unit makes for a different species among numbers. But it is impossible for numerically one and the same form to belong to diverse species."[62]

Zigliara argues that, based on the Aristotelian metaphysical ideas of substance, species, and singularity, the very concept of transformation between species over time is untenable. It is not, however, an argument whose scope is limited to human evolution nor to Darwinian natural selection. Zigliara's metaphysical critique applies to anything and everything opposed to the doctrine of special creation (the immediate creation of every individual species).

As consultor for the Congregation of the Index, Zigliara reiterated this anti-evolutionary position when reviewing pro-evolutionary books in the late nineteenth century. For example, against Raffaello Caverni's 1877 *New Studies of Philosophy: Lectures to a Young Student*, Zigliara connects his argument against evolution with the antimodernism of the Syllabus of Errors, noting that "Darwinian evolution . . . is nothing more than the material part of total evolutionism, which is the same as Hegelian pantheism."[63] A particularly telling moment occurs when Zigliara responds to one of Caverni's arguments about Church authority. Caverni argues that the Church is not infallible when it comes to the conclusions of natural science, such as theories about the origins and development of animal life.[64] Zigliara responds that such an argument is not only fallacious but dangerous: how much would natural science be allowed to determine? Doctrines of creation itself, the immortality of the soul, and the very existence of the soul would naturally come into question. "Who, exactly, would set the boundary between the objects of science and those of faith?" Furthermore, Zigliara argues, granting such freedom to the natural sciences would mean that "the first Vatican Council . . . erred when it asserted that there are certain revealed truths that are also accessible to natural reason."[65]

With such a critique, the philosophical and theological framework of the previous chapter, which centered on the four pivotal moments in nineteenth-century Catholicism, becomes evident in the case against John Zahm. Zigliara's Neo-Scholasticism, representative of the philosophy widely accepted and employed in seminaries throughout the late nineteenth and early twentieth centuries, interpreted the combination of *Dei Filius* and *Aeterni Patris* not as opening Catholic scholarship to future dialogue with "the modern age" but as an incontrovertible call to employ the writings of Aquinas against all dogmatic threats presented by that age, be they philosophical, theological, or scientific. Indeed, Zigliara and Buonpensiere would write that most evolutionary authors erred in their natural science due to their obvious lack of understanding of metaphysical principles of dogmatic philosophy. What they considered scientific proofs, such as experiential evidence for evolutionary development, were in fact a lower form of argumentation than the metaphysical arguments of Aristotle, Aquinas, or Aquinas's interpreters.

As in the discussion of Salis-Seewis above, this is exactly what one would expect from scholars who had absorbed Kleutgen's Neo-Scholastic epistemology. One can see this from Kleutgen's third principle, described in chapter 4: "knowledge is all the more perfect the further the knowing principle is removed in its being from materiality."[66] The more removed the knower is from the observed object, the more perfect the knower's knowledge of that object could be. As such, Neo-Scholastic metaphysical arguments naturally superseded empirical evidence, as the latter was a less perfect way of understanding the world.

Buonpensiere's Many Negations of Evolution

Evolution and Dogma was not the first book dealing with evolution for which Buonpensiere recommended censure. Following the death of his longtime mentor in 1893, Buonpensiere wrote three decisive reports for the Congregation of the Index related to evolutionary theory: two on Leroy, one in 1895 and one in 1897; and one on Zahm in April 1898. While all three reports are unique in some of their critiques of the respective authors, they all show the influence of Zigliara's arguments against evolution.

In the short 1895 report—only four pages—Buonpensiere expands upon Zigliara's metaphysical argument from Aquinas, adding an "empirical" argument against evolution as well. He writes:

> Evolution, as all Catholic philosophers teach, has been resolutely condemned by *ontological* and *empirical* science. In *ontology*, it has been infallibly demonstrated that the essence of any object is an *immutable type*, that is, *incapable of any evolution, whether higher or lower.* In empirical science there is an unchangeable law of *hybridization*, which maintains the distinctness of living species such that a pairing of two living beings belonging to *different species* will either produce no fruit or will produce fruit that are *completely infertile.*[67]

As such, "evolutionism, opposed completely by the philosophical sciences, cannot even be called a *hypothesis:* it is a simple *desiderata* [derived argument] of materialism, more or less Platonic."[68] He finishes with a harsh and decisive flourish:

> Consequently, the impudence of those who attempt to harmonize evolutionism with Revealed Doctrine is reckless and anti-Christian. . . . [And if] evolutionism is contrary to Science and Faith, the impudence of Father Leroy has been *truly reckless,* both for defending such absurdities, and for pretending he believes it not opposed to Revelation. . . . For me, it would be better that this work be placed on the *Index,* in accordance with the rigor of justice.[69]

While Leroy did print a retraction, as noted earlier, his book does not get placed on the index. Instead, Leroy entered into an extensive dialogue with the congregation, offering possible emendations and changes to the text. The prefect of the congregation eventually turned to Buonpensiere again for a more complete discussion of Leroy's text and ideas. Buonpensiere rose to the occasion, producing a fifty-six-page report that evaluated ten chapters of Leroy's new work.[70] Of the many specific refutations in this 1897 report, two arguments help us understand Buonpensiere's approach to the entire discussion.

First, "even granting that the Church may not have expressed its opinion on evolutionism with complete dogmatic precision," he writes, "it is nevertheless true that the Church has persistently shown its repugnance to this doctrine."[71] Since none of Darwin's books were ever on the index, one can only presume that what Buonpensiere has in mind are discussions of evolutionary theory by other Neo-Scholastic scholars (such as Zigliara), the general antimodernist stance of Pius IX, and the Neo-Scholastic interpretation of *Dei Filius* and *Aeterni Patris,* discussed above, in considering Zigliara's critique.

Second, Buonpensiere pushes back against a claim made by Leroy, that church fathers should *not* be judged as "competent judges" because their understanding of science was different from that of the nineteenth century. While Augustine, Aquinas, and others had no knowledge of evolutionary theories today, Buonpensiere countered, their opinions should still be considered dogmatic and definitive until contrary scientific theories of the modern day have been "clearly demonstrated."[72] But this apparent concession seems to be a red herring. Buonpensiere's vision of the place of natural science, as we saw from his 1895 report, does not extend to it the competence to negate dogmatic arguments, no matter how clear the demonstration. Once again, this is precisely what one would expect of someone trained in Neo-Scholasticism.

Inevitability: Buonpensiere Considers *Evolution and Dogma*

Knowing Buonpensiere's respected place among Neo-Scholastic theologians, his tutelage under Zigliara, and his repeated refutations of Leroy's evolutionary positions, it is helpful to realize at this point that the prefect of the Congregation of the Index, upon receiving Zardetti's condemnation, would have only chosen Buonpensiere to write the report *if the desired outcome was censure or something close to censure.* Zahm's firm commitment to the benefits of modernity, including but not limited to the empirical sciences, stands against the rise of Neo-Scholasticism in nineteenth-century Catholicism, not only in its rejection of modernity and democracy but also in its clear rejection of anything resembling a modern philosophy of the natural sciences. As such, we now come to the inevitable and predictable climax of this story: Zahm's modern American scientific theology meets a master of Neo-Scholastic Thomism, and the latter holds all the power.

As noted above, while Leroy interwove theological and scientific arguments throughout his evolutionary arguments, John Zahm did not.[73] The first two hundred pages of *Evolution and Dogma* contain Zahm's interpretation of the very latest scientific arguments for and against evolutionary ideas, from Bacon to Lamarck to Darwin, from fossil records to speciation to geographical distribution. Zahm is comprehensive in his scientific approach, spending the last sixty pages of the first part discussing only objections to evolutionary theory, ending with the previously mentioned claim:

The lack of this perfected theory [of Evolution] does not imply that we have not already an adequate basis for a rational assent to the theory.... By no means. The arguments adduced in behalf of Evolution in the preceding chapter, are of sufficient weight to give the theory a degree of probability which permits of little doubt as to its truth.[74]

Buonpensiere's report on Zahm consists of sixty typed pages in Latin and Italian, but only the first twelve pages cover part 1 of Zahm's text. Of the entire first part, Buonpensiere writes that "the author sets out to prove the *reality* of evolution, not with metaphysical arguments but rather on observation and the correct interpretation of the facts of nature."[75] Zahm's arguments, however, are but "arbitrary explanations of biological phenomena that, with the same ease that Zahm proposes them, can be perfectly refuted by others, inasmuch as they lack as much philosophical as traditional theological arguments."[76] The scientific arguments are of no use to Buonpensiere. Since they aid in refuting dogmatic theological claims, Zahm's arguments necessarily represent "arbitrary explanations" of data that must be otherwise interpreted, since science cannot overturn the truths of theology and philosophy.

Moving to the second part of the text, Buonpensiere repeats many of the same objections he employed in the case against Leroy, most notably objections to the alleged misuse of historical theological figures such as Augustine and Aquinas. Additionally, writes Buonpensiere, pace Zahm, a Christian is free neither to "accept moderate evolutionism" nor to interpret Genesis with such fluidity as to consider the story of creation less than scientific truth.[77] Much of the report echoes his critique of Leroy and, as with the analysis of that earlier critique, it would be unhelpful to delve into details of the many metaphysical arguments employed by Buonpensiere. It is enough to say that Buonpensiere's critiques are succinct and, unlike Zardetti's, complete in their Neo-Scholastic understanding of the world.

One major difference between Buonpensiere's report on Zahm and his report on Leroy, however, is that at the end of his report on Zahm, Buonpensiere appears to grow quite agitated. He seems compelled to repeat himself time and time again on evolution. On page 45, he goes beyond his role as a consultor when he writes: "At this point I want to put the following beyond dispute: I CONSIDER IT CATHOLIC DOCTRINE TO AFFIRM THAT GOD IMMEDIATELY AND DIRECTLY FORMED ADAM FROM THE SOIL OF THE EARTH."[78] The next six pages are not a refutation of Zahm directly but rather a Neo-Scholastic argument to prove the truth of the above claim. Beginning with Genesis, Buonpensiere cites a list of theologians extensive enough to rival any of Zahm's lists: Plato, Philo, Basil, Chrysostum, Cyril of Alexandria, Ambrose, Augustine, Albert the Great, Thomas Aquinas, Bonaventure, Duns Scotus, Suarez, Peter Lombard, and Alexander of Hales! "The unanimous agreement of the Church Fathers and Scholastic Theologians in matters of Faith and Customs bears certain witness to Catholic Dogma . . . [and] thus the truth of the conclusion above is sustained."[79]

Buonpensiere concludes his report by simultaneously dismissing Zahm and pleading his own case: "It is necessary, once and for all, to let Catholic naturalists know publicly that it is not permitted to teach that Adam's body may not have originated immediately from the soil of the earth but from the body of an anthropomorphic brute."[80] Buonpensiere argued that the Congregation of the Index should issue a formal statement stating exactly this, as it would clear up the misconceptions of modern science that led to authors like Zahm writing such blatantly pro-evolution books. While a few members of the Congregation of the Index wondered if the Congregation of the Holy Office (precursor to the Congregation for the Doctrine of the Faith) should consider precisely this question, there is no record of either congregation seriously considering publishing such a definitive doctrinal statement against human evolution.[81]

This Thing We Call Science

The rest of the story, as laid out in chapter 2, is known. The members of the Congregation of the Index voted to notify and then censure Zahm's book; the notification and submission occurred, the censure did not. Zahm's political connections fought hard to keep the censure out of the press, even appealing to Pope Leo XIII, which seems to have eventually won the day. The note in the congregation diary from February 3, 1899, remains the last official record of Zahm's case: "the Pope ordered that the publication of the decree . . . be suspended . . . until Father Zahm, who will soon come to Rome from

America, can be heard."[82] Zahm never did travel again to Rome; the decree was never published; and Zahm never again wrote on matters of evolution and faith.[83]

———

The board was set and pieces were moved, but checkmate was never really in doubt. Zahm the empirical scientist increasingly saw the probability of the evolutionary hypotheses, while Zahm the theologian consistently argued for the consonance of evolution and faith. But Zahm the theologian could not and did not fully account for the problematic theological and philosophical ideas that followed his evolutionary study to Rome. In the end, while Zahm the scientist could have stood toe-to-toe with any cleric in the Vatican, Zahm the theologian was no match for the depth and power of the Neo-Scholastic minds at the end of the nineteenth century. But Zahm's story is not just about evolution and not just about theology. It concerns each of those things but it is not limited to them. Zahm's story is one of revolutions, of philosophies, of Church councils, and of the very idea of *science*. In this light, it is my hope that this study will not only illuminate the complexities of Catholic theological discussions about science in the late nineteenth century but that it will also spur conversations on how we consider science, theologically and otherwise, today. We live in a time when new scientific discoveries appear almost hourly that call into question any simple theological approaches to the modern sciences. When such questions inevitably arise, I hope and pray that we discuss not only the results of every new experiment, but that we ask each other, time and time again, what is the nature of this thing we call modern science, and what, perhaps, should this thing be?

A New Translation of the 1864 Syllabus of Modern Errors

SYLLABUS[1]

COMPLECTENS PRÆCIPUOS NOSTRÆ ÆTATIS ERRORES QUI
NOTANTUR IN ENCYCLICIS ALIISQUE APOSTOLICIS LITTERIS
SANCTISSIMI DOMINI NOSTRI PII PAPÆ IX

§ I. PANTHEISMUS, NATURALISMUS ET RATIONALISMUS ABSOLUTUS

1. Nullum supremum, sapientissimum, providentissimumque Numen divinum exsistit ab hac rerum universitate distinctum, et Deus idem est ac rerum natura et iccirco immutationibus obnoxius, Deusque reapse fit in homine et mundo, atque omnia Deus sunt et ipsissimam Dei habent substantiam; ac una eademque res est Deus cum mundo, et proinde spiritus cum materia, necessitas cum libertate, verum cum falso, bonum cum malo, et justum cum injusto.

Alloc. *Maxima quidem* 9 iunii 1862.

2. Neganda, est omnis Dei actio in homines et mundum.

Alloc. *Maxima quidem* 9 iunii 1862.

3. Humana ratio, nullo prorsus Dei respectu habito, unicus est veri et falsi, boni et mali arbiter, sibi ipsi est lex et naturalibus suis viribus ad hominum ac populorum bonum curandum sufficit.

Alloc. *Maxima quidem* 9 iunii 1862.

4. Omnes religionis veritates ex nativa humanæ rationis vi derivant; hinc ratio est princeps norma, qua homo cognotionem: omnium cujuscumque generis veritatum assequi possit ac debeat.

---

1. The original Latin text of the Syllabus is from *Acta Santae Sedis* 3 (1867): 167–76, http://www.vatican.va/archive/ass/index_sp.htm.

SYLLABUS[1]

of the sum of the principal errors of our time which have been
noted in the encyclicals and other apostolic letters of our
most holy lord, Pope Pius IX

§ I. PANTHEISM, NATURALISM, AND
ABSOLUTE RATIONALISM (1–7)

1. There exists no supreme, most wise, and most provident divine being
distinct from the universe; and God is none other than nature and is
therefore subject to changes. In truth, God is created in man and in the
world, and all things are God and have the very substance of God. Thus
God is one and the same thing as the world, and, in the same manner,
spirit is the same as matter, necessity as liberty, truth as falsehood, good
as evil, and justice as injustice.

Alloc.[2] *Maxima quidem*, June 9, 1862.

2. One must deny every action of God in humanity and in the world.

Alloc. *Maxima quidem*, June 9, 1862.

3. Human reason, with entirely no regard for God, is the sole arbiter of
truth and falsehood, of good and evil; it is a law unto itself and is inherently sufficient in providing for the well-being both of people and of nations.

Alloc. *Maxima quidem*, June 9, 1862.

4. All truths of religion derive from the inherent strength of human reason. As such, reason is the foremost standard by which humans attain
knowledge: all truths, of every sort and kind, can and should follow
from it.

---

1. My English translation of the Syllabus is a significantly revised translation of
the Latin/English side-by-side translation in Pope Pius IX, "Text and Translation of
the Encyclical and Syllabus," *Dublin Review* 4, no. 56 (1865): 512–29. When slight dis-
crepancies in the Latin appeared between the two sources, the *Acta Santae Sedis* edition, provided here in appendix A, has been favored.

2. The descriptor *allocution* is a delineation used to describe papal addresses
given in secret when only a select group of cardinals were present. See William Fanning, "Allocution," in *The Catholic Encyclopedia*, vol. 1 (New York: Robert Appleton
Co., 1907), http://www.newadvent.org/cathen/01325c.htm.

Epist. encycl. *Qui pluribus* 9 novembris 1846.
Epist. encycl. *Singulari quidem* 17 martii 1856.
Alloc. *Maxima quidem* 9 iunii 1862.

5. Divina revelatio est imperfecta et iccirco subjecta continuo et indefinito progressui, qui humanæ rationis progressioni respondeat.

Epist. encycl. *Qui pluribus* 9 novembris 1846.
Alloc. *Maxima quidem* 9 iunii 1862.

6. Christi fides humanæ refragatur rationi; divinaque revelatio non solum nihil prodest, verum etiam nocet hominis perfectioni.

Epist. encycl. *Qui pluribus* 9 novembris 1846.
Alloc. *Maxima quidem* 9 iunii 1862.

7. Prophetiæ et miracula in Sacris Litteris exposita et narrata sunt poetarum commenta, et Christianæ fidei mysteria philosophicarum investigationum summa; et utriusque Testamenti libris mythica continentur inventa; ipseque Jesus Christus est mythica fictio.

Epist. encycl. *Qui pluribus* 9 novembris 1846.
Alloc. *Maxima quidem* 9 iunii 1862.

§ II. RATIONALISMUS MODERATUS

8. Quum ratio humana ipsi religioni æquiparetur, iccirco theologicæ disciplinæ perinde ac philosophicæ tractandæ sunt.

Alloc. *Singulari quadam perfusi* 9 decembris 1854.

9. Omnia indiscriminatim dogmata religionis Christianæ sunt objectum naturalis scientiæ seu philosophiæ; et humana ratio historice tantum exculta potest ex suis naturalibus viribus et principiis ad veram de omnibus etiam reconditioribus dogmatibus scientiam pervenire, modo hæc dogmata ipsi rationi tamquam objectum proposita fuerint.

Epist. ad Archiep. Frising. *Gravissimas* 11 decembris 1862.
Epist. ad eumdem *Tuas libenter* 21 decembris 1863.

10. Quum aliud sit philosophus, aliud philosophia, ille jus et officium habet se submittendi auctoritati, quam veram ipse probaverit; at philosophia neque potest, neque debet ulli sese submittere auctoritati.

Epist. ad Archiep. Frising. *Gravissimas* 11 decembris 1862.
Epist. ad eumdem *Tuas libenter* 21 decembris 1863.

Encyc. *Qui pluribus*, Nov. 9, 1846.

Encyc. *Singulari quidem*, Mar. 17, 1856.

Alloc. *Maxima quidem*, June 9, 1862.

5. Divine revelation is imperfect and therefore subject to a continual and indefinite advancement which corresponds with the advancement of human reason.

Encyc. *Qui pluribus*, Nov. 9, 1846.

Alloc. *Maxima quidem*, June 9, 1862.

6. Christian faith opposes human reason. As such, divine revelation not only fails to benefit human perfection, but it, in truth, injures it.

Encyc. *Qui pluribus*, Nov. 9, 1846.

Alloc. *Maxima quidem*, June 9, 1862.

7. The prophecies and miracles set forth and narrated in the Sacred Scriptures are the fictions of poets, and the mysteries of the Christian faith are the result of philosophical investigations. The books of the Old and New Testaments contain mythical inventions. Jesus Christ is himself a mythical fiction.

Encyc. *Qui pluribus*, Nov. 9, 1846.

Alloc. *Maxima quidem*, June 9, 1862.

§ II. MODERATE RATIONALISM (8–14)

8. Because human reason is equaled to religion, theological disciplines must be treated in the same manner as philosophical ones.

Alloc. *Singulari quadam perfusi*, Dec. 9, 1854.

9. All dogmas of Christian religions are, without exception, the object of scientific knowledge or philosophy. Human reason, historically developed thus far, can perceive, by its inherent strength and principles, true understanding of even the most obtuse dogmas, as long as such dogmas had been proposed in terms of rationality.

Letter to Archbp. Frising. *Gravissimas*, Dec. 11, 1862.

To the same, *Tuas libenter*, Dec. 21, 1863.

10. While the philosopher may be one thing, philosophy is another. While it is the right and duty of philosophers to submit to the authority they consider true, philosophy neither can nor should submit to any authority.

Letter to Archbp. Frising. *Gravissimas*, Dec. 11, 1862.

To the same, *Tuas libenter*, Dec. 21, 1863.

11. Ecclesia non solum non debet in philosophiam unquam animadvertere, verum etiam debet ipsius philosophiæ tolerare errores, eique relinquere ut ipsa se corrigat.

 Epist. ad Arcbiep. Frising. *Gravissimas* 11 decembris 1862.

12. Apostolicæ Sedis, Romanarumque Congregationum decreta liberum scientiæ progressum impediunt.

 Epist. ad Archiep. Frising. *Tuas libenter* 21 decembris 1863.

13. Methodus et principia, quibus antiqui Doctores scholastici Theologiam excoluerunt, temporum nostrorum necessitatibus scientiarumque progressui minime congruunt.

 Epist. ad Archiep. Frising. *Tuas libenter* 21 decembris 1863.

14. Philosophia tractanda est, nulla supernaturalis revelationis habita ratione.

 Epist. ad Archiep. Frising. *Tuas libenter* 21 decembris 1863.

 N.B.—Cum rationalismi systemate cohærent maximam partem errores Antonii Günther, qui damnantur in Epist. ad Card. Archiep. Coloniensem *Eximiam tuam* 15 iunii 1857, et in Epist. ad Episc. Wratislaviensem *Dolore haud mediocri* 30 aprilis 1860.

§ III. INDIFFERENTISMUS, LATITUDINARISMUS

15. Liberum cuique homini est eam amplecti ac profiteri religionem, quam rationis lumine quis ductus veram putaverit.

 Litt. Apost. *Multiplices inter* 10 iunii 1851.

 Alloc. *Maxima quidem* 9 iunii 1862.

16. Homines in cujusvis religionis cultu viam æternæ salutis reperire æternamque salutem assequi possunt.

 Epist. encycl. *Qui pluribus* 9 novembris 1846.

 Alloc. *Ubi primum* 17 decembris 1847.

 Epist. encycl. *Singulari quidem* 17 martii 1856.

17. Saltem bene sperandum est de æterna illorum omnium salute, qui in vera Christi Ecclesia nequaquam versantur.

 Alloc. *Singulari quadam* 9 decembris 1854.

 Epist. encycl. *Quanto conficiamur* 17 augustii 1863.

11. Not only should the Church never judge philosophy, but it should also tolerate the errors of philosophy, relinquishing correction to philosophy itself.

> Letter to Archbp. Frising. *Gravissimas*, Dec. 11, 1862.

12. The decrees of the Apostolic See and of the Roman Congregations impede the unconstrained progress of knowledge.

> Letter to Archbp. Frising. *Tuas libenter*, Dec. 21, 1863.

13. The method and principles by which the antiquated scholastic doctors developed sacred theology are no longer adaptable to the needs of our age and the progress of knowledge.

> Letter to Archbp. Frising. *Tuas libenter*, Dec. 21, 1863.

14. Philosophy should be discussed without taking account of supernatural revelation.

> Letter to Archbp. Frising. *Tuas libenter*, Dec. 21, 1863.
>
> NB—To the system of rationalism belong, for the most part, the errors of Anton Günther, condemned in the Letter to Card. Archbp. of Cologne, *Eximiam tuam*, June 15, 1857, and in the Letter to Bishop of Breslau, *Dolore haud mediocri*, Apr. 30, 1860.

§ III. INDIFFERENTISM, LATITUDARIANISM (15–18)

15. Everyone is free to embrace and profess the religion which he or she believes true as guided by the light of reason.[3]

> Apost. Letter, *Multiplices inter*, June 10, 1851.
>
> Alloc. *Maxima quidem*, June 9, 1862.

16. People of any religion can discover the way of, and gain, eternal salvation.

> Encyc. *Qui pluribus*, Nov. 9, 1846.
>
> Alloc. *Ubi primum*, Dec. 17, 1847.
>
> Encyc. *Singulari quidem*, Mar. 17, 1856.

17. At the very least, we should rightly hope for the eternal salvation of all those who in no way dwell in the true Church of Christ.

> Alloc. *Singulari quadam*, Dec. 9, 1854.
>
> Encyc. *Quanto conficiamur*, Aug. 17, 1863.

---

3. The Latin here does not include "he or she," but neither does it include a specific male form. As such, I have followed contemporary guidelines of referring to all people by the moniker "he or she" when necessary.

18. Protestantismus non aliud est quam diversa veræ ejusdem Christianæ religionis forma, in qua æque ac in Ecclesia Catholica Deo placere datum est.

Epist. encycl *Noscitis et Nobiscum* 8 decembris 1849.

§ IV. SOCIALISMUS, COMMUNISMUS, SOCIETATES CLANDESTINÆ, SOCIETATES BIBLICÆ, SOCIETATES CLERICO-LIBERALES

Ejusmodi pestes sæpe gravissimisque verborum formulis reprobantur in Epist. encycl. *Qui pluribus* 9 novembris 1846; in Alloc. *Quibus quantisque* 20 april. 1849; in Epist. encycl. *Noscitis et Nobiscum* 8 dec. 1849; in Alloc. *Singulari quadam* 9 dec. 1854; in Epist. encycl. *Quanto conficiamur mœrore* 10 augusti 1863.

§ V. ERRORES DE ECCLESIA EJUSQUE JURIBUS

19. Ecclesia non est vera perfectaque societas plane libera, nec pollet suis propriis et constantibus juribus sibi a divino suo fundatore collatis, sed civilis potestatis est definire quæ sint Ecclesiæ jura ac limites, intra quos eadem jura exercere queat.

Alloc. *Singulari quadam* 9 decembris 1854.
Alloc. *Multis gravibusque* 17 decembris 1860.
Alloc. *Maxima quidem* 9 iunii 1862.

20. Ecclesiastica potestas suam auctoritatem exercere non debet absque civilis gubernii venia et assensu.

Alloc. *Meminit unusquisque* 30 septembris 1861.

21. Ecclesia non habet potestatem dogmatice definiendi, religionem Catholicæ Ecelesiæ esse unice veram religionem.

Litt. Apost. *Multiplices inter* 10 iunii 1851.

22. Obligatio, qua Catholici magistri et scriptores omnino adstringuntur, coarctatur in iis tantum, quæ ab infallibili Ecclesiæ judicio veluti fidei dogmata ab omnibus credenda proponuntur.

Epist. ad Archiep. Frising. *Tuas libenter* 21 decembris 1863.

23. Romani Pontifices et Concilia œcumenica a limitibus suæ potestatis recesserunt, jura principum usurparunt, atque etiam in rebus fidei et morum definiendis errarunt.

Litt. Apost. *Multiplices inter* 10 iunii 1851.

18. Protestantism is nothing more than another form of the same true Christian religion, in which it is possible to be equally pleasing to God as in the Catholic Church.

Encyc. *Noscitis et Nobiscum*, Dec. 8, 1849.

§ IV. SOCIALISM, COMMUNISM, CLANDESTINE SOCIETIES, BIBLICAL SOCIETIES, LIBERAL CLERICAL SOCIETIES

Pests of this description are frequently rebuked in the severest terms in the Encyc. *Qui pluribus*, Nov. 9, 1846; Alloc. *Quibus quantisque*, Apr. 20, 1849; Encyc. *Noscitis et Nobiscum*, Dec. 8, 1849; Alloc. *Singulari quadam*, Dec. 9, 1854; Encyc. *Quanto conficiamur mærore*, Aug. 10, 1863.

§ V. ERRORS ABOUT THE CHURCH AND HER RIGHTS (19–38)

19. The Church is not a true and perfect society of equal liberty, nor does it enjoy special and immovable rights conferred upon it by its Divine Founder, but, instead, the civil power can define the rights and limits within which the Church may exercise its authority.

Alloc. *Singulari quadam*, Dec. 9, 1854.

Alloc. *Multis gravibusque*, Dec. 17, 1860.

Alloc. *Maxima quidem*, June 9, 1862.

20. Ecclesiastical power must not exercise its authority without the permission and assent of the civil government.

Alloc. *Meminit unusquisque*, Sept. 30, 1861.

21. The Church does not have the power to define as dogma that the religion of the Catholic Church is the only true religion.

Apost. Letter, *Multiplices inter*, June 10, 1851.

22. The obligation, which binds all Catholic teachers and authors, applies only to those things which are proposed by the infallible judgment of the Church as dogmas of the faith for universal belief.

Letter to Archbp. Frising. *Tuas libenter*, Dec. 21, 1863.

23. The Roman Pontiffs and Ecumenical Councils have exceeded the limits of their power, have usurped the rights of civil leaders, and have even erred in defining matters of faith and morals.

Apost. Letter, *Multiplices inter*, June 10, 1851.

24. Ecclesia vis inferendæ potestatem non habet, neque potestatem ullam temporalem directam vel indirectam.

Litt. Apost. *Ad apostolicæ* 22 augusti 1851.

25. Præter potestatem Episcopatui inhærentem, alia est attributa temporalis potestas a civili imperio vel expresse vel tacite concessa, revocanda propterea, cum libuerit, a civili imperio.

Litt. Apost. *Ad apostolicæ* 22 augusti 1851.

26. Ecclesia non habet nativum ac legitimum jus acquirendi ac possidendi.

Alloc. *Nunquam fore* 15 decembris 1856.

Epist. encycl. *Incredibili* 17 septembris 1863.

27. Sacri Ecclesiæ ministri Romanusque Pontifex ab omni rerum temporalium cura ac dominio sunt omnino excludendi.

Alloc. *Maxima quidem* 9 iunii 1862.

28. Episcopis, sine gubernii venia, fas non est vel ipsas apostolicas litteras promulgare.

Alloc. *Nunquam fore* 15 decembris 1856.

29. Gratiæ a Romano Pontifice concessæ existimari debent tamquam irritæ, nisi per gubernium fuerint imploratæ.

Alloc. *Nunquam fore* 15 decembris 1856.

30. Ecclesiæ et personarum ecclesiasticarum immunitas a jure civili ortum habuit.

Litt. Apost. *Multiplices inter* 10 iunii 1851.

31. Ecclesiasticum forum pro temporalibus clericorum causis sive civilibus sive criminalibus omnino de medio tollendum est, etiam inconsulta et reclamante Apostolica Sede.

Alloc. *Acerbissimum* 27 septembris 1852.

Alloc. *Nunquam fore* 15 decembris 1856.

32. Absque ulla naturalis juris et æquitatis violatione potest abrogari personalis immunitas, qua clerici ab onere subeundæ exercendæque militiæ eximuntur; hanc vero abrogationem postulat civilis progressus maxime in societate ad formam liberioris regiminis constituta.

Epist. ad Epistc. Montisregal. *Singularis Nobisque* 29 septembris 1864.

33. Non pertinet unice ad ecclesiasticam jurisdictionis potestatem proprio ac nativo jure dirigere theologicarum rerum doctrinam.

Epist. ad Archiep. Frising. *Tuas libenter* 21 decembris 1863.

24. The Church neither has the power to avail herself of military force, nor any other direct or indirect temporal power.

Apost. Letter, *Ad apostolicæ*, Aug. 22, 1851.

25. Prior to any authority claimed by the Episcopate, a temporal power is granted to it by the civil authority, either expressly or tacitly. Thus, such power is revocable by the civil authority whenever it pleases.

Apost. Letter, *Ad apostolicæ*, Aug. 22, 1851.

26. The Church does not have an innate and legitimate right of acquisition and possession.

Alloc. *Nunquam fore*, Dec. 15, 1856.

Encyc. *Incredibili*, Sept. 17, 1863.

27. The sacred ministers of the Church, including the Pope, should be excluded from all charge and dominion over temporal affairs.

Alloc. *Maxima quidem*, June 9, 1862.

28. Bishops do not have the right of promulgating even their apostolic letters without the permission of the civil government.

Alloc. *Nunquam fore*, Dec. 15, 1856.

29. Dispensations granted by the Pope must be considered null unless they have been requested by the civil government.

Alloc. *Nunquam fore*, Dec. 15, 1856.

30. The immunity of the Church and ecclesiastical persons derives its authority from civil law.

Apost. Letter, *Multiplices inter*, June 10, 1851.

31. Ecclesiastical courts for temporal causes of the clergy, whether civil or criminal, should be abolished by any means, including either without the agreement or against the protest of the Holy See.

Alloc. *Acerbissimum*, Sept. 27, 1852.

Alloc. *Nunquam fore*, Dec. 15, 1856.

32. The personal immunity exonerating the clergy from military service may be abolished without violation either of natural rights or of equity. Its abolition is called for by civil progress, especially in a community constituted upon principles of liberal government.

Letter to Archbp. Montreal, *Singularis nobisque*, Sept. 29, 1864.

33. The direction of the instruction of theological things does not exclusively concern ecclesiastical jurisdiction by any particular and inherent right.

Letter to Archbp. Frising. *Tuas libenter*, Dec. 21, 1863.

34. Doctrina, comparantium Romanum Pontificem principi libero et agenti in universa Ecclesia doctrina est quæ media ævo prævaluit.

Litt. Apost. *Ad apostolicæ* 22 augusti 1851.

35. Nihil vetat, alicujus concilii generalis sententia aut universorum populorum facto, summum Pontificatum ab Romano Episcopo atque Urbe ad alium Episcopum aliamque civitatem transferri.

Litt. Apost. *Ad apostolicæ* 22 augusti 1851.

36. Nationalis consilii definitio nullam aliam admittit disputationem, civilisque administratio rem ad hosce terminos exigere potest.

Litt. Apost. *Ad apostolicæ* 22 augusti 1851.

37. Institui possunt nationales Ecclesiæ ab auctoritate Romani Pontificis subductæ planeque divisæ.

Alloc. *Multis gravibusque* 17 decembris 1860.

Alloc. *Iamdudum cernimus* 18 martii 1861.

38. Divisioni Ecclesiæ in orientalem atque occidentalem nimia Romanorum Pontificum arbitria contulerunt.

Litt. Apost. *Ad apostolicæ* 22 augusti 1851.

§ VI. ERRORES DE SOCIETATE CIVILI TUM IN SE, TUM IN SUIS AD ECCLESIAM RELATIONIBUS SPECTATA

39. Reipublicæ status, utpote omnium jurium origo et fons, jure quodam pollet nullis circumscripto limitibus.

Alloc. *Maxima quidem* 9 iunii 1862.

40. Catholicæ Ecclesia doctrina humanæ societatis bono et commodis adversatur.

Epist. encycl. *Qui pluribus* 9 novembris 1846.

Alloc. *Quibus quantisque* 20 aprilis 1849.

41. Civili potestati vel ab infideli imperante exercitæ competit potestas indirecta negativa in sacra; eidem proinde competit nedum jus quod vocant exequatur, sed etiam jus appellationis, quam nuncupant, ab abusu.

Litt. Apost. *Ad apostolicæ* 22 augusti 1851.

42. In conflictu legum utriusque potestatis jus civile prævalet.

Litt. Apost. *Ad apostolicæ* 22 augusti 1851.

34. The doctrine which compares the Pope to a free sovereign acting on behalf of the universal Church is a doctrine which prevailed in the Middle Ages.

Apost. Letter, *Ad apostolicæ*, Aug. 22, 1851.

35. There would be no obstacle to the sentence of a general council or an act of the universal population which sought to transfer the Pope's sovereignty from the Bishopric and City of Rome to some other bishopric and city.

Apost. Letter, *Ad apostolicæ*, Aug. 22, 1851.

36. The definition of a national council does not admit subsequent discussion, and a civil administration can regard as settled an affair decided by such a national council.

Apost. Letter, *Ad apostolicæ*, Aug. 22, 1851.

37. National churches can be established after being withdrawn and plainly separated from the authority of the Pope.

Alloc. *Multis gravibusque*, Dec. 17, 1860.

Alloc. *Jamdudum cernimus*, Mar. 18, 1861.

38. Popes have contributed to the division of the Church into eastern and western by their excessive arbitrary conduct.

Apost. Letter, *Ad apostolicæ*, Aug. 22, 1851.

§ VI. ERRORS ABOUT CIVIL SOCIETY ON ITS OWN AND IN RELATIONSHIP WITH THE CHURCH (39–55)

39. The republic is the origin and source of all rights, and it possesses rights which are not circumscribed by any limits.

Alloc. *Maxima quidem*, June 9, 1862.

40. The doctrine of the Catholic Church is opposed to the well-being and interests of human society.

Encyc. *Qui pluribus*, Nov. 9, 1846.

Alloc. *Quibus quantisque*, Apr. 20, 1849.

41. Civil power, even when exercised by an unbelieving sovereign, possesses an indirect inhibitive power over religious affairs. It therefore possesses not only the right called that of *exequatur*, but that of the *appellatio ab abusu*.

Apost. Letter, *Ad apostolicæ*, Aug. 22, 1851.

42. In legal conflicts between the two powers, civil law prevails.

Apost. Letter, *Ad apostolicæ*, Aug. 22, 1851.

43. Laica potestas auctoritatem habet rescindendi, declarandi ac faciendi irritas solemnes conventiones (vulgo Concordata) super usu jurium ad ecclesiasticam immunitatem pertinentium cum Sede Apostolica initas, sine hujus consensu, immo et ea reclamante.

Alloc. *In Consistoriali* 1 novembris 1850.

Alloc. *Multis gravibusque* 17 decembris 1860.

44. Civilis auctoritas potest se immiscere rebus quæ ad religionem, mores et regimen spiritual pertinent. Hinc potest de instructionibus judicare, quas Ecclesiæ pastores ad conscientiarum normam pro suo munere edunt, quin etiam potest de divinorum sacramentorum administratione et dispositionibus ad ea suscipienda necessariis decernere.

Alloc. *In Consistoriali* 1 novembris 1850.

Alloc. *Maxima quidem* 9 iunii 1862.

45. Totum scholarum publicarum regimen, in quibus juventus Christianæ alicujus reipublicæ instituitur, episcopalibus dumtaxat seminariis aliqua ratione exceptis, potest ac debet attribui auctoritati civili, et ita quidem attribui, ut nullam alii cuicumque auctoritati recognoscatur jus immiscendi se in disciplina scholarum, in regimine studiorum, in graduum collatione, in dilectu aut approbatione magistrorum.

Alloc. *In Consistoriali* 1 novembris 1850.

Alloc. *Quibus luctuosissimis* 5 septembris 1851.

46. Immo in ipsis clericorum seminariis methodus studiorum adhibenda civili auctoritati subjicitur.

Alloc. *Nunquam fore* 15 decembris 1856.

47. Postulat optima civilis societatis ratio, ut populares scholæ, quæ patent omnibus cujusque e populo classis pueris, ac publica universim instituta, quæ litteris severioribusque disciplinis tradendis et educationi juventutis curandæ sunt destinata, eximantur ab omni Ecclesiæ auctoritate, moderatrice vi et ingerentia, plenoque civilis ac politicæ auctoritatis arbitrio subjiciantur ad imperantium placita et ad communium ætatis opinionum amussim.

Epist. ad Archiep. Friburg. *Quum non sine* 14 julii 1864.

43. The civil power has a right to break and to declare and render null the solemn conventions (commonly called Concordats) concluded by the Apostolic See, relative to the use of rights pertaining to ecclesiastical immunity, without the consent of the Apostolic See, and even contrary to its protest.

> Alloc. *In Consistoriali*, Nov. 1, 1850.
> Alloc. *Multis gravibusque*, Dec. 17, 1860.

44. The civil authority may interfere in matters relating to religion, morality, and spiritual government. As such it has control over the instructions for the guidance of consciences issued, conformably with their mission, by the pastors of the Church. Further, it possesses power to decree, in the matter of administering the divine sacraments, as to the dispositions necessary for their reception.

> Alloc. *In Consistoriali*, Nov. 1, 1850.
> Alloc. *Maxima quidem*, June 9, 1862.

45. The entire direction of public schools, in which the youth of Christian states are educated, except to a certain extent the case of seminaries, may and must be under the jurisdiction of the civil power and belong to it such that no other authority whatsoever shall be recognized as having any right to interfere in the discipline of the schools, the arrangement of the studies, the taking of degrees, or the choice and approval of the teachers.

> Alloc. *In Consistoriali*, Nov. 1, 1850.
> Alloc. *Quibus luctuosissimis*, Sept. 5, 1851.

46. Furthermore, in seminaries themselves, the method of study to be adopted is subject to civil authority.

> Alloc. *Numquam fore*, Dec. 15, 1856.

47. The best theory of civil society requires that popular schools open to the children of all classes, and, generally, all public institutes intended for instruction in letters and philosophy, and for conducting the education of the young, should be freed from all ecclesiastical authority, government, and interference, and should be fully subject to civil and political power, in conformity with the will of rulers and the prevalent opinions of the age.

> Letter to Archbp. Fribourg, *Quum non sine*, July 14, 1864.

48. Catholicis viris probari potest ea juventutis instituendæ ratio, quæ sit a Catholica fide et ab Ecclesiæ potestate sejuncta, quæque rerum dumtaxat naturalium scientiam ac terrenæ socialis vitæ fines tantummodo vel saltem primario spectet.

Epist. ad Archiep. Friburg. *Quum non sine* 14 julii 1864.

49. Civilis auctoritas potest impedire quominus sacrorum antistites et fideles populi cum Romano Pontifice libere ac mutuo communicent.

Alloc. *Maxima quidem* 9 iunii 1862.

50. Laica auctoritas habet per se jus præsentandi episcopos et potest ab illis exigere, ut ineant diœcesium procurationem, antequam ipsi canonicam at S. Sede institutionem et apostolicas litteras accipiant.

Alloc. *Nunquam fore* 15 decembris 1856.

51. Immo laicum gubernium habet jus deponendi ab exercitio pastoralis ministerii episcopos, neque tenetur obedire Romano Pontifici in iis quæ episcopatuum et episcoporum respiciunt institutionem.

Litt. Apost. *Multiplices inter* 10 iunii 1851.

Alloc. *Acerbissimum* 27 septembris 1852.

52. Gubernium potest suo jure immutare ætatem ab Ecclesia præscriptam pro religiosa tam mulierum quam virorum professione, omnibusque religiosis familiis indicere, ut neminem sine suo permissu ad solemnia vota nuncupanda admittant.

Alloc. *Nunquam fore* 15 decembris 1856.

53. Abrogandæ sunt leges quæ ad religiosarum familiarum statum tutandum, earumque jura et officia pertinent; immo potest civile gubernium iis omnibus auxilium præstare, qui a suscepto religiosæ vitæ instituto deficere ac solemnia vota frangere velint; pariterque potest religiosas easdem familias perinde ac collegiatas Ecclesias, et beneficia simplicia etiam juris patronatus penitus extinguere, illorumque bona et reditus civilis potestatis administrationi et arbitrio subjicere et vindicare.

Alloc. *Acerbissimum* 27 septembris 1852.

Alloc. *Probe memineritis* 22 januarii 1855.

Alloc. *Cum sæpie* 26 julii 1855.

54. Reges et principes non solum ab Ecclesiæ jurisdictione eximuntur, verum etiam in quæstionibus jurisdiotionis dirimendis superiores sunt Ecclesia.

Litt. Apost. *Multiplices inter* 10 iunii 1851.

48. This system of instructing youth, which consists in separating it from the Catholic faith and from the power of the Church, and in teaching exclusively, or at least primarily, the knowledge of natural things and the earthly ends of social life alone, may be approved by Catholics.

Letter to Archbp. Fribourg, *Quum non sine*, July 14, 1864.

49. Civil power has the right to prevent ministers of religion, and the faithful, from communicating freely and mutually with each other as well as with the Pope.

Alloc. *Maxima quidem*, June 9, 1862.

50. Lay authority possesses the right of installing and removing bishops, and may require that they take possession of dioceses before having received canonical institution and the Apostolic Letters from the Holy See.

Alloc. *Nunquam fore*, Dec. 15, 1856.

51. And, further, secular government has the right to depose bishops from their pastoral functions, and is not bound to obey the Pope in those things which relate to episcopal sees and the institution of bishops.

Apost. Letter, *Multiplices inter*, June 10, 1851.
Alloc. *Acerbissimum*, Sept. 27, 1852.

52. The government has in itself the right to alter the age prescribed by the Church for religious profession, both of men and women; and it may force all religious establishments not to admit anyone to take solemn vows without its permission.

Alloc. *Nunquam fore*, Dec. 15, 1856.

53. Laws for the protection of religious establishments, and for securing their rights and duties, ought to be abolished. Furthermore, civil government may lend its assistance to all who desire to quit the religious life they have undertaken and to break their vows. The government may also suppress religious orders, collegiate churches, and simple charities, even those belonging to private persons, and submit their goods and revenues to the administration and disposal of the civil power.

Alloc. *Acerbissimum*, Sept. 27, 1852.
Alloc. *Probe memineritis*, Jan. 22, 1855.
Alloc. *Cum sæpe*, July 26, 1855.

54. Kings and princes are not only exempt from the jurisdiction of the Church, but are superior to the Church in legal questions of jurisdiction.

Apost. Letter, *Multiplices inter*, June 10, 1851.

55. Ecclesia a Statu, Statusque ab Ecclesia sejungendus est.

Alloc. *Acerbissimum* 27 septembris 1852.

§ VII. ERRORES DE ETHICA NATURALI ET CHRISTIANA

56. Morum leges divina haud egent sanctione, minimeque opus est ut humanæ leges ad naturæ jus confirmentur aut obligandi vim a Deo accipiant.

Alloc. *Maxima quidem* 9 iunii 1862.

57. Philosophicarum rerum morumque scientia, itemque civiles leges possunt et debent a divina et ecclesiastica auctoritate declinare.

Alloc. *Maxima quidem* 9 iunii 1862.

58. Aliæ vires non sunt agnoscendæ nisi illæ quæ in materia positæ sunt, et omnis morum disciplina honestasque collocari debet in cumulandis et augendis quovis modo divitiis ac in voluptatibus explendis.

Alloc. *Maxima quidem* 9 iunii 1862.

Epist. encycl. *Quanta conficiamur* 10 augusti 1863.

59. Jus in materiali facto consistit, et omnia hominum officia sunt nomen inane, et omnia humana facta juris vim habent.

Alloc. *Maxima quidem* 9 iunii 1862.

60. Auctoritas nihil aliud est nisi numeri et materialium virium summa.

Alloc. *Maxima quidem* 9 iunii 1862.

61. Fortunata facti injustitia nullum juris sanctitati detrimentum affert.

Alloc. *Iamdudum cernimus* 18 martii 1861.

62. Proclamandum est et observandum principium quod vocant de non-interventu.

Alloc. *Novos et ante* 28 septembris 1860.

63. Legitimis principibus obedientiam detrectare, immo et rebellare licet.

Epist. encycl. *Qui pluribus* 9 novembris 1846.

Alloc. *Quisque vestrum* 4 octobris 1847.

Epist. encycl. *Noscitis et Nobiscum* 8 decembris 1849.

Litt. Apost. *Cum catholica* 26 martii 1860.

55. The Church should be separated from the State, and the State from the Church.

> Alloc. *Acerbissimum*, Sept. 27, 1852.

§ VII. ERRORS ABOUT NATURAL AND CHRISTIAN ETHICS (56–64)

56. Moral laws do not stand in need of divine sanction, and there is no need for human laws to be conformable to the laws of nature and to receive their sanction from God.

> Alloc. *Maxima quidem*, June 9, 1862.

57. Knowledge of philosophical and moral ideas, and even civil laws, may and must depart from divine and ecclesiastical authority.

> Alloc. *Maxima quidem*, June 9, 1862.

58. No other forces are to be recognized than those which reside in material things. All moral teaching and moral excellence should be made to consist in the accumulation and increase of riches by every possible means as well as in the enjoyment of pleasure.

> Alloc. *Maxima quidem*, June 9, 1862.
> Encyc. *Quanto conficiamur*, 10th Aug. 1863.

59. Rights consist of material acts. All human obligations are empty words, and all human acts have the force of rights.

> Alloc. *Maxima quidem*, June 9, 1862.

60. Authority is nothing other than the result of greater numbers and material force.

> Alloc. *Maxima quidem*, June 9, 1862.

61. A successfully unjust act inflicts no injury upon the sanctity of rights.

> Alloc. *Jamdudum cernimus*, Mar. 18, 1861.

62. The principle of nonintervention, as it is called, ought to be proclaimed and held.

> Alloc. *Novos et ante*, Sept. 28, 1860.

63. One may refuse obedience to legitimate leaders; indeed, one may even revolt against them.

> Encyc. *Qui pluribus*, Nov. 9, 1846.
> Alloc. *Quisque vestrum*, Oct. 4, 1847.
> Encyc. *Noscitis et Nobiscum*, Dec. 8, 1849.
> Apost. Letter, *Cum catholica*, Mar. 26, 1860.

64. Tum cujusque sanctissimi juramenti violatio, tum quælibet scelesta flagitiosaque actio sempiternæ legi repugnans, non solum haud est improbanda, verum etiam omnino licita, summisque laudibus efferenda, quando id pro patriæ amore agatur.

Alloc. *Quibus quantisque* 20 aprilis 1849.

§ VIII. ERRORES DE MATRIMONIO CHRISTIANO

65. Nulla ratione ferri potest, Christum evexisse matrimonium ad dignitatem sacramenti.

Litt. Apost. *Ad apostolicæ* 22 augusti 1851.

66. Matrimonii sacramentum non est nisi quid contractui accessorium ab eoque separabile, ipsumque sacramentum in una tantum nuptiali benedictione situm est.

Litt. Apost. *Ad apostolicæ* 22 augusti 1851.

67. Jure naturæ matrimonii vinculum non est indissolubile et in variis casibus divortium proprie dictum auctoritate civili sanciri potest.

Litt. Apost. *Ad apostolicæ* 22 augusti 1851.

Alloc. *Acerbissimum* 27 septembris 1852.

68. Ecclesia non habet potestatem impedimenta matrimonium dirimentia inducendi, sed ea potestas civili auctoritati competit, a qua impedimenta existentia tollenda sunt.

Litt. Apost. *Multiplices inter* 10 iunii 1851.

69. Ecclesia sequioribus sæcutis dirimentia impedimenta inducere cœpit, non jure proprio, sed illo jure usa, quod a civili potestate mutuata erat.

Litt. Apost. *Ad apostolicæ* 22 augusti 1851.

70. Tridentini canones, qui anathematis censuram illis inferunt, qui facultatem impedimenta dirimentia inducendi Ecclesiæ negare audeant, vel non sunt dogmatici vel de hac mutuata potestate intelligendi sunt.

Litt. Apost. *Ad apostolicæ* 22 augusti 1851.

71. Tridentini forma sub infirmitatis pœna non obligat, ubi lex civilis aliam formam præstituat, et velit hac nova forma interveniente matrimonium valere.

Litt. Apost. *Ad apostolicæ* 22 augusti 1851.

64. The violation of a solemn oath, including every accursed and dissolute action repugnant to eternal law, is not only not blamable, but quite lawful and worthy of the highest praise, when done for the love of country.

Alloc. *Quibus quantisque,* Apr. 20, 1849.

§ VIII. ERRORS ABOUT CHRISTIAN MARRIAGE (65–74)

65. It cannot be tolerated by any means to maintain that Christ raised marriage to the dignity of a sacrament.

Apost. Letter, *Ad apostolicæ,* Aug. 22, 1851.

66. The sacrament of marriage is only an accessory of the contract and separable from it, and the sacrament itself consists in the nuptial blessing alone.

Apost. Letter, *Ad apostolicæ,* Aug. 22, 1851.

67. By the law of nature, the marriage tie is not indissoluble, and in many cases divorce, as it is called, may be pronounced by the civil authority.

Apost. Letter, *Ad apostolicæ,* Aug. 22, 1851.

Alloc. *Acerbissimum,* Sept. 27, 1852.

68. The Church does not have the power to lay aside impediments to marriage that may result in nullification of the marriage. The civil authority possesses such power, and can do away with existing impediments to marriage.

Apost. Letter, *Multiplices inter,* June 10, 1851.

69. The Church only began to bring in nullifying impediments in later ages, and then she availed herself of a right not her own, but borrowed from the civil power.

Apost. Letter, *Ad apostolicæ,* Aug. 22, 1851.

70. The canons of the Council of Trent, which pronounce censure of anathema against those who deny to the Church the right of declaring nullifying impediments, either are not dogmatic or must be understood as referring only to borrowed power.

Apost. Letter, *Ad apostolicæ,* Aug. 22, 1851.

71. The Tridentine form of solemnizing marriage under penalty of nullity does not bind in cases where the civil law has appointed another form and where it decrees that this new form shall effectuate a valid marriage.

Apost. Letter, *Ad apostolicæ,* Aug. 22, 1851.

72. Bonifacius VIII. votum castitatis in ordinatione emissum nuptias nullas reddere primus asseruit.

Litt. Apost. *Ad apostolicæ* 22 augusti 1851.

73. Vi contractus mere civilis potest inter Christianos constare veri nominis matrimonium; falsumque est, aut contractum matrimonii inter Christianos semper esse sacramentum, aut nullum esse contractum, si sacramentum excludatur.

Litt. Apost. *Ad apostolicæ* 22 augusti 1851.

Lettera di S. S. PIO IX. al Re di Sardegna 9 settembre 1852.

Alloc. *Acerbissimum* 27 septembris 1852.

Alloc. *Multis gravibusque* 17 decembris 1860.

74. Caussæ matrimoniales et sponsalia suapte natura ad forum civile pertinent.

Litt. Apost. *Ad apostolicæ* 22 augusti 1851.

Alloc. *Acerbissimum* 27 septembris 1852.

N.B.—Huc facere possunt duo alii errores de clericorum cælibatu abolendo et de statu matrimonii statui virginitatis anteferendo. (Confodiuntur, prior in Epist. Encycl. *Qui pluribus* 9 novembris 1846, posterior in litteris apost. *Multiplices inter* 10 iunii 1851.)

§ IX. ERRORES DE CIVILI ROMANI PONTIFICIS PRINCIPATU

75. De temporalis regni cum spirituali compatibilitate disputant inter se Christianæ et Catholicæ Ecclesiæ filii.

Litt. Apost. *Ad apostolicæ* 22 augusti 1851.

76. Abrogatio civilis imperii, quo Apostolica Sedes potitur, ad Ecclesiæ libertatem felicitatemque vel maxime conduceret.

Alloc. *Quibus quantisque* 20 aprilis 1849.

N.B.—Præter hos errores explicite notatos, alii complures implicite reprobantur, proposita et asserta doctrina, quam Catholici omnes firmissime retinere debeant, de civili Romani Pontificis principatu. (Ejusmodi doctrina luculenter traditur in Alloc. *Quibus quantisque* 20 aprilis 1849; in Alloc. *Si semper antea* 20 maii 1850; in Litt. apost. *Quum Catholica Ecclesia* 26 martii 1860; in Alloc. *Novos* 28 septembris 1860; in Alloc. *Iamdudum* 18 martii 1861; in Alloc. *Maxima quidem* 9 iunii 1862.

72. Boniface VIII is the first who declared that the vow of chastity pronounced at ordination annuls a marriage act.

> Apost. Letter, *Ad apostolicæ*, Aug. 22, 1851.

73. A civil contract may constitute a true marriage among Christians. It is false either that the marriage contract between Christians is always a sacrament, or that the contract is null if the sacrament be excluded.

> Apost. Letter, *Ad apostolicæ*, Aug. 22, 1851.
>
> Letter from Pope Pius IX to the King of Sardinia, Sept. 9, 1852.
>
> Alloc. *Acerbissimum*, Sept. 27, 1852.
>
> Alloc. *Multis gravibusque*, Dec. 17, 1860.

74. Matrimonial causes and weddings belong by their very nature to civil jurisdiction.

> Apost. Letter, *Ad apostolicæ*, Aug. 22, 1851.
>
> Alloc. *Acerbissimum*, Sept. 27, 1852.
>
> NB—Two other errors may tend in this direction, those upon the abolition of the celibacy of priests, and the preference due to the state of marriage over that of virginity. These have been proscribed; the first in the Encyc. *Qui pluribus*, Nov. 9, 1846; the second in the Apost. Letter *Multiplices inter*, June 10, 1851.

§ IX. ERRORS ABOUT THE CIVIL SUPREMACY OF THE ROMAN PONTIFF (75–77)

75. The children of the Christian and Catholic Church are not agreed upon the compatibility of the temporal with the spiritual power.

> Apost. Letter, *Ad apostolicæ*, Aug. 22, 1851.

76. The abolition of the political power possessed by the Apostolic See would be of greatest advantage to the liberty and prosperity of the Church.

> Alloc. *Quibus quantisque*, Apr. 20, 1849.
>
> NB—Besides these errors, explicitly noted, many others are implicitly rebuked by the proposed and asserted doctrine, which all Catholics are bound most firmly to hold, touching the temporal sovereignty of the Roman Pontiff. These doctrines are clearly stated in the Alloc. *Quibus quantisque*, Apr. 20, 1849, and *Si semper antea*, May 20, 1850; Apost. Letter, *Quum Catholica Ecclesia*, Mar. 26, 1860; Alloc. *Novos*, Sept. 28, 1860; *Jamdudum*, Mar. 18, 1861; and *Maxima quidem*, June 9, 1862.

§ X. ERRORES QUI AD LIBERALISMUM HODIERNUM REFERUNTUR

77. Ætate hac nostra non amplius expedit, religionem Catholicam haberi tamquam unicam Status religionem, ceteris quibuscumque cultibus exclusis.

Alloc. *Nemo vestrum* 26 julii 1855.

78. Hinc laudabiliter in quibusdam Catholici nominis regionibus lege cautum est, ut hominibus illuc immigrantibus liceat publicum proprii cujusque cultus exercitium habere.

Alloc. *Acerbissimum* 27 septembris 1852.

79. Enimvero falsum est, civilem cujusque cultus libertatem, itemque plenam potestatem omnibus attributam quaslibet opiniones cogitationesque palam publiceque manifestandi conducere ad populorum mores animosque facilius corrumpendos ac indifferentismi pestem propogandam.

Alloc. *Nunquam fore* 15 decembris 1856.

80. Romanus Pontifex potest ac debet cum progressu, cum liberalismo et cum recenti civilitate sese reconciliare et componere.

Alloc. *Iamdudum cernimus* 18 martii 1861.

§ X. ERRORS WHICH REFERENCE MODERN LIBERALISM (78–80)

77. In the present day, it is no longer expedient that the Catholic religion shall be held as the only religion of the State to the exclusion of all other modes of worship.

Alloc. *Nemo vestrum*, July 26, 1855.

78. Thus it has been wisely provided by law, in some countries called Catholic, that persons coming to reside therein shall enjoy the public exercise of their own worship.

Alloc. *Acerbissimum*, Sept. 27, 1852.

79. Moreover, it is false that the civil liberty of every mode of worship and the full power given to all of overtly and publicly manifesting their opinions and their ideas, of all kinds whatsoever, conduces more easily to corrupt the morals and minds of the people and to the propagation of the pest of indifferentism.

Alloc. *Nunquam fore*, Dec. 15, 1856.

80. The Pope can and should reconcile himself to, and agree with, progress, liberalism, and new modes of government.

Alloc. *Jamdudum cernimus*, Mar. 18, 1861.

APPENDIX B

An English Translation of Otto Zardetti's Condemnation

Eminentissimus DD SRE Cardinalibus S. Congregationi Indicis librorum prohibitorum praepositis debitam reverentiam.[1]

Quoniam Episcoporum maxime est libros perniciosus Apostolicae Sedi denunciare, liceat mihi EE. PP.[2] attentos reddere ad librum aliquem, qui utique doctrinae catholicae sat perniciosus videtur.

Paucis ab hinc mensibus editum fuit opus lingua anglica conscriptum a Rdo. D. J. A. Zahm et, approbante auctore, in linguam italicam versum a D. Alfonso M. Galea. Hujus operis exemplar hisce EE. PP. examinandum trado.

Puncta vero ob quae, examine diligenti instituto, librum denunciatione atque censura S. L. C. [Severae Luci Caeli] digrum indico illa praecipae sunt quae capitibus VI, VII et VIII Partis secundae euisdem operis continentur, quaeque amexis foliis breviter indicantur.

Ceterum humiliter, uti par est, indicium meum quoad hanc rem EE^{um} PP^{um} sententiae subiicio.

EE^{um} PP^{um}
Servus in Domino L. C.
Otto Zardetti
Datum Romae dic 5 Novembris 1897.

NB Titulus operis de quo hic agitur est "Evoluzione e Domma" pel J A Zahm CSC. . . .Versio ne autorizzata dall'Autore per Alforese M. Galea. Siena 1896.

---

1. The original text of Zardetti's letter is from Zardetti to the cardinals of the Congregation of the Index, Index, Protocolli, 1897–99, fol. 179, ACDF.

2. The abbreviation EE PP or EE^{um} PP^{um} was a shorthand for writing, literally, "most eminent principals," an honorific for the persons that would have been reading the letter and deciding the matter, whomever they might be. I translate it as "most holy eminences," a similar honorific sometimes used today, although still a bit antiquated, as EE PP was even in 1897.

To the most holy eminences and doctors, due reverence given
to the leaders of the Cardinals of the Sacred Congregation
of Prohibited Books.

Because it is chiefly the role of bishops to denounce dangerous books to
the Apostolic See, it is my duty to bring the attention of your most holy
eminences to another book which seems of sufficient danger to Catholic
doctrine.

A few months after the book was originally written in the English
language by Rev. Dr. John A. Zahm, an Italian version, approved by
the author, was written by Dr. Alfonso M. Galea. I hand over a copy
of this work for examination by the most holy eminences.

Having made a careful examination, I declare this book worthy of
denunciation and censure of the Harsh Light of Heaven as a consequence of certain points contained in chapters 6, 7, and 8 of the second part of the work, which is divided into two shorter sections.

Humble in all things, I duly submit my judgment on this matter
to the opinions of the most holy eminences.

To the most holy eminences,
Servant of God the Light of Heaven,
Otto Zardetti
Rome. November 5, 1897.

NB: The title of the work is "Evolution and Dogma" by Fr. John A Zahm,
CSC. The authorized Italian version is by Alfonso M. Galea: Siena, 1896.

Puncta excerpta ex opera <u>Evoluzione e Domma.</u> auctore P. J. A. Zahm.

1. Scopo del libro è dimstrare, che il <u>Sistema dell'Evoluzione</u> ci dà un concetto dell'Ente Divine "di gran lunga pui mobile di quello che ce lo rappresenta quasi in atto di fare delle esperienze con materio prima, e riuscire, solo dopo molti vani tentativi a produrre l'organismo proposti. Immaginarsi la Divinità in atto di adoperarsi a quel modo, è un concetto antropomorfico del Creatore, e nè il Dogma cattolico nè la sana scienza possono mai ritenerlo per buono." Pag. 11 e Pag. 285.[3]

2. Tutto il libro inoltre è ma difesa della <u>risposta affermativa</u> data alla domanda che l'Autore si propone nell' "Introduzione": "può un Cattolico, può un Cristiano di qualsiasi denominazione, essere coerente colla fede che ha cara ed essere evoluzionista nel tempo stesso?" Pag. 16.

3. L'Autore sostiene il Sistema dell'evoluzione non solo per le piante e per gli animali inferiori; ma altresì per l'uomo <u>quoad corpus.</u> "Abbiamo già imparato che come cattolici, siamo liberi di accettare la teoria dell'Evoluzione quanto alle molteplici forme di animali e di piante; chè, certo, è dessa più probabile, se non anzi la teoria più probabile, e che lungi dal menomare la sapienza e l'onnipotenza de Dio, <u>essa all'opposto, ci dà un concetto più nobile della Divinità che non l'opinione</u> tradizionale della creazione speciale." Pagg. 284–285.

3. Very few copies of the Italian version of the book still exist today. Saint Mary's College in Notre Dame, Indiana, possesses one of five copies of the book of which I am aware. Three others are listed on the website www.worldcat.org, and I have seen and perused the copy in the ACDF in Vatican City. I am extremely grateful to Jill Hobgood and the librarians at Saint Mary's College for facilitating my many hours to work with the rare text.

Excerpted points from the work *Evolution and Dogma*, authored by Fr. J. A. Zahm.

1. The purpose of the book is to demonstrate that the <u>system of Evolution</u>[1] gives us a concept of the Divine Authority "[which] is a nobler conception of the Creator than that which represents Him as experimenting, as it were, with crude materials, and succeeding, only after numerous attempts, in producing the organism which He is supposed to have had in view from the beginning. To picture the Deity thus working tentatively is an anthropomorphic view of the Creator, which is as little warranted by Catholic dogma as it is by genuine science." (p. 122)[2]

2. Additionally, the whole book is a defense of <u>the affirmative answer</u> to the question that the author poses in the Introduction: "Can a Catholic, can a Christian of any denomination, consistently with the faith he holds dear, be an evolutionist; or is there something in the theory that is so antagonistic to faith and Scripture as to render its acceptance tantamount to the denial of the fundamental tenets of religious belief?" (p. 14)

3. The author supports the system of evolution not only for plants and lower animals but also for man <u>with respect to the body</u> [Latin]: "We have seen that, as Catholics, we are at liberty to accept the theory of Evolution as to all the multifarious forms of animal and plant life, that it is, indeed, a probable, if not the most probable, theory, and that far from derogating from the wisdom and omnipotence of God, <u>it affords us, on the contrary, a nobler conception of the Deity than does the traditional view of Special Creation</u>." (p. 350)

---

1. All emphases are original. Furthermore, when Zardetti emphasizes words in Zahm's texts, I distinguish between Zahm's emphases and Zardetti's in that Zahm's emphases are italicized and Zardetti's emphases are underlined. Zardetti at times double underlined certain words in the original handwritten script.

2. All page numbers in the English translation are from the original English version of *Evolution and Dogma* (Chicago: McBride, 1896). This first point comes from the foreword to the Italian translation, *Evoluzione e dogma* (Siena: Presso l'Ufficio della Biblioteca del clero, 1896), written by the translator himself, Alfonso M. Galea, which in turn cites p. 122 in the English version. Zardetti also cites p. 285 in the Italian version for a similar quote, detailed under the third point below.

4. Quindi prosegue: "Supposta l'impossibilità di scoprire unquemai questo anello mancante tra l'uomo e la scimmia . . . potremo noi, nondimeno, in quanto teoria, credere che un tale anello sia esistito, e che corporalmente, l'uomo è genealogicamente affine a qualche specie sconosciuta di scimmia o di babbuino? L'analogia e la congruità scientifica, vuolsi affermare, richiedono il nostro assenso alla teoria evolutiva per quanto alla forma corporea dell'uomo, se gli animali inferiori furono mai soggetti a questa legge. La scienza biologica non eccettuerebbe il corpo umano dall'azione di questa legge; ma, intanto, v'è nulla in fatto di Dogma e della metafisica, che si opporrebbe salva fide, a quest'opinione, patrocinata con tanto ardore dalla maggioranza degli evoluzionisti contemporonei?" Pagg. 285–286.

5. A dimostrare che "nulla nè in fatto di Domma e di metafisica" che si opponga alla teoria "dell'affirmità geneologica dell'uomo con qualche specie di scimmia o di babbuino," l'Autore cita anzilutto l'autorità del "distinto biologo e filosofo" inglese Georgio Mivart, il quale in un duo libro difese l'anzidetta teoria. Parlando di questo libro, l'Autore dà ad intedere (contra la verità), ch'esso "denunziato con veemenza straordimaria", non solo non fur condarmato, ma approvato dalla Santa Sede. Pagg. 286–287.

Si avverta che il Prof. Mivart, di cui que si parla con tanta lode, è quel medesimo i cui scritti sulla natura ed eternità delle pene dell'Inferno furono condamati dal Santo Ufficio con Decreto del 19 luglio 1893. Scrivendo dopo questa condemna, lo Zahm propone a suoi lettori il Mivart come teologo di nota abilita. Pag. 303.

6. A ribadire la sua tesi, l'Autore insegna che "l'opimo ne della origine derivative del Corpo di Adamo (da una scrimmia o da un babbuino) è in perfetta armonia con altri principii emessi dai due grandi luminari della Chiesa, Sant'Agostino e San Tommaso." Pag. 288. Questa asserzione è stata confutata della Civiltà Cattolica nell'opuscolo qui annesso.

4. He thus continues: "But granting that the search for the link connecting man with the ape has so far been futile . . . may we not, nevertheless, believe, as a matter of theory, that there has been such a link, and that, corporeally, man is genetically descended from some unknown species of ape or monkey? Analogy and scientific consistency, we are told, require us to admit that man's bodily frame has been subject to the same law of Evolution, if an Evolution there has been, as has obtained for the lower animals. There is nothing in biological science that would necessarily exempt man's corporeal structure from the action of this law. Is there, then, anything in Dogma or sound metaphysics, which would make it impossible for us, *without faith*, to hold a view which has found such favor with the great majority of contemporary evolutionists?" (p. 352)

5. To show that "nothing in Dogma or sound metaphysics" is opposed to the theory "that man is genetically descended from some unknown species of ape or monkey," the author cites an additional authority in "the distinguished biologist and philosopher" [St.] George Mivart, who defended the aforementioned theory in a pair of books. Speaking of this book, the author led us to understand that, contrary to the truth, the book, which was "denounced with extraordinary vehemence," was not only not condemned, but was approved by the Holy See. (p. 352)

Be advised that Prof. Mivart, of whom he speaks with so much praise, is the same whose writings on the nature and eternity of the pains of hell were condemned by the Holy Office with the Decree of July 19, 1893. Writing after this condemnation, Zahm presents Mivart to his readers as a "theologian of recognized ability." (p. 374)

6. To emphasize his argument, the author teaches that "this view of the derivative origin of Adam's body [Zardetti inserts the above quote here ('either from ape or monkey')] is also quite in harmony with other principles laid down both by the great Bishop of Hippo and the Angel of the Schools."[3] (p. 356) This assertion has been refuted in the article from *Civiltà Cattolica* attached here.

3. Here the Italian translation of the original English book is significant. Galea translates "quite in harmony" to, in Italian, "in perfect harmony," exaggerating, if only slightly, Zahm's claim of unity between Augustine, Aquinas, and Zahm. Knowing Zahm's use of superlatives, however, Galea's translation was probably quite close to Zahm's own thinking. Were it not for the condemnation, I doubt Zahm would have minded the adjustment. Cf. Zahm, *Evoluzione e dogma*, 288.

7. In fine conferma la sua tesi con l'autorità del Padre Leroy O.P. "Per tacere di un buon dato di altri scrittori cattolici, la teoria mivartiana è nobilmente difesa dall'illustre domenicano francese, Pére Leroy . . . . [Questi] sostiene la sua tesi con validi argomenti, e la sua opera L'Èvolution Restreinte des Espèces Organiques, oltre ad essere provveduta dello imprimatur del provinciale e del censor librorum del suo Ordine, gode il cordiale senso dell'autorevole geologo cattolico Lapparent e di altri." Pagg. 293–294.

Ora questa tesi del P. Leroy, esaminata a Roma dall'autorità competente fu giudicata insostenibile e incompatibile coi testi della S. Scrittura e coi principii dell sana filosofia. In consegnenza di questo autorevole giudizio il P. Leroy fu richiesto di fare una pubblica ritrattazione e la fece, mandando ai giornali una sua lettera del 26 febbraio 1895, da cui qui si aggiungi una copia.

Lo Zahm faceva l'elogio della tesi del Leroy un anno e puì dopo che questo si fosse ritrattato. Ignorando il giudizio dell'autorità competente, egli sostiene nel suo libro la compatibilità della medesima tesi con la Scrittura e coi principii dell sana filosofia.

8. Nel capitolo VIII ed ultimo lo Zahm parla ancora con più franchezza. Per lui "l'Evoluzione sarà il propugnacolo, la rocca, il puì naturale alleato della Religione," Pag. 314; "L'evoluzione dà maggior risalto al disegno, senza che non vi sarebbe 'altro che un caos tenebroso di forze capardie e capricciose,'" Pag. 334; "L'evoluzione venne condannata come antipatristica ed antiscolastica; eppure S. Gregorio Nisseno, St. Agostino, e San Tommaso fanno esplicita dichiarazione di principii che sono in perfetta armonia colle legittime esigenze dell'Evoluzione," Pag. 335[-36]; "L'Evoluzione di fronte alla Creazione speciale, ha questo di buono, che essa spiega è coordina i fatti ed i fenomeni della natura in tutta la loro semplicità e bellezza; mentre la teoria della Creazione speciale non solo non spiega alcuna cosa, nè saprebbe spiegarne alcuna, ma di sua stessa natura, tende a impacciare le ricerche, a ostruire la via al progresso," Pag. 338; "L'evoluzione, non che essere una teoria che vada di pari passo colla scienza e colla Scrittura, colla teologia patristica e scolasatica, promette pure di essere tosto un'opinione generalmente accettata; opinione che si raccomanda da sè non solo alla filosofia cristiana, ma sì ancora all'apologeta cattolico." Pag. 341.

7. In the end, he confirms his thesis with the authority of Fr. Leroy, O.P. "Not to mention a number of other Catholic writers who might be named, Mivart's theory has an able defender in the learned French Dominican, Fr. Leroy. . . . The argument of the author is well sustained, and his work, entitled *L'Évolution Restreinte des Espèces Organiques*, besides having the *imprimatur* of the provincial and *censor librorum* of his order, has the cordial endorsement of such distinguished authorities as the eminent Catholic geologist Lapparent [and others]." (p. 363)

Now this thesis of Fr. Leroy, having been examined by the competent authority in Rome, was considered unsustainable and incompatible with the texts of Holy Scripture and with the principles of sound philosophy. In consideration of this authoritative judgment on Fr. Leroy, he was asked to make a public retraction and did, sending to newspapers the letter of 26 February 1895, of which I have attached a copy.

Thus Zahm praises the thesis of Leroy more than a year after it had been retracted. Ignoring the judgment of the competent authority, he maintains in his book the compatibility of the same argument with Scripture and with the principles of sound philosophy.

8. In the final chapter, chapter 8, Zahm speaks with even more frankness. For him, "far from being an enemy of religious, [evolution] is, on the contrary, its strongest and most natural ally." (p. 388); "Evolution accentuates design, without which all were 'only a dark chaos of obstinate and capricious forces.'" (p. 414); "Evolution has been condemned as anti-Patristic and anti-Scholastic, although Saints Gregory of Nyssa, Augustine and Thomas Aquinas, are most explicit in their assertion of principles that are in perfect accord with all the legitimate demands of theistic Evolution." (p. 416); "Evolution, as against special creation, has this in its favor, that it explains and coordinates the facts and phenomena of nature in a most beautiful and simple manner; whereas the theory of special creation not only explains nothing and is incapable of explaining anything, but, by its very nature, tends to impede research, to bar progress" (p. 419); "But not only is Evolution a theory which is in perfect accordance with science and Scripture, with Patristic and Scholastic theology; it is likewise a theory which promises soon to be the generally accepted view; the view which will specially commend itself not only to Christian philosophy, but also to Christian apologetics as well." (p. 424)

9. La seguente proposizione dello Zahm merita di essere notate: "Sentiamo spesso ripeterci che la discendenza dell'uomo dalla scimmia degrada l'uomo. Ma che! E perchè non dire piuttosto che siffatta discendenza nobilita la scimmia? A parte il sentimentalismo, che importa al cristiano 'che egli tracci il suo lignaggio direttamente o indirettamente dalla polvere.' San Francesco d'Assisi, 'chiamava suoi fratelli gli uccelli.' Commune si fosse egli creduto in diritto di farlo, per ragioni teologiche o zoologiche, egli era affatto libero da vani timori d'essere preso per una scimmia." Pag. [345–]346. "L'evoluzione . . . intesa nel vero senso, riesce essa un'alleata utile e strenua del Dogma Cattolico," Pag. 349.

10. Alla Pag. 341, Lo Zahm ripete e raccomanda la sua tesi come conforme alla Scrittura e alla teologia patristica, dicturando che "tanto più confidiamo che sia cosi in quanto vediamo eminenti scienziati cattolici esprimersi in questo senso, come un Monsabré, un D. Hulst, un Leroy, un De Lapparent, un Mivart."

La tesi difesa prima dal Mivart e poscia dal Leroy ed ora dallo Zahm si trova teologicamente confutata in tutti i suoi particolari nel trattato De Deo Creante, pubblicato dall'Emm Cardinale Mazzella.

Dal resoconto del Congresso tenuto quest'anno a Friburgo apparisce che molto attiva è la propaganda che si fa dallo Zahm del sistema evoluzionista. Di questo sistema l'Emō Card Satolli cosi scrive nell'ultima sua opera De habitibus (p. 237) "Eadem caret quaris factorum comprobatione, repugnant undique principiis et conclusionibus Metaphysicae nec non naturalium scientiarum."

9. The following proposition of Zahm deserves to be noticed: "But the derivation of man from the ape, we are told, degrades man. <u>Not at all. It would be truer to say that such derivation ennobles the ape.</u>[4] Sentiment aside, it quite unimportant to the Christian 'whether he is to trace back his pedigree directly or indirectly to the dust.' St. Francis of Assisi, as we learn from his life, 'called the birds his brothers.' Whether he was correct, <u>either theologically or zoologically [biologically]</u>, he was plainly free from that fear of being mistaken for an ape which haunts so many in these modern times." (p. 430); "evolution . . . , when properly understood, is found to be a strong and useful ally of Catholic Dogma." (p. 434)

10. On page 341, Zahm repeats and urges that his thesis conforms to both Scripture and patristic theology, saying that "we have seen some indications of this in the already quoted opinions of such <u>eminent Catholic authorities</u> as Monsabré, D'Hulst, <u>Leroy</u>, De Lapparent and <u>Mivart</u>."

The defense of the thesis, first from Mivart, then by Leroy, and now by Zahm has been <u>theologically</u> refuted in all its details in the treatise *De Deo Creante*, published by the Eminent Cardinal Mazzella.

The report of the congress held this year at Freiburg appears to be a highly charged piece of propaganda for Zahm's evolutionary system. It is this system that the Eminent Cardinal Satolli writes about in his latest work, *De habitibus* (p. 237): [Latin] "Thus, in recognition of the facts, [evolution] remains incompatible with all the principles and conclusions of metaphysics as well as the natural sciences."

---

4. The Italian translation turns this statement into a question, but the meaning remains nearly the same.

NOTES

Introduction

1. Many have written on the different visions of science in different eras. See, for example, Thomas S. Kuhn, *The Structure of Scientific Revolutions* (Chicago: University of Chicago Press, 1962); Thomas S. Kuhn, "What Are Scientific Revolutions?" in *The Road Since Structure: Philosophical Essays, 1970–1993, with an Autobiographical Interview*, ed. James Conant and John Haugeland (Chicago: University of Chicago Press, 2002), 13–32; and Peter Harrison, *The Territories of Science and Religion* (Chicago: University of Chicago Press, 2017).

ONE. Setting the Stage

1. For the novice, the general theory of biological evolution consists of "inherited changes in populations of organisms over time leading to differences among them." Human evolution is a subset of this theory that applies the theory of evolution to the human species. This should be differentiated from Darwin's theory of natural selection, which was his way of explaining the method by which evolutionary changes occur. See Brian K. Hall and Benedikt Hallgrímsson, *Strickberger's Evolution*, 4th ed. (Sudbury, MA: Jones and Bartlett Publishers, 2008), 3.

2. Pope Francis, *Laudato Si': On Care for Our Common Home*, Encyclical Letter (May 24, 2015), para. 81, http://w2.vatican.va/content/francesco/en/encyclicals/documents/papa-francesco_20150524_enciclica-laudato-si.html; Pope John Paul II, "Message to the Pontifical Academy of Sciences on Evolution," October 22, 1996, https://www.ewtn.com/library/papaldoc/jp961022.htm; Pope Pius XII, *Humani Generis*, Encyclical Letter (December 8, 1950), http://w2.vatican.va/content/pius-xii/en/encyclicals/documents/hf_p-xii_enc_12081950_humani-generis.html.

3. Pope Pius XII, *Humani Generis*, para. 36–37.

4. Michael Sheehan, *Apologetics and Catholic Doctrine: A Two Years' Course of Religious Instruction for Schools and Colleges* (Dublin: M. H. Gill and Son, 1937), 54.

5. John L. Morrison, "A History of American Catholic Opinion on the Theory of Evolution, 1859–1950" (PhD diss., University of Missouri, 1951), 265.

6. John O'Brien, *The Origin of Man: Light from Modern Science* (New York: Paulist, 1947), 26.

7. Ralph Edward Weber, *Notre Dame's John Zahm; American Catholic Apologist and Educator* (Notre Dame, IN: University of Notre Dame Press, 1961).

8. R. Scott Appleby, "American Catholic Modernism at the Turn of the Century" (PhD diss., University of Chicago, 1985). The dissertation later became part of Appleby's 1992 book *"Church and Age Unite!": The Modernist Impulse in American Catholicism* (Notre Dame, IN: University of Notre Dame Press, 1992). Appleby also reworked the first chapter of the book for an essay on the wider debates in the Catholic Church hierarchy around evolution, published as "Exposing Darwin's 'Hidden Agenda': Roman Catholic Responses to Evolution, 1875–1925," in *Disseminating Darwinism*, ed. Ronald Numbers and John Stenhouse (Cambridge: Cambridge University Press, 1999), 173–207.

9. See "Americanism" entry in *A Concise Dictionary of Theology*, ed. Gerald O'Collins and Edward G. Farrugia (New York: Paulist, 2000). There were other arguments within the Americanist movement that have not been accepted by the Church, such as a democratic organization of the Church (anti-monarchy, anti-infallibility), married priests, increased power to local bishops, and others. It is difficult to conceive that the Church today was firmly against democracy and individual freedom of expression in the past, but such was unquestionably the case in the nineteenth and early twentieth centuries.

10. Mariano Artigas, Thomas F. Glick, and Rafael A. Martínez, *Negotiating Darwin: The Vatican Confronts Evolution, 1877–1902* (Baltimore, MD: Johns Hopkins University Press, 2006); Barry Brundell, "Catholic Church Politics and Evolution Theory, 1894–1902," *British Journal for the History of Science* 34, no. 1 (2001): 81–95.

11. Edward Heinle, "Religion and Evolution: John Zahm's Reconciliation" (master's thesis, University of Notre Dame, 1987); Phillip R. Sloan, "Bringing Evolution to Notre Dame: Father John Zahm, C.S.C. and Theistic Evolutionism," *American Midland Naturalist* 161, no. 2 (2009): 189–205.

12. Morrison, "A History of American Catholic Opinion," 361. Though Morrison defended the dissertation in 1951, he gives no mention of the encyclical. The most recent scholarly reference in his study is May 1950.

13. Ibid., 12.

14. "The Evolution of Life," *Catholic World* 17, no. 98 (1873): 145–57. All articles in *Catholic World*, and in many other popular journals, were published anonymously until the 1880s. This was done, the editors argued, to ensure the wide range of free speech on controversial topics.

15. Morrison, "A History of American Catholic Opinion," 13. Cf. "The Evolution of Life," 155.

16. Morrison, "A History of American Catholic Opinion," 14.

17. Due to the Italian Revolution, the council ended prematurely after publishing only two documents, *Dei Filius*, on the interaction of faith and reason, and *Aeterni Patris*, on the infallibility of the pope.

18. John W. Draper, *A History of the Conflict between Religion and Science* (New York: Appleton, 1874).

19. Index, Protocolli, 1875–78 (126), fol. 240, Archives of the Congregation for the Doctrine of the Faith, Vatican City (hereafter cited as ACDF).

20. Morrison, "A History of American Catholic Opinion," 97.

21. John Gmeiner, *Modern Scientific Views and Christian Doctrines Compared* (Milwaukee, WI: Yewdale, 1884).

22. Ibid., 152–207.

23. "The usual branches of profane learning, not omitting the natural sciences, as well as music and the Gregorian chant are to be part of the curriculum." William Fanning, "Third Plenary Council of Baltimore," in *The Catholic Encyclopedia*, vol. 2 (New York: Robert Appleton Co., 1907), http://www.newadvent.org/cathen/02235a.htm.

24. While some have used the terms *liberal* and *conservative* to describe these two groups, this study refers to them as Americanist and anti-Americanist due to the continued and muddled use of the words *liberal* and *conservative* today.

25. Morrison, "A History of American Catholic Opinion," 153.

26. Ibid., 177.

27. Ibid., 197.

28. Ibid., 198–99.

29. Ibid., 205.

30. Ibid., 206.

31. Ibid., 212.

32. Ibid., 223.

33. Ibid., 251.

34. Ibid., 252–53.

35. Ibid., 263. Cf. "A New Theory of Evolution Applied to Man," *Catholic Fortnightly Review* 13 (1906): 137–38.

36. Morrison, "A History of American Catholic Opinion," 264. Cf. Bertram C. A. Windle, *The Church and Science* (London: Catholic Truth Society, 1918), 386–87.

37. While Weber's book is readily available, his dissertation is only accessible through the University of Notre Dame Archives. For the most part, however, the material in the published form is more concise and of better use to this study and is thus referenced throughout. When necessary, the dissertation is cited independently.

38. Weber, *Notre Dame's John Zahm*, 196.

39. Ibid., 26–27.

40. Ibid., 54.

41. Ibid., 48–49.

42. Ibid., 49–51.

43. Ibid., 83, 85n78.

44. Ibid., 112–13; Français to Zahm, November 10, 1898, John Zahm Papers, University of Notre Dame Archives, Notre Dame, IN (hereafter cited as JZA, UNDA). Cf. Morrison, "A History of American Catholic Opinion," 243–44.

45. Français to Zahm, November 10, 1898, JZA, UNDA.

46. Weber, *Notre Dame's John Zahm*, 116–19.

47. Ibid., 124.

48. Ibid.

49. Ibid., 156, 172.

50. One must recall that Weber's book was published a decade into Fr. Theodore Hesburgh's tenure as the president of Notre Dame. Fr. Hesburgh's vision of Notre Dame was very similar to Zahm's, thus even while Zahm was rejected because of this vision at the turn of the century, Hesburgh would lift him up as one who foresaw the grandeur of the university. As proof of this, Hesburgh named a newly constructed dormitory after John Zahm, which still stands today.

51. Appleby, "American Catholic Modernism," 102–79.

52. See "modernism" entry in O'Collins and Farrugia, *A Concise Dictionary of Theology*.

53. Appleby, "American Catholic Modernism," 116.

54. Ibid., 102–80.

55. Ibid., 179–80.

56. Appleby, "Between Americanism and Modernism: John Zahm and Theistic Evolution," *Church History* 56, no. 4 (1987): 474–90.

57. Appleby, "American Catholic Modernism," 199.

58. Brundell, "Catholic Church Politics"; Barry Brundell, review of *Negotiating Darwin: The Vatican Confronts Evolution, 1877–1902*, by Mariano Artigas, Thomas F. Glick, and Rafael A. Martínez, *Isis* 99, no. 2 (2008): 415–16.

59. Artigas, Glick, and Martínez, *Negotiating Darwin*, 279.

60. Ibid., 279.

61. Ibid., 143–58.

62. Ibid., 202.

63. Brundell, "Catholic Church Politics," 89.

64. Brundell's position was not without controversy. *Negotiating Darwin* devotes two pages to refute Brundell's thesis, claiming that his reasoning "does not constitute proof" and that his conclusions were "inexact because, as we have seen, the matter was quite a bit more complex" (Artigas, Glick, and Martínez, *Negotiating Darwin*, 200–201). Brundell responded to this claim in his review of *Negotiating Darwin*, noting that he was not unaware of the complexities of the case but merely wanted to ensure the role of the journal's editors was not undervalued. See Brundell, review of *Negotiating Darwin*, 415–16.

65. Heinle, "Religion and Evolution," 52–53.

66. Ibid., 52.

67. Ibid., 54.

68. Ibid.

69. Phillip R. Sloan, "Bringing Evolution to Notre Dame: Father John Zahm, C.S.C. and Theistic Evolutionism," *American Midland Naturalist* 161, no. 2 (2009): 189–205.

70. Ibid., 199. For more information on Zahm's evolutionary arguments, see chapter 3 in this volume.

71. Ibid., 202.

72. Ibid.

73. Hubert Wolf, ed., *Römische Inquisition und Indexkongregation. Grundlagenforschung: 1814–1917*, 3 vols. (Munich: Schöningh, 2005), 1:232.

74. The three volumes of Wolf's *Römische Inquisition und Indexkongregation. Grundlagenforschung: 1814–1917* are divided into seven books: an introduction (one book, including translations into English, Spanish, and Italian), an index (one book, including a register of accused persons and administrative persons), a copy of every published decree by the Congregation of the Index and the Congregation of the Holy Office during the time period (vol. 1, one book), a detailed listing of nearly all the cases brought before the Index and Holy Office (vol. 2, two books), and brief timelines and biographies of nearly every member of both congregations involved (vol. 3, two books). Wolf also organized a previous series, in the same format, covering the years 1701–1813. See Hubert Wolf et al., eds., *Römische Inquisition und Indexkongregation. Grundlagenforschung: 1701–1813*, 3 vols. (Paderborn: Ferdinand Schöningh, 2009).

75. Wolf, *Römische Inquisition und Indexkongregation. Grundlagenforschung: 1814–1917*, 1:256. While most of Wolf's volumes are only in German, the

introduction includes within it translations of the German into French, Spanish, and English.

TWO. The Rise and Fall of John Zahm, CSC

1. On the first page of Weber's biography *Notre Dame's John Zahm*, Zahm's birth date has been wrongly listed as June 11, 1851. This error seems to be that of the publisher, however, as Weber's dissertation lists the correct date of June 14, 1851. See Ralph Weber, "The Life of Reverend John A. Zahm, C.S.C.: American Catholic Apologist and Educator" (PhD diss., University of Notre Dame, 1956), 1, Book Collection, UNDA. This unfortunate mistake has gone unchecked in every mention of Zahm since the 1950s! The correct date of June 14 has been corroborated with multiple sources, including a passport application filled out by Zahm in 1889 (JZA, UNDA); Zahm's tombstone in the Holy Cross Community Cemetery, Notre Dame, Indiana (image accessible at http://www.findagrave.com/cgi-bin/fg.cgi?page=gr&GRid=89368849); and a card for prayer intentions issued by the superior general of the Congregation of Holy Cross upon Zahm's death (G. Français, CSC, November 12, 1921, JZA, UNDA).

2. *Scholastic* 1, no. 14 (1867): 1. Fortunately for the writing of this book, this student magazine began the same year Zahm arrived on campus, offering details and opinions otherwise generally not recorded in the first twenty-five years of the university. It is helpful to realize that the magazine has changed its name a few times, going back and forth between *The Notre Dame Scholastic, The Scholastic, Scholastic,* and *Notre Dame Scholastic* from 1867 to the present day. For purposes of simplicity, I refer to the publication as *Scholastic.*

3. See table 3.1, "A Comprehensive List of Zahm's University Coursework" in chapter 3 of this volume.

4. University of Notre Dame, *Annual Catalogue of the University of Notre Dame,* vols. 24–29 (Notre Dame, IN: Ave Maria Press, 1867–73), Digital Collections, UNDA, http://www.archives.nd.edu/bulletin/.

5. University of Notre Dame, *Annual Catalogue of the University of Notre Dame,* vols. 30–31 (Notre Dame, IN: Ave Maria Press, 1873–75), Digital Collections, UNDA, http://www.archives.nd.edu/bulletin/.

6. Weber, *Notre Dame's John Zahm,* 9.

7. *Scholastic* 2, no. 35 (1868): 1.

8. Arthur J. Hope, CSC, *Notre Dame: One Hundred Years* (Notre Dame, IN: University of Notre Dame Press, 1978), 150–51.

9. Weber, *Notre Dame's John Zahm,* 6.

10. James M. Schmidt, *Notre Dame and the Civil War: Marching Onward to Victory* (Charleston, SC: History Press, 2010), 35. Cf. Howard Thomas

[anon.], *A Brief History of the University of Notre Dame du Lac: From 1842–1892. Prepared for the Golden Jubilee* (Chicago: Werner Co., 1895), 89, Digital Collections, UNDA, http://archives.nd.edu/Anniversary/Golden.pdf.

11. Schmidt, *Notre Dame and the Civil War*, 36–37.

12. Thomas, *A Brief History of the University of Notre Dame du Lac*, 120.

13. Hope, *Notre Dame: One Hundred Years*, 225–28.

14. William Dunn, CSC, "Holy Cross at St. Mary's College, Galveston: A Short Story of the 1870s," paper presented at the Conference of the History of the Congregations of Holy Cross, Notre Dame, IN, July 5–7, 1991, 15; *Scholastic* 10, no. 2 (1876): 26.

15. The University of Notre Dame *Annual Catalogue* is publicly searchable via the Digital Collections of the UNDA, http://archives.nd.edu/bulletin/.

16. University of Notre Dame, *Annual Catalogue of the University of Notre Dame*, vol. 35 (Notre Dame, IN: Scholastic Press, 1879), 70, Digital Collections, UNDA, http://archives.nd.edu/bulletin/AC_35.pdf.

17. *Scholastic* 4, no. 5 (1870): 4; no. 11 (1871): 3; no. 6 (1870): 8.

18. *Scholastic* 6, no. 19 (1873): 147.

19. Ibid.

20. Ibid.

21. Joseph Carrier Collection, Archives Province Canadienne de la Congrégation de Sainte-Croix, Montréal, Quebec (hereafter cited as JCC, APC).

22. These are labeled "1st Lecture" through "13th Lecture" and do not have page numbers, dates, or places attached (JCC, APC).

23. Joseph Carrier, "2nd Lecture," pp. 10, 9, JCC, APC. Original emphasis.

24. *Scholastic* 6, no. 19 (1873): 147.

25. JCC, APC.

26. Augustine, *The Literal Meaning of Genesis*, trans. John Hammond Taylor (New York: Newman Press, 1982), 19–22.

27. "From these words of the Genesis we may derive many useful and interesting instructions: When God creates the elements, the sun, the stars, the planets, the animals, he speaks words of command: 'Let the light be; let there be two great luminaries in the heavens, etc.' But when he is about to create man, he expresses himself differently: 'Let us make man to our image and likeness; and let him [illegible] the fishes of the sea and fowls of the air, etc.'; God says in the form plural—'Let us make man to our image,' and to whom does he say that? To himself because he is one of many; the Father says it to the Son and the Spirit and by this is the mystery, of the Adorable Trinity proved. . . . Man was not, therefore, created to the image of any other creature but to that of God himself, not even to the image of the Angels; this is clear from the text of Moses; when he repeats himself twice in employing the same phrase: 'God created, then, man to his own image, and to the image of God he created him.'" Joseph Carrier,

"11th Lecture," p. 2, JCC, APC. See also Augustine, *The Literal Meaning of Genesis*, 22.

28. Carrier to James F. Edwards, March 3, 1895, JZA, UNDA.

29. Ibid.

30. Thomas, *A Brief History of the University of Notre Dame du Lac*, 119–22.

31. In his 1922 biographical sketch on Zahm, John Cavanaugh would write of the two: "He was Father Sorin's intimate friend, his trusted counselor; I saw him hold the venerable founder in his arms as he lay a-dying." John Cavanaugh, CSC, "Father Zahm," *Catholic World* 114, no. 683 (1922): 577.

32. Weber, *Notre Dame's John Zahm*, 12.

33. Ibid., 14–16.

34. Ibid., 16–17.

35. Ibid., 18.

36. Ibid., 19.

37. John Zahm, "Catholic Church and Modern Science," *Ave Maria* 19 (1883): 241–48, 261–68.

38. Weber, *Notre Dame's John Zahm*, 47–50; John Zahm, *Sound and Music* (Chicago: A. C. McClurg, 1893).

39. Weber, *Notre Dame's John Zahm*, 49.

40. Certainly, as provincial of the Congregation of Holy Cross, Zahm would still exert significant influence over the university. The year 1892, however, marked the last time that Zahm would impact the direction of the university, one might say, from the inside.

41. As a small example, see laudatory reviews in *Nature* 47 (1893): 222–23; *Music: A Monthly Magazine* 3 (1892–April 1893): 214–18; *Christian Union* 47 (1893): 523.

42. Zahm to Sorin, September 6, 1893, John Augustine Zahm Collection, Archives of the United States Province of the Congregation of Holy Cross, Notre Dame, IN (hereafter cited as JZC, CSCA).

43. Zahm's master's degree included courses in theology and philosophy, of course, but he was only as educated as the average Holy Cross priest in 1892 on these disciplines. Such an education began to show itself in his increasingly complex publications in discussions of evolution and Catholicism in the 1890s.

44. Cavanaugh, "Father Zahm," 581.

45. John Zahm, *Evolution and Dogma* (Chicago: McBride, 1896), 5.

46. John Zahm, *Scientific Theory and Catholic Doctrine* (Chicago: McBride, 1896), 7.

47. "The Catholic Summer School movement grew out of the desire of a group of thoughtful Catholics, clerical and lay, to provide an opportunity for serious minded Catholics to meet together during the summer months to fos-

ter intellectual culture in harmony with Christian faith by means of lectures and special courses along university extension lines. The first session was held at New London, Connecticut, in 1892. The 1893 session was held at Plattsburg, New York, where, at nearby Cliff Haven, a permanent foundation was eventually made under the name of the Catholic Summer School of America. The Columbian Summer School was founded at Madison, Wisconsin, in 1895, and a Winter School at New Orleans in 1896. The Cliff Haven School continued in operation until the outbreak of World War II." Thomas F. O'Connor, "John A. Zahm, C.S.C.," *The Americas* 7, no. 4 (1951): 441n34.

48. Zahm to James Burns, August 13, 1893, JZA, UNDA. Cf. Weber, *Notre Dame's John Zahm*, 55–56.

49. Clipping in Zahm scrapbook, JZC, CSCA. Cf. Weber, *Notre Dame's John Zahm*, 56–57.

50. Weber, *Notre Dame's John Zahm*, 71.

51. Ibid., 73.

52. Ibid.

53. Quoted in ibid., 74.

54. Weber, *Notre Dame's John Zahm*, 75.

55. A copy of the certificate of bestowal of the degree is on file in JZC, CSCA.

56. For just a few examples, see John Zahm, "A Distinguished Orientalist, Monsignor Charles De Harlez," *Rosary* 5 (1895): 262–71; Zahm, "A Galaxy of Catholic Scientists," *Donahue's Magazine* 32 (1894): 595–610; Zahm, "A New System of Writing for the Blind," *Catholic World* 61 (1895): 32–43; Zahm, "Leo XIII and Science," *Catholic University Bulletin* 2 (1896): 21–38; and Zahm "Leo XIII and the Social Question," *North American Review* 61 (1895): 200–214.

57. Morrison notes, among others, *Catholic Reading Circle Review, American Catholic Quarterly Review*, and *Catholic World*. Morrison, "A History of American Catholic Opinion," 198–99.

58. Cavanaugh, "Father Zahm," 582.

59. Weber, *Notre Dame's John Zahm*, 67–73; Morrison, "A History of American Catholic Opinion," 223–34. Weber takes pains, however, to point out that these accusations of liberalism were nothing but baseless accusations. Morrison, on the other hand, is quite comfortable placing Zahm amid the liberal faction, pointing out the highly political rise of Americanism with the rise of Zahm's own provocative views on evolution.

60. Appleby, "Between Americanism and Modernism," 484.

61. Appleby, "American Catholic Modernism," 144.

62. Ibid.

63. Zahm to Fr. Joseph H. McMahon, May 19, 1892, JZA, UNDA.

64. Zahm to Augustine F. Hewit, October 2, 1895, JZA, UNDA.

65. Zahm mailed several sections of *Evolution and Dogma* to Hewit on October 2, 1875, writing that "I wish to have your comforting opinion that I am 'safe' & not temerarious" (Zahm to Hewit, JZA, UNDA). Hewit replied negatively, stating that not only did he believe that Zahm's line of reasoning was impossible to prove, but that "he feared Zahm's ideas might well awaken opposition and, unless it was very important, he suggested it should not be published" (Hewit to Zahm, October 7, 1895, JZA, UNDA). Cf. Weber, *Notre Dame's John Zahm*, 78–79.

66. While *Sound and Music* was also well received around the world, the reception of *Evolution and Dogma* was immediate and resounding, dwarfing the success of any previous title.

67. Previous studies have covered these responses in detail. See Weber, *Notre Dame's John Zahm*, 82–85; Morrison, "A History of American Catholic Opinion," 211–19; and Artigas, Glick, and Martínez, *Negotiating Darwin*, 134–39.

68. John Zahm, *Evoluzione e dogma*, trans. Alfonso M. Galea (Siena: Presso l'Ufficio della Biblioteca del clero, 1896); Zahm, *L'évolution et le dogme*, trans. Abbé J. Flageolet (Paris: Lethielleux, 1897). In 1905 the book was also translated into Spanish as *La evolución y el dogma*, trans. Miguel Asúa (Madrid: Sociedad Editorial Española, 1905).

69. A much more detailed outline of the correspondence related to the case can be found in Artigas, Glick, and Martínez, *Negotiating Darwin*, 143–99.

70. Zardetti to the cardinals of the Congregation of the Index, Index, Protocolli, 1897–99, fol. 179, ACDF.

71. Buonpensiere wrote two reports during the trial of the evolutionist Marie-Dalmace Leroy (Index, Protocolli, 1894–96, fol. 117, ACDF; Index, Protocolli, 1897–99, fol. 55, ACDF) and one concerning scientific methods generally in 1897 (Index, Protocolli, 1897–99, fol. 38, ACDF). Buonspensiere's reports are discussed in depth in chapter 5.

72. Index, Protocolli, 1897–99, fol. 180, p. 52, ACDF.

73. Index, Protocolli, 1897–99, fol. 181, ACDF.

74. Index, Protocolli, 1897–99, fol. 181, p. 2, ACDF: "Attesta di avere fatto tale confronto diligentemente, e che la detta versione è fedelissima, anzi, per quanto permette la frase italiana, *ad litteram*." Original emphasis.

75. There are three versions of the meeting of the Preparatory Congregation in the ACDF. One seems to be a draft of the final version, of which there are two copies—assumedly one draft and one to copy into the congregation diary. Folio 190 of the Protocolli contains a printed version of the proceedings. The printed version, however, is identical to the copy from the diary. See Artigas,

Glick, and Martínez, *Negotiating Darwin*, 153–54; Index, Protocolli, 1897–99, fols. 190–92, ACDF; and Index, Diari, vol. 22, fol. 39r–v, August 5, 1898, ACDF.

76. Index, Protocolli, 1897–99, fols. 193–95, ACDF. Folio 194 contains the copy of the *Decretum* for distribution, while folio 195 contains the banner version, to be placed on the doors, one presumes, of churches. The decree is dated September 1, coordinating with the day of the decision from the General Congregation. However, the diary of the Congregation of the Index (Diari, vol. 22, fol. 39v) records the decree as not being published until September 5, after presenting the cases to the pope on September 3. One can find a copy of the decree in Wolf, *Römische Inquisition und Indexkongregation. Grundlagenforschung: 1814–1917*, 1:509–10.

77. September 1, 1898, Index, Diari, vol. 22, fol. 39v, ACDF.

78. Index, Protocolli, 1897–99, fol. 193, p. 4, ACDF; Artigas, Glick, and Martínez, *Negotiating Darwin*, 155.

79. Index, Protocolli, 1897–99, fol. 193, p. 4, ACDF; Artigas, Glick, and Martínez, *Negotiating Darwin*, 155.

80. Office of the Secretary of the Congregation of the Index, Rome, to Français. September 10, 1898, JZC, CSCA. Permission to send the letter, September 9, 1898, Index, Diari, vol. 22, fol. 41r, ACDF. Cf. Weber, *Notre Dame's John Zahm*, 107–8; Artigas, Glick, and Martínez, *Negotiating Darwin*, 156.

81. Français to Zahm, September 11, 1898, JZC, CSCA. Français to the cardinal prefect of the Congregation of the Index, September 18, 1898, Index, Protocolli, 1897–99, fol. 277, ACDF.

82. Weber, *Notre Dame's John Zahm*, 109; Index, Protocolli, 1897–99, fol. 179, ACDF. For a detailed timeline, see table 5.1 in this volume.

83. Index, Diari, vol. 22, fol. 42r, ACDF.

84. Leo XIII's instructions are noted February 3, 1889, Index, Diari, vol. 22, fol. 48r, ACDF. Cf. Artigas, Glick, and Martínez, *Negotiating Darwin*, 158. This is not quite the whole story, as Morrison relates. Archbishop John Ireland was assured of the pope's acquiescence as early as November 1898, which a Fr. Legrand assured Zahm of separately. However, in April 1899, Ireland was granted an audience with the pope, and was told the new order for Zahm, which lines up with the ACDF account from February 3: that Zahm needed to go to Rome to explain himself, and only then would the prohibition not be published. See Morrison, "A History of American Catholic Opinion," 244–48. Cf. Ireland to Zahm, November 9, 1898; Legrand to Zahm, November 11, 1898; Ireland to Zahm, December 13, 1898; Denis O'Connell to Zahm, April 12, 1899, JZA, UNDA.

85. These factors can be seen in the detailed accounts outlined in Weber, *Notre Dame's John Zahm*, 107–24; Artigas, Glick, and Martínez, *Negotiating*

Darwin, 156–202; Morrison, "A History of American Catholic Opinion," 240–52; and Appleby, "American Catholic Modernism," 175–77. Morrison, particularly, encapsulates the connections Zahm had with the Americanist movement and their influence over the pope. Bishop Keane wrote, "The Holy Father has had his eyes opened to the mistaken measurings toward which extremists were pushing him in their hostility to Americanism. No such measures need now be feared" (Keane to Zahm, November 9, 1898, JZA, UNDA). While the pope would indeed act hostile toward Americanism in 1899 with the publication of the encyclical *Testem Benevolentiae,* Ireland and Keane seem to have been partially correct in their understanding of the situation concerning Zahm.

86. Declaration of Alfonso M. Galea, published, alongside Zahm's letter, in the newspaper *Gazzetta di Malta,* May 31, 1899, quoted in Artigas, Glick, and Martínez, *Negotiating Darwin,* 196.

87. *New York Daily Tribune,* July 2, 1899.

88. Mariano Artigas, Thomas F. Glick, and Rafael A. Martínez, *Negotiating Darwin: The Vatican Confronts Evolution, 1877–1902* (Baltimore: Johns Hopkins University Press, 2006).

89. As mentioned, and as will be seen in chapter 5, there were some who still desired more from the Vatican. Buonpensiere was among those who explicitly called for the Holy Office, or the pope himself, to issue a decree stating that Adam's body was formed immediately according to Genesis, but such a decree was never published. This is the basis for the claim that the Vatican was a neutral party, held by the authors of *Negotiating Darwin,* but it is the opinion of this author that focusing such a claim on this technicality diminishes the damage done to the conversation concerning evolution and Catholicism by the Congregation of the Index upon the mindset of so many Catholics around the world.

90. Office of the Secretary of the Congregation of the Index, Rome, to Français. September 10, 1898, JZC, CSCA.

91. Weber, *Notre Dame's John Zahm,* 106–9, 129–32.

92. Zahm to O'Connell, February 5, 1898, JZA, UNDA.

93. In short, the brothers complained that Zahm's vision of greatness for Notre Dame left him incapable of managing the concerns of the individual brothers around the country and world. While Notre Dame benefitted from Zahm's ardor, many working in other educational institutions felt neglected and chastised by Zahm's brash manner. Weber argues that some of these complaints were more about personality than substance, noting that the brothers were struggling with morale even before Zahm entered the scene in 1898. Nevertheless, Zahm was voted out of office in 1906. See Weber, *Notre Dame's John Zahm,* 156–70.

94. Zahm to Français, January 12, 1906, JZC, CSCA. Cf. Weber, *Notre Dame's John Zahm*, 168–70.

95. John Zahm [H. J. Mozans], *Following the Conquistadores: Up the Orinoco and Down the Magdalena* (New York: Appleton, 1910); Zahm [H. J. Mozans], *Along the Andes and Down the Amazon* (New York: Appleton, 1911).

96. John Zahm [H. J. Mozans], *Woman in Science* (New York: Appleton, 1913); *Madison Journal* (Wisconsin), December 10, 1913; *Women's Journal* (Boston): December 20, 1913; Weber, *Notre Dame's John Zahm*, 193–94.

97. Weber, *Notre Dame's John Zahm*, 194; John Zahm, *Great Inspirers* (New York: Appleton, 1917).

98. John Zahm, *The Quest of El Dorado: The Most Romantic Episode in the History of South American Conquest* (New York, Appleton, 1917).

99. John Zahm, *From Berlin to Bagdad and Babylon* (New York: Appleton, 1922).

100. John Zahm death certificate, JZA, UNDA.

101. Weber, *Notre Dame's John Zahm*, 173, 173nn123, 124.

THREE. The Scientific Mind of John Zahm, CSC

1. John Zahm, *Catholic Church and Modern Science* (Notre Dame, IN: Ave Maria Press, 1886), 18, 22; Zahm, *Evolution and Dogma*, 138–39.

2. John Zahm, "Thoughts on Science and the Age in Which We Live," *Scholastic* 4, no. 19 (1871): 1–2.

3. Zahm, "Thoughts on Science," 1.

4. Such a description clearly does not excuse Zahm's blatant racism against, at least, people of Asia and Native Americans. It is not clear how he may have acted on this racism specifically, but it is clear that his views of cultural progress assume the cultural superiority of the West as compared with primitive peoples such as Native Americans and those—Zahm guessed—in Asia.

5. Zahm, "Thoughts on Science," 1.

6. Ibid.

7. Ibid.

8. Ibid.

9. Ibid., 2.

10. Ibid.

11. Weber, *Notre Dame's John Zahm*, 7.

12. Zahm, "Thoughts on Science," 1.

13. Zahm writes in "Thoughts on Science," "Far different is the modern system of philosophy, of which Bacon is one of the chief exponents, and far

different is the light in which science is considered. . . . Instead of teaching him [*sic*] to be indifferent in sickness and distress, to consider them as necessary evils, modern science and philosophy have made the greatest possible efforts to assuage his [*sic*] pains and comfort him [*sic*] in his [*sic*] afflictions" (1).

14. George H. Daniels, *History of American Science and Technology: American Science in the Age of Jackson* (Tuscaloosa: University of Alabama Press, 1968), 63.

15. Jefferson to John Trumbull, February 15, 1789, Thomas Jefferson Papers, series 1: general correspondence, 1651–1827, Library of Congress, Washington DC, http://hdl.loc.gov/loc.mss/mtj.mtjbib004110.

16. Daniels, *History of American Science*, 65.

17. Ibid., 65–67. Cf. Herbert Hovenkamp, *Science and Religion in America, 1800–1860* (Philadelphia: University of Pennsylvania Press, 1978), 24.

18. Daniels, *History of American Science*, 66.

19. Ibid., 66–67. Cf. George J. Chace, "Of the Divine Agency in the Production of Material Phenomena," *Bibliotheca Sacra* 5 (1848): 347.

20. Hovenkamp, *Science and Religion*, 27. Cf. John H. Roberts, *Darwinism and the Divine in America* (Notre Dame, IN: University of Notre Dame Press, 1988), 41.

21. Daniels takes note of three Catholic arguments in the 1840s: Joseph De Maistre, *Examen de la Philosophie de Bacon* (Lyon, 1845), especially tome 2, p. 313; "Brande's Encyclopedia," *United States Catholic Monthly Review* 3 (January 1844): 3; "Utility of Physical Sciences," *The Catholic Expositor and Literary Magazine* 2 (1842): 251. Daniels, *History of American Science*, 68–85.

22. Daniels, *History of American Science*, 135.

23. Hovenkamp, *Science and Religion*, 209.

24. Roberts, *Darwinism and the Divine*, 69.

25. Ibid., 17. Cf. George Marsden, *Fundamentalism and American Culture*, 2nd ed. (New York: Oxford University Press, 2006), 19–20.

26. Charles Hodge, *What Is Darwinism?* (New York: Scribner and Armstrong, 1874), 173.

27. See, for example, Orestes Augustus Brownson, "Darwin's Descent of Man," *Brownson's Quarterly Review* (July 1873): 340–51, http://orestesbrownson.org/24.html.

28. Roberts, *Darwinism and the Divine*, 18. Cf. Hovenkamp, *Science and Religion*, 209.

29. Kuhn, *The Structure of Scientific Revolutions*, 19–20.

30. University of Notre Dame, *Annual Catalogue of the University of Notre Dame*, vol. 21 (Notre Dame, IN: Ave Maria Press, 1865), Digital Collections, UNDA, http://www.archives.nd.edu/bulletin/AC_21.pdf.

31. Steven Jay Gould, *Time's Arrow, Time's Cycle: Myth and Metaphor in the Discovery of Geological Time* (Cambridge, MA: Harvard University Press, 1987), 105, see also 99–179.

32. Ibid., 105–7.

33. An examination of Zahm's 1894 *Bible, Science, and Faith*, for example, shows a significant amount of time spent on Noah's Flood and geological timelines. Undoubtedly the evolution question was more pressing for both Zahm and Church authorities, but the question of biblical events such as the Garden of Eden and Noah's Flood were still hotly debated. John Zahm, *Bible, Science, and Faith* (Baltimore: John Murphy, 1894). Cf. Charles Lyell, *Principles of Geology*, 10th ed. (London: John Murray, 1866), 79, 293.

34. Gould, *Time's Arrow*, 111.

35. Ibid.

36. Sanborn Tenney, *Natural History: A Manual of Zoology for Schools, Colleges, and the General Reader* (New York: Scribner, 1866), 532.

37. Roberts, *Darwinism and the Divine*, 50–51.

38. Tenney, *Natural History*, 534–45.

39. Asa Gray, *Manual of the Botany of the Northern United States, Including Virginia, Kentucky, and All East of the Mississippi*, 3rd ed. (New York: Ivison, Phinney and Co., 1862).

40. Gerry Moore, James Macklin, and Lisa DeCesare, "A Brief History of Asa Gray's *Manual of Botany*," *Harvard Papers in Botany* 15, no. 2 (2010): 277–86.

41. Zahm, *Evolution and Dogma*, 211–12.

42. Benjamin Silliman, *Principles of Physics, or Natural Philosophy*, 2nd ed. (Philadelphia: Theodore Bliss, 1866).

43. It is helpful to know that Silliman also played a large role in the debate over geology and the Book of Genesis in the early nineteenth century, arguing vehemently for the "long day" interpretation of the seven days of creation. In his text on geology which he co-wrote with Robert Bakewell, Silliman writes, "The great convulsions which have, at distant periods, changed the ancient surface of the globe, and reduced it from a chaotic to its present habitable state, were not, it is reasonable to believe, effected by the blind fury of tumultuous and conflicting elements, but were the result of determined laws, directed by the same wisdom which regulates every part of the external universe. Compared with the ephemeral existence of man on the earth, the epochs of these changes may appear of almost inconceivable duration; but we are expressly told, 'that with the Creator a thousand years are as one day, and one day as a thousand years.'" Robert Bakewell and Benjamin Silliman, *An Introduction to Geology* (New Haven, CT: Hezekiah Howe, 1833), 16. Cf. Hovenkamp, *Science and Religion*, 126–31.

44. Silliman, *Principles of Physics*, 2.

45. Weber, *Notre Dame's John Zahm*, 26–29.

46. Zahm to O. A. Brownson, October 14, 1875, JZC, CSCA.

47. See numerous letters between Brownson and Sorin in UNDA's Digital Collections, http://archives.nd.edu/search/.

48. Carrier to O. A. Brownson, October 12, 1872, Orestes Augustus Brownson Papers, UNDA.

49. Ibid.

50. Orestes Augustus Brownson, "True and False Science," in *The Works of Orestes A. Brownson*, vol. 9, *Scientific Theories*, ed. Henry Brownson (Detroit: Thorndike Nourse, 1884), 529, quoted in Morrison, "A History of American Catholic Opinion," 46–47. Brownson's essay was originally printed in *Brownson's Quarterly Review*, l.s., 1 (1873): 367–98.

51. John W. Draper, *A History of the Conflict between Religion and Science* (New York: Appleton, 1874).

52. Orestes Augustus Brownson, "The Roman Church and Modern Society," *Brownson's Quarterly Review* (January 1846): 123–24, http://orestes brownson.org/313; *Brownson's Quarterly Review* is also available through the HathiTrust, https://catalog.hathitrust.org/Record/000061068.

53. Notebook titled, "Brownson Works, Vol. 9," JZC, CSCA. Cf. Orestes Augustus Brownson, "Science and the Sciences," in Brownson, *The Works of Orestes A. Brownson*, vol. 9, *Scientific Theories*, 265.

54. Orestes Brownson, "Kant's Critique of Pure Reason—Part 1," *Brownson's Quarterly Review* (April 1844): 167–69, http://orestesbrownson.org/172 .html; *Brownson's Quarterly Review* is also available through the HathiTrust, https://catalog.hathitrust.org/Record/000061068.

55. Zahm, *Catholic Church and Modern Science*, 52–53. This text was first printed in a short form as "Catholic Church and Modern Science," *Ave Maria* 19 (1883): 241–48, 261–68. All references refer to the book form, however, published in 1886.

56. Zahm, *Catholic Church and Modern Science*, 52–53. It is somewhat surprising that Zahm did not refer to *Dei Filius* at this juncture, but such an omission will prove to be a predictable parcel of his corpus. Zahm, first and foremost, is an orator and popularizer of science, not a dogmatic theologian.

57. Zahm, *Catholic Church and Modern Science*, 18–22.

58. Ibid.

59. Ibid., 22.

60. Ibid., 57.

61. Ibid., 56.

62. See, for example, John Zahm, "The Reckless Skepticism of Modern Scientists," *Scholastic* 19 (1885): 146–47; and Zahm, "Notice of a Lecture on the Teachings of Some Scientists," *Scholastic* 20 (1887): 540.

63. Compare, for example, Zahm, *Catholic Church and Modern Science*, 32–40, 54.

64. John Zahm, "The Church and Science: Text of a Lecture," *Scholastic* 22 (1889): 414–15. Cf. Zahm, "What the Church Has Done for Science," *Scholastic* 18 no. 26 (1885): 405–11; no. 27 (1885): 421–26; no. 28 (1885): 437–40.

65. John Zahm, "Catholic Dogma and Scientific Dogmatism," *American Catholic Quarterly Review* 15 (1890): 439.

66. Ibid.

67. Zahm, *Catholic Church and Modern Science*, 25.

68. An affection further demonstrated by two of Mivart's books appearing on Zahm's "A List of One Hundred Best Books," *Scholastic* 20 (1887): 588–90. Cf. Sloan, "Bringing Evolution to Notre Dame."

69. Weber, *Notre Dame's John Zahm*, 47–49. Zahm also kept a large collection of accolades and congratulations from the publication of *Sound and Music*, which can be found in the 1890–92 folder, JZC, CSCA.

70. Zahm writes romantically in the introduction:

> A period of remarkable intellectual activity in every department of natural and physical science, the latter half of the nineteenth century must ever remain memorable. Never in the world's history has so much been accomplished in the same space of time. The fauna and flora of every continent and of every sea have been studied and compared; the forms of life of the dim and distant past have been unearthed and assigned their places in the scheme of creation. Aided by appliances he never dreamed of a few decades ago, the astronomer has penetrated the depths of stellar space, and can now literally unfold to us the story of the heavens in the light of the radiant orbs that are the constant objects of his nightly vigils. Worlds of untold magnitude and atoms of inconceivable minuteness—the infinitely great and the infinitely small—are alike the subjects of earnest quest and patient investigation. It would be difficult indeed to say in which department of knowledge the most work has been accomplished, and in which line of research the most energy has been expended. The facts observed and the discoveries made are almost incredible to one who has not made an attempt to keep abreast with the advance of science; and they show, in a most striking manner, what can be accomplished by unity of action and persistence in properly directed effort.

Zahm, *Sound and Music*, 15–16. Cf. Weber, *Notre Dame's John Zahm*, 48–49.

71. Review of *Sound and Music*, by John Zahm, *Chicago Tribune*, February 18, 1893.

72. Review of *Sound and Music*, by John Zahm, *North-Western Chronicle*, May 13, 1893.

73. Zahm states as much in his introduction to the reproduction of the lectures in *Scientific Theory and Catholic Doctrine*: "The present little work embraces my recent lectures before the Madison and Plattsburgh Summer Schools, and the Winter School of New Orleans. . . . The following chapters, it may also be remarked, cover essentially the same ground as Part II of my more extended work on 'Evolution and Dogma'" (7).

74. John Zahm, "The Age of the Human Race According to Modern Science and Biblical Chronology," *American Catholic Historical Review* 18 (1893): 225–49, 562–87, 719–34; 19 (1894): 260–75.

75. Zahm, *Scientific Theory and Catholic Doctrine*, 7.

76. As far as I have been able to discern, however, all published versions are nearly identical.

77. Clipping in Zahm scrapbook, JZC, CSCA. Cf. Weber, *Notre Dame's John Zahm*, 56–57.

78. Bishop Sebastian G. Messmer to Zahm, JZA, UNDA, January 20, 1896.

79. Zahm, *Scientific Theory and Catholic Doctrine*, 37.

80. Ibid., 113.

81. Ibid., 181.

82. Rudolph Virchow, "Anthropology in the Last Twenty Years," in *Annual Report of the Board of Regents of the Smithsonian Institution* (Washington, DC: Government Printing Office, 1890), 563, https://books.google.com/books?id=Ons3AQAAIAAJ, quoted in Zahm, *Scientific Theory and Catholic Doctrine*, 198.

83. Zahm, *Scientific Theory and Catholic Doctrine*, 199–201.

84. Ibid., 201–2.

85. Ibid., 207. Cf. St. George Jackson Mivart, *On the Genesis of Species* (New York: Appleton, 1871).

86. Zahm, *Scientific Theory and Catholic Doctrine*, 215–18.

87. Sloan, "Bringing Evolution to Notre Dame," 202. Cf. Artigas, Glick, and Martínez, *Negotiating Darwin*, 248ff.

88. Artigas, Glick, and Martínez, *Negotiating Darwin*, 260–62.

89. Zahm, *Scientific Theory and Catholic Doctrine*, 241–42.

90. Ibid., 246–47, 256.

91. Ibid., 303.

92. Zahm, *Evolution and Dogma*, 5: prefatory note, December 18, 1895. There are several good overviews of *Evolution and Dogma* in scholarship today, including Morrison, "A History of American Catholic Opinion," 206–11; Artigas, Glick, and Martínez, *Negotiating Darwin*, 126–34; and Weber, *Notre Dame's John Zahm*, 79–83.

93. Zahm, *Evolution and Dogma*, 84.

94. Ibid., 134. Zahm considers "geographical classification and geological succession" to be a single class of argumentation.

95. Ibid.

96. Ibid., 135.

97. Zahm, *Catholic Church and Modern Science*, 18, 22.

98. Zahm, *Evolution and Dogma*, 138–39.

99. Ibid., 196.

100. Ibid., 200.

101. Ibid., 201.

102. Sloan, "Bringing Evolution to Notre Dame," 198. For more on Sloan's position, see "Edward Heinle and Phillip Sloan" in chapter 1.

103. Zahm, *Evolution and Dogma*, 305.

104. Sloan, "Bringing Evolution to Notre Dame," 199. Cf. Zahm, *Evolution and Dogma*, 313.

105. Sloan, "Bringing Evolution to Notre Dame," 199.

106. Ibid.

107. Ibid., 200–201. Cf. Mivart, *On the Genesis of Species*, 300.

108. Sloan, "Bringing Evolution to Notre Dame," 204.

109. Zahm, *Evolution and Dogma*, 340–54.

110. While I could talk much more about Zahm's detailed and varying evolutionary positions in *Evolution and Dogma*, I refrain from doing so for two reasons. First, it is tangential to the central goals of this study, as the latter chapters will show that the Congregation of the Index cared far more about Zahm's general approach to science than about his specific evolutionary ideas. Second, excellent overviews of *Evolution and Dogma* exist in the aforementioned scholarly literature, the most notable being the second chapter of David Burrell's *When Faith and Reason Meet: The Legacy of John Zahm, CSC* (Notre Dame, IN: Corby Books, 2009), 15–35. The first chapter of Burrell's book also provides a nice overview of Zahm's *Bible, Science, and Faith*. I do not include Burrell's work in this study, however, because it is more of an excellent summation than a novel analysis on Zahm's case.

FOUR.   The Development of Catholic Teachings on Science, Faith, and Reason in the Nineteenth Century

1. Owen Chadwick, *A History of the Popes, 1830–1914* (New York: Oxford University Press, 1998), 168–75. In contrast to my hesitancy to use the word *liberal* to define the Americanist movement of the Church, the ecclesial documents in this chapter explicitly use the word *liberal* to define such ideas as democracy and individual freedoms, as well as atheism, agnosticism, acceptance of non-Catholics, acceptance of evolution, and other ideas deemed corrosive to the Church. When possible, I employ the term *antiliberal* instead of *conservative*

to discuss the resistance to nineteenth-century liberalism as I attempt to be historically precise.

2. Over two dozen encyclicals against culture were written by Popes Pius IX, Gregory XVI, Leo XII, and Pius VII.

3. Pope Pius IX, *Quanta Cura*, Encyclical Letter (December 8, 1864), para. 1. The English translation is my revised version of the English translations promulgated with the encyclical at the time, as seen in Pope Pius IX, "Text and Translation of the Encyclical and Syllabus," *Dublin Review* 4, no. 56 (1865): 500–511. The official Latin text can be found in *Acta Santae Sedis* 3 (1867): 160–67, http://www.vatican.va/archive/ass/documents/ASS-03-1867-ocr.pdf. Hereafter cited in text as *QC*.

4. Chadwick, *A History of the Popes*, 180.

5. Pope Pius IX, Syllabus of Modern Errors (December 8, 1864), in *Acta Santae Sedis* 3 (1867): 167–76, http://www.vatican.va/archive/ass/index_sp.htm. My English translation is revised from Pope Pius IX, "Text and Translation of the Encyclical and Syllabus," in *Dublin Review* 4, no. 56 (1865): 512–529, https://babel.hathitrust.org/cgi/pt?id=umn.31951002148591d;view=1up;seq=526. Hereafter cited in text by section number. For the full English translation and original Latin text, see appendix A in this volume.

6. Gerald McCool, *Nineteenth-Century Scholasticism: The Search for a Unitary Method* (New York: Fordham University Press, 1989) [Originally published as *Catholic Theology in the Nineteenth Century* by Seabury Press, 1977], 129.

7. Ibid.

8. Cf. Francis S. Fiorenza, "Presidential Address: Foundations of Theology: A Community's Tradition of Discourse and Practice," *Proceedings of the Catholic Theological Society of America* 41 (1986): 111.

9. Georg Wilhelm Friedrich Hegel, *Phenomenology of Spirit* (New York: Oxford University Press, 1977), 438.

10. Ludwig Feuerbach, *The Fiery Brook: Selected Writings of L. Feuerbach*, trans. Zawar Hanfi (New York: Doubleday, 1972), 101–2.

11. The Catholic priest and theologian Antonio Rosmini Serbati exemplified a version of these arguments, and his influence within European Catholicism was likely one of the key reasons for Pius placing this section in the Syllabus. For a good overview of his involvement, see Richard Malone, "Historical Overview of the Rosmini Case," *L'Osservatore Romano*, July 25, 2001, https://www.ewtn.com/library/theology/rosmini.htm.

12. McCool, *Nineteenth-Century Scholasticism*, 108.

13. Ibid. Cf. Joseph Pritz, *Glauben und Wissen bei Anton Günther* (Vienna: Herder, 1963), 117–48; and Pritz, *Wegweisung zur Theologie* (Vienna: Wiener Domverlag, 1971), 26–28.

14. McCool, *Nineteenth-Century Scholasticism*, 108.

15. Chadwick, *A History of the Popes*, 182.

16. Henry Edward Manning, *The True Story of the Vatican Council* (London: Henry S. King, 1877), 1–2, https://books.google.com/books?id=Fv ENAAAAYAAJ.

17. Giovan Domenico Mansi, Philippe Labbe, Jean Baptiste Martin, eds., *Sacrorum Conciliorum Nova, et Amplissima Collectio*, 53 vols. (Paris: H. Welter, 1901–27), 49:9–10.

18. Manning, *The True Story of the Vatican Council*, 4.

19. Hermann Josef Pottmeyer, *Der Glaube vor dem Anspruch der Wissenschaft: Die Konstitution über den katholischen Glauben "Dei Filius" des 1. Vatikanischen Konzils und der unveröffentlichten theologischen Voten der vorbereitenden Kommission* (Vienna: Herder, 1968), 45.

20. McCool, *Nineteenth-Century Scholasticism*, 219–20. Cf. Fiorenza, "Presidential Address," 110; Pottmeyer, *Der Glaube*, 47. Franzelin's *Definitio* was largely based on his own 1868 votum, "De Erroribus Nonnullis circa Cognitionem Naturalem et Supernaturalem," which was itself explicitly based on Pius's 1864 Syllabus. Both are available in Pottmeyer, *Der Glaube*, *29–*89 ("De Erroribus") and *90–*115 ("Definitio").

21. McCool, *Nineteenth-Century Scholasticism*, 220. See discussions of the document in Mansi et al., *Sacrorum Conciliorum Nova*, 49:719–25.

22. McCool, *Nineteenth-Century Scholasticism*, 220–21. Without doubt, Pottmeyer's *Der Glaube* remains the authority on the transition and theological approach to *Dei Filius*. Of particular interest to any study on the construction of the document is Pottmeyer's appendix in which he compares the four official drafts of the document (469–98). Furthermore, the discussion of each schema is presented in Mansi et al., *Sacrorum Conciliorum Nova*, as follows: schemas I, II, 49:617–740; schema III, 50:59–212; schema IV, 51:31–426; final version with signatures and introduction, 51:427–50.

23. Chadwick, *A History of the Popes*, 208.

24. Ibid. Cf. Dom Cuthbert Butler, *The Vatican Council: The Story Told from Inside in Bishop Ullathorne's Letters*, 2 vols. (New York: Longmans, Green, and Co., 1930), 1:270–73; and Mansi et al., *Sacrorum Conciliorum Nova*, 51:72f.

25. This assessment of *Dei Filius* closely follows Pottmeyer's. Pottmeyer argues in multiple works that *Dei Filius* reached a point of brilliance through its insistence on openness in theology and philosophy and through its hesitation to employ specific metaphysical terms in describing the relationship of faith and reason. The argument is perhaps most succinctly captured in Hermann Josef Pottmeyer, "Die Konstitution 'Dei Filius' des 1. Vatikanischen Konzils zwischen Abwehr und Rezeption der Moderne," in *Wege der Theologie: an der Schwelle zum dritten Jahrtausend*, ed. Günter Riße, Heino Sonnemans, and Burkhard Theß (Paderborn: Bonifatius, 1996), 73–86.

26. While the canons of the document—those that declare unbelievers *anathema*—could perhaps be better compared with the Syllabus, they lack the philosophical breadth of the chapters themselves. As such, this analysis focuses on the chapters instead of the canons, which are essentially the chapters in shortened form.

27. This analysis uses a modern translation of *Dei Filius* in *Decrees of the Ecumenical Councils*, 2 vols., ed. Norman P. Tanner, SJ, 1:804–11 (Washington, DC: Georgetown University Press, 1990). For the original Latin text see First Vatican Council, *Dei Filius*, Dogmatic Constitution (April 24, 1870), in *Acta Santae Sedis* 5 (1869–70): 484–90, http://www.vatican.va/archive/ass/documents/ASS-05-1869-70-ocr.pdf. Any deviations from Tanner's translation are marked as such. Hereafter cited in text as *DF*.

28. Pottmeyer, *Der Glaube*, 158.

29. McCool, *Nineteenth-Century Scholasticism*, 216.

30. Pottmeyer, *Der Glaube*, 167.

31. My translation. "Deum . . . naturali humanae rationis lumine e rebus creates certo cognosci posse."

32. Bernard Lonergan, "Natural Knowledge of God," in *A Second Collection*, ed. William Ryan and Bernard Tyrrell (Westminster: Philadelphia, 1974), 117–33.

33. Ibid., 119.

34. My translation.

35. Pottmeyer, "Die Konstitution 'Dei Filius.'"

36. Lonergan, "Natural Knowledge of God," 120.

37. Ibid.

38. Ibid. This should not be confused with the possibility of rationality to attain *some* knowledge of God—for example, God's existence. Lonergan is well known for his philosophical proof of God's existence in *Insight: A Study of Human Understanding*, vol. 3 of *Collected Works of Bernard Lonergan*, ed. by Frederick E. Crowe and Robert M. Doran (Toronto: University of Toronto Press, 1992), see esp. 695. However, following Thomas Aquinas, Lonergan does not argue that philosophical or scientific argumentation can lead people to full knowledge of God.

39. See Stephen Jay Gould, *Rocks of Ages: Science and Religion in the Fullness of Life* (New York: Ballantine, 1999).

40. "Hoc quoque perpetuus Ecclesiæ Catholicæ consensus tenuit et tenet, duplicem esse ordinem cognitionis, non solum principio, sed objecto etiam distinctum: principio quidem, quia in altero naturali ratione, in altero fide divina cognoscimus; objecto autem, quia præter ea, ad quæ naturalis ratio pertingere potest, credenda nobis proponuntur mysteria in Deo abscondita, quæ, nisi revelata divinitus, innotescere non possunt."

41. While McCool quite clearly blames *Dei Filius* for the imposition of Neo-Thomism in the last decades of the nineteenth century, Pottmeyer praises the document as one of the most open and forward-thinking Catholic philosophical and theological works of the era. See McCool, *Nineteenth-Century Scholasticism*, 218–26; and Pottmeyer, "Die Konstitution 'Dei Filius,'" 82–86.

42. Butler, *The Vatican Council*, 300.

43. Pottmeyer, "Die Konstitution 'Dei Filius,'" 77–78.

44. Ibid.

45. Fifth Lateran Council, *Apostolici Regiminis*, December 8, 1513, in Tanner, *Decrees of the Ecumenical Councils*, 2:605–16. Cf. Luca Bianchi, *Pour Une Histoire de La Double Vérité* (Paris: J. Vrin, 2008), 119–34; Eric A. Constant, "A Reinterpretation of the Fifth Lateran Council Decree 'Apostolici Regiminis' (1513)," *Sixteenth Century Journal* 33, no. 2 (2002): 353–79; Tanner, *Decrees of the Ecumenical Councils*, 1:605. I cannot help but note that the original 1520 publication of the conciliar text is now freely available online thanks to digitalization efforts at the Bavarian State Library in Germany. See Fifth Lateran Council, *Apostolici Regiminis* (December 8, 1513), in *Concilium Sanctum Lateranense Novissimum* (Rome, 1520), 239–41, https://reader.digitale-sammlungen .de/de/fs1/object/display/bsb10141706_00239.html.

46. Chadwick, *A History of the Popes*, 143–44.

47. Ibid., 215.

48. Ibid., 217.

49. One may argue against my use of the term *overthrow*, since modern Italians see this event as the liberation of Rome. As this chapter focuses on the view from the papacy, however, I label it as Pius IX saw it, an unlawful overthrow of an existing power structure.

50. Frank Coppa, *The Modern Papacy* (New York: Longman, 1998), 116.

51. Pope Pius IX, "Pius IX on Liberal Catholicism," *Dublin Review* 26, n.s. (1876): 489.

52. Ibid., 489–90. Cf. Coppa, *The Modern Papacy*, 116.

53. Chadwick, *A History of the Popes*, 247.

54. Bernard O'Reilly, *Life of Leo XIII* (New York: Charles L. Webster, 1887), 306–7.

55. Ibid.. Cf. Chadwick, *A History of the Popes*, 277.

56. See Umberto Benigni, "Pope Leo XIII," in *The Catholic Encyclopedia*, vol. 9 (New York: Robert Appleton Co., 1910), http://www.newadvent.org /cathen/09169a.htm.

57. Coppa, *The Modern Papacy*, 118.

58. As far as I can tell, the German *Neuscholastiker* was the first usage of the prefix *new* with the term *Scholastic*. It was written by Georg Hermes, a critic of the new movement who later would be censured by the Congregation of the

Index. While proponents of the movement typically preferred the term *Scholastic* to connect them with the past, Hermes's typification came into regular usage—from supporters and critics—by the late 1850s, and became increasingly common after the publication of *AP* in 1879. See Georg Hermes, *Hermes, oder, Kritisches Jahrbuch der Literatur*, vol. 32 (Leipzig: Brodhaus, 1829), 48. Employing Google analytics, which analyzes the texts of millions of books in their database, one can get a general sense of the term's usage. While the main analytics website can be accessed at http://books.google.com/ngrams, specific instances of this philological trend can be traced with the graphs found at http://goo.gl /HefPfl and http://goo.gl/dYGfeG. These graphs were made by, respectively, searching for the terms "Neuscholastik, Neuscholastiker" in the German database, and the terms "Neoscholastic, Neo-Scholastic, Neothomist, Neo-Thomist, Neo-Scholasticism, Neo-Thomism" in the English database.

59. Wolf confirms the date of July 11, 1850, in Index, Diari 19 (1807–65), fol. 98, ACDF. Wolf, *Römische Inquisition und Indexkongregation. Grundlagenforschung: 1814–1917*, 3:807.

60. The camerlengo of the Church historically has managed the pope's property and finances.

61. John Inglis points to similar movements toward recovering medieval philosophy in France and Germany in the nineteenth century, not all of which could be labeled Neo-Scholasticism, but all of which had similar goals of defeating the Enlightenment and raising up Aquinas as the exemplary counterexample for Catholicism. Similarly, Thomas O'Meara writes that from the 1840s on, "more and more bishops and seminary professors were convinced of the value of a Thomist restoration, and in Mainz, Münster, Rome, and Louvain centers were committed to uncovering and expounding Thomas Aquinas." O'Meara, *Aquinas, Theologian* (Notre Dame, IN: University of Notre Dame Press, 1997), 153–80. Cf. Inglis, *Spheres of Philosophical Inquiry and the Historiography of Medieval Philosophy* (Boston: Brill, 1998), 57–61.

62. Pope Leo XIII himself would be one example, of course. Another would be Gaetano Sanseverino (1811–65), a Dominican priest who published a five-volume philosophical treatise in the 1850s outlining a new philosophy of Thomas Aquinas. James A. Weisheipl points to Sanseverino as one of the five most influential members of the nineteenth-century movement. Weisheipl, "The Revival of Thomism: An Historical Survey" (lecture, Mount Saint Bernard Seminary, Dubuque, IA, 1962), http://opcentral.org/resources/2014/02/17 /the-revival-of-thomism/.

63. This remains a significant difference between Inglis's and McCool's interpretation of the same era. McCool—and many others, for that matter—see the explosion of beneficial Catholic studies known as the *ressourcement* in the early twentieth century as relying heavily on the popularity of Neo-

Scholasticism, whereas Inglis sees the same work as a continuation of an already-growing trend of turning back to medieval and other ancient sources to recover a philosophical tradition decried by modern philosophy.

64. Excepting certain times, of course. The reinstatement of the Jesuits and the rise of Neo-Scholasticism in the first half of the nineteenth century brought Thomism back into the picture of education generally as well as specifically. See O'Meara, *Aquinas, Theologian*, 169.

65. See, for example, Thomas Aquinas, *Summa contra gentiles*, I, 1–9.

66. This study does not consider Neo-Scholasticism and Neo-Thomism after Leo XIII. The perceived character of Neo-Scholasticism changed much with the policies and theologies of Pius X, both in his harsh critiques of modernism and in his support of so-called manualist theology. One could argue that it also changed much in the pontificate of Leo XIII, but Leo's own scholarly approach to theology and philosophy, as well as his engagement with modern culture, separates him from the contentious political moves of both Pius IX and Pius X. As the character of the curia often reflects the character of the pope, Leo's Neo-Scholasticism was enforced in a manner far more consistent with a desire to show the world the beauties of Aquinas's scholarship than to decry, yet again, the evils of modernity.

67. McCool, *Nineteenth-Century Scholasticism*, 232–33.

68. Ibid., 186–87.

69. One such nuance—epistemological realism—is discussed below in the section on Joseph Kleutgen.

70. Compare this to Pope John Paul II's *Fides et Ratio* from 1998, which was over twenty-five thousand words in Latin and thirty-two thousand in English. Pope John Paul II, *Fides et Ratio*, Encyclical Letter (September 14, 1998), http://w2.vatican.va/content/john-paul-ii/la/encyclicals/documents/hf_jp-ii _enc_14091998_fides-et-ratio.html.

71. Pope Leo XIII, *Aeterni Patris*, Encyclical Letter (August 4, 1879), para. 6, http://w2.vatican.va/content/leo-xiii/en/encyclicals/documents/hf_l -xiii_enc_04081879_aeterni-patris.html. For the official Latin text, see *Acta Sanctae Sedis* 12 (1879): 97–115, http://www.vatican.va/archive/ass/documents /ASS-12-1879-ocr.pdf. This analysis follows the paragraph numbering and English translation from the Vatican website. Any deviations from that translation are noted. Hereafter cited in text as *AP*.

72. Cf. *DF*, chap. 4, para. 3.

73. Inglis, *Spheres*, 157.

74. McCool, *Nineteenth-Century Scholasticism*, 167. Outside of McCool and Inglis, many other works consider Kleutgen's place in the history of nineteenth-century Catholic thought. While Inglis, McCool, and Pottmeyer serve as the main reference points for my discussion of Kleutgen, the following

works are referenced to varying degrees in this chapter: Aidan Nichols, *Conversation of Faith and Reason: Modern Catholic Thought from Hermes to Benedict XVI* (Chicago: Hillenbrand, 2009); Johann Hertkens and P. Ludwig Lercher, *P. Joseph Kleutgen, sein Leben und seine literarishce Wirksamkeit* (Regensburg: F. Pustet, 1910); Franz Lakner, "Kleutgen und die kirchliche Wissenschaft Deutschland sim 19. Jahrhundert," *Zeitschrift für katholische Theologie* 57 (1933): 161–214; J. Sachs, "Kleutgen, Joseph," *Kirchliches Handlexikon* 2 (1912): 411; Konrad Deufel, *Kirche und Tradition. Ein Beitrag zur Geschichte der theologischen Wende im 19. Jahrhundert am Beispiel des kirchlich-theologischen Kampfprogramms P. Joseph Kleutgen S.J.* (Munich: Ferdinand Schöningh, 1976); Leonard E. Boyle, OP, "A Remembrance of Pope Leo XIII: The Encyclical *Aeterni Patris*," in *One Hundred Years of Thomism: Aeterni Patris and Afterwards: A Symposium*, ed. Victor B. Brezik, CSB (Houston: Center for Thomistic Studies, 1981): 7–22; and Weisheipl, "The Revival of Thomism."

75. McCool, *Nineteenth-Century Scholasticism*, 167. McCool does not have a specific date for Kleutgen's entry into the Congregation of the Index, but documents in the ACDF confirm McCool's timeline. See note 59, above, for details.

76. In "The Revival of Thomism," Weisheipl is convinced Kleutgen did not have a hand in the document. In *Nineteenth-Century Scholasticism*, McCool is convinced of the exact opposite (168), but offers little evidence.

77. Inglis, *Spheres*, 157.

78. Ibid. Many studies (including McCool's) have carried this tradition, although there is no proof to confirm it. Cf. Hertkens and Lercher, *P. Joseph Kleutgen*, 90; Lakner, "Kleutgen und die kirchliche Wissenschaft Deutschland sim 19. Jahrhundert," 199; and Sachs, "Kleutgen, Joseph," 411.

79. Inglis, *Spheres*, 156–57.

80. Kleutgen to Christoph Bernhard Schlüter, October 19, 1879, in Deufel, *Kirche und Tradition*, 383–84, quoted in Inglis, *Spheres*, 157–58.

81. Inglis, *Spheres*, 158.

82. McCool, *Nineteenth-Century Scholasticism*, 232–33.

83. Both McCool and Inglis point to similarities between the *Aeterni Patris* and Kleutgen's work, but neither include more specifics than have been outlined here, excepting the aforementioned note about objective universality. Cf. McCool, *Nineteenth-Century Scholasticism*, 228; and Inglis, *Spheres*, 158–60.

84. Inglis, *Spheres*, 85.

85. Ibid., 84–86. Cf. Joseph Kleutgen, *Die Philosophie der Vorzeit vertheidigt*, 2 vols. (Münster: Theissingsche Buchhandlung, 1860–63), 1:567–69.

86. Inglis, *Spheres*, 86.

87. Kleutgen, *Die Philosophie*, 1:569, quoted in ibid.

88. Kleutgen, *Die Philosophie*, 1:614. My emphasis.

89. Inglis, *Spheres*, 86–90. Inglis subsequently argues that Kleutgen misread Kant on this precise issue, noting that Kant himself could be understood as a realist in a certain sense: "Kleutgen thinks that, for Kant, we each have our own personal structures with which to interpret experience. This would imply a lack of objectivity, since each individual might redefine knowledge according to how she or he is 'constituted.'... But this is not what Kant is saying. For Kant, '*Subjekt*,' like the regulative ideal of soul, refers to what is required for any experience, and not to an individual subject as the source of experience.... His terms '*Subjekt*' and '*subjektiv*' refer to conditions for the possibility of any experience and not to individual beings. Therefore Kleutgen's concern that Kant is opening the door to a type of philosophical individualism and skepticism is unfounded. Both Kant and Kleutgen had the same philosophical purpose, namely, to account for objective knowledge" (ibid.).

90. Ibid., 91.

91. Kleutgen, *Die Philosophie*, 1:26.

92. Inglis, *Spheres*, 41.

93. Ibid., 92. This has ties to popular conceptions of Platonic metaphysical dualism, but Kleutgen's metaphysics were actually more founded upon Aristotelian metaphysics as they were based strongly in Aquinas's thought.

94. Kleutgen, *Die Philosophie*, 1:120, quoted in ibid.

95. Inglis, *Spheres*, 93. My emphasis.

96. Zahm, "Leo XIII and Science," 30.

FIVE. Trials and Tribulations

1. See Artigas, Glick, and Martínez, *Negotiating Darwin*, 9. Cf. Niccolò Del Re, *La Curia romana. Lineamenti storico-giuridici*, 3rd ed. (Rome: Edizioni di Storia e Letteratura, 1970), 325–29.

2. Del Re, *La Curia romana*, 325–29.

3. Jesús Martínez de Bujanda, *Index de Rome, 1557, 1559, 1564. Les premiers index romains et l'index du Concile de Trente* (Québec: Éditions de l'Université de Sherbrooke, 1990), 13–44.

4. Ibid., 13.

5. Pope Paul VI, *Integrae Servandae* (December 7, 1965), in *Acta Apostolicae Sedis* 57 (1965): 952–55. Paul VI shortly after created the Congregation for the Doctrine of the Faith to handle matters that were previously dealt with by the Congregation of the Index. See *Acta Apostolicae Sedis* 58 (1966): 445, http://www.vatican.va/archive/aas/documents/AAS-58-1966-ocr.pdf.

6. Marquis de Nadaillac and Jean-François-Albert du Pouget, review of *L'évolution et le dogme*, by John A. Zahm, *Revue des Questions Scientifiques* 40

(July 1896): 229–46; David Fleming, review of *Evolution and Dogma*, by John A. Zahm, *Dublin Review* 119 (July–October 1896): 245–55; Francesco Salis-Seewis, "*Evoluzione e Dogma* pel Padre J. A. Zahm," *La Civiltà Cattolica*, 16th ser., 10, no. 1118 (1897): 201–4, https://babel.hathitrust.org/cgi/pt?id=ucl.a0003520319 ;view=1up;seq=137. Nearly every major journal reviewed the book, including *Popular Science Monthly* 49 (July 1895): 414–15; *Ave Maria* 42 (April 1896): 468–69; *Catholic World* 63 (April 1896): 130–33; *American Ecclesiastical Review* 14 (June 1896): 568–70; *Catholic University Bulletin* 2 (April 1896): 237–38; and *Freeman's Journal*, May 16, 1896, 4–6.

7. M. D. Leroy, "Monsieur le Directeur," February 26, 1895, *Le Monde*, March 4, 1895; and Salis-Seewis, "*Evoluzione e Dogma* pel Padre J. A. Zahm." Cf. Index, Protocolli, 1897–99, fol. 179, ACDF.

8. Vincent A. Yzermans, *Frontier Bishop of Saint Cloud* (Waite Park, MN: Park Press, 1988), 3.

9. Ibid.

10. Joseph P. Chinnici, OFM, *Devotion to the Holy Spirit in American Catholicism* (New York: Paulist, 1985), 64.

11. Quoted in Yzermans, *Frontier Bishop*, 7.

12. Yzermans, *Frontier Bishop*, 141.

13. Quoted in ibid. Cf. *Der Wanderer*, February 26, 1891.

14. Cf. Robert Emmett Curran, *Michael Augustine Corrigan and the Shaping of Conservative Catholicism in America, 1878–1902* (New York: Arno, 1978), 322–445.

15. Quoted in Yzermans, *Frontier Bishop*, 154–55. Cf. Zardetti to McQuaid, July 17, 1892, Archives of the Diocese of Rochester, Rochester, New York.

16. Yzermans, *Frontier Bishop*, 159–60.

17. Quoted in ibid., 175. Cf. Zardetti to Hudson, October 11, 1895, JZA, UNDA.

18. Yzermans, *Frontier Bishop*, 173.

19. See, for example, Zardetti to Hudson, January 19, 1900, JZA, UNDA.

20. Yzermans, *Frontier Bishop*, 175.

21. Ibid., 175–76. Cf. Franz Xaver Wetzel, *Dr. Otto Zardetti, Erzbischof von Mocissus* (Einsiedeln: Benziger, 1902), 34.

22. Curran, *Michael Augustine Corrigan*, 489–90.

23. Artigas, Glick, and Martínez, *Negotiating Darwin*, 152.

24. Ibid., 168.

25. Curran, *Michael Augustine Corrigan*, 490.

26. Ibid., 490n70.

27. Ibid., 490–91.

28. I confirmed this both through the internal computer system of the ACDF and through Wolf, *Römische Inquisition und Indexkongregation*. The

ACDF's computer system has rather extensively indexed every letter, paper, and folder in the centuries of documents. There is no real way to cite this index, as it is neither publicly available online nor in any book. The nearest is the collection of indices in the multivolume series edited by Wolf, as discussed in chapter 1.

29. Curran, *Michael Augustine Corrigan*, 495.

30. Yzermans, *Frontier Bishop*, 176–77.

31. Otto Zardetti, *Pius der Große: Immortellenkränze auf den Sarkophag Papst Pius IX* (Frankfurt: Fösser, 1879), 66. My translation.

32. Ibid., 69.

33. Ibid., 72.

34. Otto Zardetti, *Special Devotion to the Holy Ghost: A Manual* (Milwaukee: Hoffmann, 1888), 55–56.

35. Chinnici, *Devotion to the Holy Spirit*, 68.

36. Ibid., 70–71.

37. Zardetti, *Special Devotion*, 125.

38. Chinnici, *Devotion to the Holy Spirit*, 72.

39. Otto Zardetti, *Westlich! oder Durch den fernen Westen Nord-Amerikas* (Mainz: Verlag von Franz Kirchheim, 1897), https://archive.org/details/westli choderdur00zardgoog.

40. Zardetti, *Westlich!* 22. My translation.

41. Ibid., 22. My translation.

42. Index, Protocolli, 1897–99, fol. 179, ACDF; Artigas, Glick, and Martínez, *Negotiating Darwin*, 101.

43. Salis-Seewis, "*Evoluzione e Dogma* pel Padre J. A. Zahm," 201–4. Cf. Artigas, Glick, and Martínez, *Negotiating Darwin*, 137–39.

44. Salis-Seewis, "*Evoluzione e Dogma* pel Padre J. A. Zahm," 202. My translation.

45. Joseph Louis Perrier, *The Revival of Scholastic Philosophy in the Nineteenth Century* (New York: Columbia University Press, 1909), 171–72; Cf. Alberto Gómez Izquierdo, *Historia de la filosofía del siglo XIX* (Zarasoga: Gasca, 1903), 450–51; and Francesco Salis-Seewis, *Della Conoscenza Sensitiva* (Prato: Giachetti, 1881).

46. Index, Protocolli, 1897–99, fol. 179, ACDF.

47. Ibid.

48. It is worth a concluding moment to reflect upon the analysis of this report in the only other scholarly text to consider the document, Artigas, Glick, and Martínez's *Negotiating Darwin*. "Zardetti's denunciation," they write, "was clear, complete, and ordered." Zardetti was fairly clear, and certainly ordered, but that one can consider Zardetti's denunciation *complete* seems wrong given the focus of Zardetti's claims on the last part of Zahm's book. Such a statement reveals a clear tendency by Artigas, Glick, and Martínez to misunderstand the

power of the *appearance* of doctrine, as their study fails to take into account that both scientists around the world as well as the highest members of the Vatican hierarchy felt strongly that special creation was, indeed, the doctrine of the Church from the late nineteenth century into the early twentieth. Artigas, Glick, and Martínez, *Negotiating Darwin*, 144, 270–83.

49. Gero Grassi and Maria Teresa de Scisciolo, "Frate Enrico Buonpensiere," in *Per Ricordare: 347 Donne e Uomini di avantieri, di ieri e di oggi della nostra Terlizzi 1300–2013* (Terlizzi: Cooperativa Culturale RTS, 2013), 90–91, http://www.gerograssi.it/cms2/images//libro%20gero%20per%20ricordare.pdf.

50. See "Pontifical Academy of St. Thomas Aquinas," http://www.vatican.va/roman_curia/pontifical_academies/san-tommaso/index.htm. For an extended history of the academy, see Abelardo Lobato, "The Pontifical Academy of St. Thomas Aquinas: History and Mission," *Anuario Filosófico* 39, no. 2 (2006): 309–27, 317–18, and 229–30, 329–49, https://web.archive.org/web/20140108144628/http://dspace.unav.es/dspace/bitstream/10171/16163/1/1.%20LOBATO.pdf.

51. The Sacred Congregation of Studies organized and approved curricula and charters of Catholic universities and seminaries around the world. It is now known as the Congregation for Catholic Education. See "Congregation for Catholic Education (for Educational Institutions)," http://www.vatican.va/roman_curia/congregations/ccatheduc/index.htm.

52. Charles Callan, "Tommaso Maria Zigliara," in *The Catholic Encyclopedia*, vol. 15 (New York: Robert Appleton Co., 1912), http://www.newadvent.org/cathen/15759a.htm.

53. The apostolic datary was largely an honorific position that was one of the five "curial offices" before being abolished by Pope Paul VI in 1967. The main task of dataries in the late nineteenth century was to respond on behalf of the pope to letters from around the world, especially those regarding indulgences and graces. Wolf, *Römische Inquisition und Indexkongregation. Grundlagenforschung: 1814–1917*, 3:224–25. Cf. Hubert Jedin, *The Church in the Modern Age* (London: Burns and Oates, 1999), 16, 169.

54. Tomus Alter, ed., *De Religiosis Institutis & Personis: Supplementa et Monumenta* (Rome: Brugis, 1907), Supplementa, pp. 166–67, https://archive.org/details/dereligiosisins01vermgoog. The pope officially named St. Thomas a pontifical college on May 26, 1906, as the above book details, but the official papal pronouncement was not issued until two years later, on November 8, 1908. Cf. Pope Pius X, *Domum Delectis* (November 8, 1908), in *Acta Apostolicae Sedis* 11, no. 2 (1909): 137–38, http://w2.vatican.va/content/pius-x/la/letters/documents/hf_p-x_let_19081108_domum-delectis.html.

55. Grassi and Scisciolo, "Frate Enrico Buonpensiere," 91.

56. Enrico Buonpensiere, *Commentaria in I. P. Summae Theologicae S. Thomae Aquinatis, O.P., a Q. I ad Q. XXIII (De Deo uno)* (Romae: F. Pustet, 1902); Buonpensiere, *Commentaria in I. P. Summae Theologicae S. Thomae Aquinatis, O.P.: a Q. XXVII ad Q. XLIII (De Deo trino)* (Vergarae: "El Santísimo Rosario," 1930).

57. Cf. Angelus Walz, "The 'Angelicum' Celebrates Its Fiftieth Anniversary," *Dominicana* 44, no. 3 (Fall 1959): 273, http://www.dominicanajournal .org/wp-content/files/old-journal-archive/vol44/no3/dominicanav44n3roman jubileeangelicumcelebrates.pdf.

58. "Cloister Chronicle," *Dominicana* 12, no. 1 (1927): 88, http://www .dominicanajournal.org/wp-content/files/old-journal-archive/vol12/no1 /dominicanav12n1cloisterchronicle.pdf.

59. Reginald Garrigou-Lagrange, *Reality: A Synthesis of Thomistic Thought* (St. Louis: Herder, 1950), chap. 3, https://www.ewtn.com/library/theology /reality.htm. My emphasis.

60. Artigas, Glick, and Martínez, *Negotiating Darwin*, 40.

61. Thoma Maria Zigliara, *Summa philosophica in usum scholarum*, 3 vols., 12th ed. (Paris: Briguet, 1900), 2:149.

62. Ibid., 2:150. Original emphasis. Cf. Thomas Aquinas, *Summa theologicae* I, Q. 118, A. 2, ad 2.

63. Index, Protocolli, 1878–81, fol. 71, ACDF; Artigas, Glick, and Martínez, *Negotiating Darwin*, 43–44. See also "Syllabus of Modern Errors (1864)" in chapter 4 of this volume.

64. Artigas, Glick, and Martínez, *Negotiating Darwin*, 42.

65. Index, Protocolli, 1878–81, fol. 71, ACDF; Artigas, Glick, and Martínez, *Negotiating Darwin*, 42–43.

66. Kleutgen, *Die Philosophie*, 1:41.

67. Index, Protocolli, 1895–96, fol. 118, p. 3, ACDF, original emphasis; Artigas, Glick, and Martínez, *Negotiating Darwin*, 92, updated translation.

68. Index, Protocolli, 1895–96, fol. 118, p. 4, ACDF; Artigas, Glick, and Martínez, *Negotiating Darwin*, 93, updated translation.

69. Index, Protocolli, 1895–96, fol. 118, p. 8, ACDF; Artigas, Glick, and Martínez, *Negotiating Darwin*, 95–96.

70. Index, Protocolli, 1897–99, fol. 55, ACDF; Artigas, Glick, and Martínez, *Negotiating Darwin*, 108–12.

71. Index, Protocolli, 1897–99, fol. 55, p. 5, ACDF; Artigas, Glick, and Martínez, *Negotiating Darwin*, 108.

72. Artigas, Glick, and Martínez, *Negotiating Darwin*, 108. Cf. Index, Protocolli, 1897–99, fol. 55, p. 23, ACDF.

73. To see this easily, compare the table of contents in *Evolution and Dogma* to the table of contents of Leroy's contested work, *L'Évolution restriente*

aux Espèces organiques (Paris: Briguet, 1891), 285, http://books.google.com/books?id=1CA7AQAAMAAJ.

74. Zahm, *Evolution and Dogma*, 201.

75. Index, Protocolli, 1897–99, fol. 80, p. 8, ACDF; Artigas, Glick, and Martínez, *Negotiating Darwin*, 146, updated translation.

76. Index, Protocolli, 1897–99, fol. 80, p. 8, ACDF; Artigas, Glick, and Martínez, *Negotiating Darwin*, 146, updated translation.

77. Artigas, Glick, and Martínez, *Negotiating Darwin*, 148. Cf. Index, Protocolli, 1897–99, fol. 80, pp. 25–35, ACDF.

78. "Mi sembra essere dottrina cattolica lo affermare che Dio abbia immediatamente e direttamente formato Adamo dal limo della terra." Index, Protocolli, 1897–99, fol. 80, p. 45, ACDF.

79. Index, Protocolli, 1897–99, fol. 80, p. 51, ACDF.

80. Index, Protocolli, 1897–99, fol. 80, p. 53, ACDF.

81. Artigas, Glick, and Martínez, *Negotiating Darwin*, 151. Cf. Index, Diari, vol. 22, fol. 39r, ACDF.

82. Index, Diari, vol. 22, fol. 42r, ACDF. Cf. Artigas, Glick, and Martínez, *Negotiating Darwin*, 158.

83. Though, as chapter 2 indicates, there was a good year of continued fireworks around Zahm's book, including a delayed retraction from the Italian translator and further negative reviews in *Civiltà Cattolica*. In terms of official notices, however, the line in the diary remains the last official word in the historical record.

BIBLIOGRAPHY

Archives

Archives of the Congregation for the Doctrine of the Faith (ACDF), Vatican City.

Archives of the Diocese of Rochester, Rochester, New York.

Archives of the United States Province of the Congregation of Holy Cross (CSCA), Notre Dame, Indiana.

Archives Province Canadienne de la Congrégation de Sainte-Croix (APC), Montréal, Quebec.

University of Notre Dame Archives (UNDA), Notre Dame, Indiana.

Sources

Alsteens, André. "Science et foi dans le chapitre IV de la Constitution *Dei Filius* au Concile du Vatican." *Ephemerides Theologicae Lovanienses* 38, no. 2 (1962): 461–503.

Alter, Tomus, ed. *De Religiosis Institutis & Personis: Supplementa et Monumenta.* Rome: Brugis, 1907. https://archive.org/details/dereligiosisins01 vermgoog.

Appleby, R. Scott. "American Catholic Modernism at the Turn of the Century." PhD diss., University of Chicago, 1985.

———. "Between Americanism and Modernism: John Zahm and Theistic Evolution." *Church History* 56, no. 4 (1987): 474–90.

———. *"Church and Age Unite!": The Modernist Impulse in American Catholicism.* Notre Dame, IN: University of Notre Dame Press, 1992.

———. "Exposing Darwin's 'Hidden Agenda': Roman Catholic Responses to Evolution, 1875–1925." In *Disseminating Darwinism,* edited by Ronald

Numbers and John Stenhouse, 173–207. Cambridge: Cambridge University Press, 1999.

Artigas, Mariano, Thomas F. Glick, and Rafael A. Martínez. *Negotiating Darwin: The Vatican Confronts Evolution, 1877–1902*. Baltimore, MD: Johns Hopkins University Press, 2006.

Augustine. *The Literal Meaning of Genesis*. Translated by John Hammond Taylor. New York: Newman Press, 1982.

Bakewell, Robert, and Benjamin Silliman. *An Introduction to Geology*. New Haven, CT: Hezekiah Howe, 1833.

Benigni, Umberto. "Pope Leo XIII." In *The Catholic Encyclopedia*, vol. 9. New York: Robert Appleton Co., 1910. http://www.newadvent.org/cathen/09169a.htm.

Bianchi, Luca. *Pour Une Histoire de La Double Vérité*. Paris: J. Vrin, 2008.

Blum, C. "St. George Mivart, Catholic Natural Philosopher." PhD diss., University of Notre Dame, 1996.

Boyle, Leonard E., OP. "A Remembrance of Pope Leo XIII: The Encyclical *Aeterni Patris*." In *One Hundred Years of Thomism: Aeterni Patris and Afterwards: A Symposium*, edited by Victor B. Brezik, CSB, 7–22. Houston: Center for Thomistic Studies, 1981.

Brownson, Orestes Augustus. "Darwin's Descent of Man." *Brownson's Quarterly Review* (July 1873): 340–51. http://orestesbrownson.org/24.html.

———. "Kant's Critique of Pure Reason—Part 1." *Brownson's Quarterly Review* (April 1844): 167–69. http://orestesbrownson.org/172.html.

———. "The Roman Church and Modern Society." *Brownson's Quarterly Review* (January 1846): 123–24. http://orestesbrownson.org/313.

———. "Science and the Sciences." In Brownson, *The Works of Orestes A. Brownson*, 9:254–67.

———. "True and False Science." In Brownson, *The Works of Orestes A. Brownson*, 9:497–527.

———. *The Works of Orestes A. Brownson*. Vol. 9, *Scientific Theories*, edited by Henry Brownson. Detroit: Thorndike Nourse, 1884.

Brundell, Barry. "Catholic Church Politics and Evolution Theory, 1894–1902." *British Journal for the History of Science* 34, no. 1 (2001): 81–95.

———. Review of *Negotiating Darwin: The Vatican Confronts Evolution, 1877–1902*, by Mariano Artigas, Thomas F. Glick, and Rafael A. Martínez. *Isis* 99, no. 2 (2008): 415–16.

Bujanda, Jesús Martínez de. *Index de Rome, 1557, 1559, 1564. Les premiers index romains et l'index du Concile de Trente*. Québec: Éditions de l'Université de Sherbrooke, 1990.

———. *Index Librorum Prohibitorum: 1600–1966*. Centre d'Études de la Renaissance, Université de Sherbrooke. Montréal: Médiaspaul, 2002.

Buonpensiere, Enrico. *Commentaria in I. P. Summae Theologicae S. Thomae Aquinatis, O.P.: a Q. I ad Q. XXIII (De Deo uno)*. Romae: F. Pustet, 1902.

———. *Commentaria in I. P. Summae Theologicae S. Thomae Aquinatis, O.P.: a Q. XXVII ad Q. XLIII (De Deo trino)*. Vergarae: El Santísimo Rosario, 1930.

Burrell, David B. *When Faith and Reason Meet: The Legacy of John Zahm, CSC*. Notre Dame, IN: Corby Books, 2009.

Butler, Dom Cuthbert. *The Vatican Council: The Story Told from Inside in Bishop Ullathorne's Letters*. 2 vols. New York: Longmans, Green and Co., 1930.

Callan, Charles. "Tommaso Maria Zigliara." In *The Catholic Encyclopedia*, vol. 15. New York: Robert Appleton Co., 1912. http://www.newadvent.org/cathen/15759a.htm.

Carroll, Patrick. "Mind in Action: John A. Zahm." *Ave Maria*, n.s., 63 (January 5–June 29, 1946); 64 (July 6–20, 1946).

Caruana, Louis, ed. *Darwin and Catholicism: The Past and Present Dynamics of a Cultural Encounter*. New York: T and T Clark, 2009.

Cavanaugh, John, CSC. "Father Zahm." *Catholic World* 114, no. 683 (1922): 577–88.

Chace, George J. "Of the Divine Agency in the Production of Material Phenomena." *Bibliotheca Sacra* 5 (1848): 347.

Chadwick, Owen. *A History of the Popes, 1830–1914*. New York: Oxford University Press, 1998.

———. *The Popes and European Revolution*. New York: Oxford University Press, 1980.

Chinnici, Joseph P., OFM. *Devotion to the Holy Spirit in American Catholicism*. New York: Paulist, 1985.

"Cloister Chronicle." *Dominicana* 12, no. 1 (1927): 88. http://www.dominicanajournal.org/wp-content/files/old-journal-archive/vol12/no1/dominicanav12n1cloisterchronicle.pdf.

Constant, Eric A. "A Reinterpretation of the Fifth Lateran Council Decree 'Apostolici Regiminis' (1513)." *Sixteenth Century Journal* 33, no. 2 (2002): 353–79.

Coppa, Frank. *The Modern Papacy*. New York: Longman, 1998.

Curran, Robert Emmett. *Michael Augustine Corrigan and the Shaping of Conservative Catholicism in America, 1878–1902*. New York: Arno, 1978.

Daniels, George H. *History of American Science and Technology: American Science in the Age of Jackson*. Tuscaloosa: University of Alabama Press, 1968.

Del Re, Niccolò. *La Curia romana. Lineamenti storico-giuridici*. 3rd ed. Rome: Edizioni di Storia e Letteratura, 1970.

Deufel, Konrad. *Kirche und Tradition. Ein Beitrag zur Geschichte der theologischen Wende im 19. Jahrhundert am Beispiel des kirchlich-theologischen*

Kampfprogramms P. Joseph Kleutgen S.J. Munich: Ferdinand Schöningh, 1976.

Draper, John W. *A History of the Conflict between Religion and Science.* New York: Appleton, 1874.

Dulles, Avery. *The Assurance of Things Hoped For: A Theology of Christian Faith.* New York: Oxford University Press, 1994.

Dunn, William, CSC. "Holy Cross at St. Mary's College, Galveston: A Short Story of the 1870s." Paper presented at the Conference of the History of the Congregations of Holy Cross, Notre Dame, IN, July 5–7, 1991.

"The Evolution of Life." *Catholic World* 17, no. 98 (1873): 145–57.

Fanning, William. "Allocution." In *The Catholic Encyclopedia*, vol. 1. New York: Robert Appleton Co., 1907. http://www.newadvent.org/cathen/01325c.htm.

———. "Third Plenary Council of Baltimore." In *The Catholic Encyclopedia*, vol. 2. New York: Robert Appleton Co., 1907. http://www.newadvent.org /cathen/02235a.htm.

Feuerbach, Ludwig. *The Fiery Brook: Selected Writings of L. Feuerbach.* Translated by Hanfi Zawar. New York: Doubleday, 1972.

Fifth Lateran Council. *Apostolici Regiminis.* December 8, 1513. In *Concilium Sanctum Lateranense Novissimum*, 239–41. Rome, 1520. https://reader .digitale-sammlungen.de/de/fs1/object/display/bsb10141706_00239.html.

———. *Apostolici Regiminis.* December 8, 1513. In Tanner, *Decrees of the Ecumenical Councils*, 2:605–16.

Fiorenza, Francis S. "Presidential Address: Foundations of Theology: A Community's Tradition of Discourse and Practice." *Proceedings of the Catholic Theological Society of America* 41 (1986): 107–34.

First Vatican Council. *Dei Filius.* Dogmatic Constitution. April 24, 1870. In *Acta Santae Sedis* 5 (1869–70): 484–90. English trans., *Dei Filius*, in *Decrees of the Ecumenical Councils*, 2 vols., edited by Norman P. Tanner, SJ, 2:804–11. Washington, DC: Georgetown University Press, 1990.

Flannery, Austin. "Vatican I." *Modern Catholic Encyclopedia*, edited by Michael Glazier and Monika K. Hellwig. Collegeville, MN: Liturgical, 2004.

Flynn, Gabriel, and Paul D. Murray, eds. *Ressourcement: A Movement for Renewal in Twentieth-Century Catholic Theology.* Oxford: Oxford University Press, 2011.

Francis, Pope. *Laudato Si': On Care for Our Common Home.* Encyclical Letter. May 24, 2015. http://w2.vatican.va/content/francesco/en/encyclicals /documents/papa-francesco_20150524_enciclica-laudato-si.html.

Garrigou-Lagrange, Reginald. *Reality: A Synthesis of Thomistic Thought.* St. Louis: Herder, 1950. https://www.ewtn.com/library/theology/reality.htm.

Gmeiner, John. *Modern Scientific Views and Christian Doctrines Compared.* Milwaukee, WI: Yewdale, 1884.

Gómez Izquierdo, Alberto. *Historia de la filosofía del siglo XIX*. Zarasoga: Gasca, 1903.

Gould, Steven Jay. *Rocks of Ages: Science and Religion in the Fullness of Life*. New York: Ballantine, 1999.

———. *Time's Arrow, Time's Cycle: Myth and Metaphor in the Discovery of Geological Time*. Cambridge, MA: Harvard University Press, 1987.

Grassi, Gero, and Maria Teresa de Scisciolo. "Frate Enrico Buonpensiere." In *Per Ricordare: 347 Donne e Uomini di avantieri, di ieri e di oggi della nostra Terlizzi 1300–2013*, 90–91. Terlizzi: Cooperativa Culturale RTS, 2013. http://www.gerograssi.it/cms2/images//libro%20gero%20per%20ricordare.pdf.

Gray, Asa. *Manual of the Botany of the Northern United States, Including Virginia, Kentucky, and All East of the Mississippi*. 3rd ed. New York: Ivison, Phinney and Co., 1862.

Gruber, J. W. *A Conscience in Conflict: The Life of St. George Mivart*. New York: Columbia University Press, 1960.

Guarino, Thomas. "Vincent of Lerins and the Hermeneutical Question: Historical and Theological Reflections." *Gregorianum* 75, no. 3 (1994): 491–524.

Hall, Brian K., and Benedikt Hallgrímsson. *Strickberger's Evolution*. 4th ed. Sudbury, MA: Jones and Bartlett Publishers, 2008.

Harrison, Peter. *The Territories of Science and Religion*. Chicago: University of Chicago Press, 2017.

Hegel, Georg Wilhelm Friedrich. *Phenomenology of Spirit*. New York: Oxford University Press, 1977.

Heinle, Edward. "Religion and Evolution: John Zahm's Reconciliation." Master's thesis, University of Notre Dame, 1987.

Hennesey, James J. *The First Council of the Vatican: The American Experience*. New York: Herder and Herder, 1963.

Hermes, Georg. *Hermes, oder, Kritisches Jahrbuch der Literatur*. Vol. 32. Leipzig: Brodhaus, 1829.

Hertkens, Johann, and P. Ludwig Lercher, *P. Joseph Kleutgen, sein Leben und seine literarishce Wirksamkeit*. Regensburg: F. Pustet, 1910.

Hodge, Charles. *What Is Darwinism?* New York: Scribner and Armstrong, 1874.

Holmes, J. Derek. *The Triumph of the Holy See: A Short History of the Papacy in the Nineteenth Century*. London: Burns and Oates, 1978.

Hope, Arthur J., CSC. *Notre Dame: One Hundred Years*. Notre Dame, IN: University of Notre Dame Press, 1978.

Hovenkamp, Herbert. *Science and Religion in America, 1800–1860*. Philadelphia: University of Pennsylvania Press, 1978.

Howard, Thomas. [anon.] *A Brief History of the University of Notre Dame du Lac: From 1842–1892*. Prepared for the Golden Jubilee. Chicago: Werner Co., 1895. Digital Collections, UNDA. http://archives.nd.edu/Anniversary/Golden.pdf.

Hull, David, ed. *Darwin and His Critics: The Reception of Darwin's Theory of Evolution by the Scientific Community.* Chicago: University of Chicago Press, 1973.

Inglis, John. "Aquinas and the Historiography of Medieval Philosophy: A Re-evaluation." PhD diss., University of Kentucky, 1993.

———. "Philosophical Autonomy and the Historiography of Medieval Philosophy." *British Journal for the History of Philosophy* 5, no. 1 (1997): 21–53.

———. *Spheres of Philosophical Inquiry and the Historiography of Medieval Philosophy.* Boston: Brill, 1998.

Jedin, Hubert. *The Church in the Modern Age.* London: Burns and Oates, 1999.

John Paul II, Pope. *Fides et Ratio.* Encyclical Letter. September 14, 1998. http://w2.vatican.va/content/john-paul-ii/la/encyclicals/documents/hf_jp-ii_enc_14091998_fides-et-ratio.html.

———. "Message to the Pontifical Academy of Sciences on Evolution." October 22, 1996. https://www.ewtn.com/library/papaldoc/jp961022.htm.

Kleutgen, Joseph. *Die Philosophie der Vorzeit vertheidigt.* 2 vols. Münster: Theissingsche Buchhandlung, 1860–1863.

Komonchak, Joseph. "Augustine, Aquinas or the Gospel *sine glossa*? Divisions over *Gaudium et Spes.*" In *Unfinished Journey: The Church 40 Years after Vatican II*, edited by Austen Ivereigh, 102–18. New York: Continuum, 2003.

Kuhn, Thomas S. *The Structure of Scientific Revolutions.* Chicago: University of Chicago Press, 1962.

———. "What Are Scientific Revolutions?" In *The Road Since Structure: Philosophical Essays, 1970–1993, with an Autobiographical Interview*, edited by James Conant and John Haugeland, 13–32. Chicago: University of Chicago Press, 2002.

Lakner, Franz. "Kleutgen und die kirchliche Wissenschaft Deutschland sim 19. Jahrhundert." *Zeitschrift für katholische Theologie* 57 (1933): 161–214.

Leo XIII, Pope. *Aeterni Patris.* Encyclical Letter. August 4, 1879. In *Acta Sanctae Sedis* 12 (1879): 97–115. English trans., http://w2.vatican.va/content/leo-xiii/en/encyclicals/documents/hf_l-xiii_enc_04081879_aeterni-patris.html.

———. *Providentissimus Deus.* Encyclical Letter. November 18, 1893. In *Acta Sanctae Sedis* 26 (1893): 269–92. English trans., http://w2.vatican.va/content/leo-xiii/en/encyclicals/documents/hf_l-xiii_enc_18111893_providentissimus-deus.html.

———. *Testem Benevolentiae Nostrae.* Encyclical Letter. January 22, 1899. In *Acta Sanctae Sedis* 31 (1898–99): 470–79. English trans., https://w2.vatican.va/content/leo-xiii/la/letters/documents/hf_l-xiii_let_18990122_testem-benevolentiae.html.

Lobato, Abelardo. "The Pontifical Academy of St. Thomas Aquinas: History and Mission." *Anuario Filosófico* 39, no. 2 (2006): 309–27, 317–18, and 229–30, 329–49. https://web.archive.org/web/20140108144628/http://dspace.unav.es/dspace/bitstream/10171/16163/1/1.%20LOBATO.pdf.

Lonergan, Bernard. *Insight: A Study of Human Understanding*. Vol. 3 of *Collected Works of Bernard Lonergan*, edited by Frederick E. Crowe and Robert M. Doran. Toronto: University of Toronto Press, 1992.

———. "Natural Knowledge of God." In *A Second Collection*, edited by William Ryan and Bernard Tyrrell, 117–33. Westminster: Philadelphia, 1974.

———. "The Transition from a Classicist World-View to Historical-Mindedness." In *A Second Collection*, edited by William Ryan and Bernard Tyrrell, 1–9. Westminster: Philadelphia, 1974.

Lyell, Charles. *Principles of Geology*. 10th ed. London: John Murray, 1866.

Malone, Richard. "Historical Overview of the Rosmini Case." *L'Osservatore Romano*, July 25, 2001. https://www.ewtn.com/library/theology/rosmini.htm.

Manning, Henry Edward. *The True Story of the Vatican Council*. London: Henry S. King, 1877. http://books.google.com/books?id=FvENAAAAYAAJ.

Mansi, Giovan Domenico, Philippe Labbe, and Jean Baptiste Martin, eds. *Sacrorum Conciliorum Nova, et Amplissima Collectio*. 53 vols. Paris: Welter, 1901–27.

Marsden, George. *Fundamentalism and American Culture*. 2nd ed. New York: Oxford University Press, 2006.

McCool, Gerald. *Nineteenth-Century Scholasticism: The Search for a Unitary Method*. New York: Fordham University Press, 1989. [Originally published as *Catholic Theology in the Nineteenth Century* (Seabury Press, 1977)].

Mettepenningen, Jürgen. *Nouvelle Théologie—New Theology: Inheritor of Modernism, Precursor of Vatican II*. New York: T and T Clark, 2010.

Mivart, St. George Jackson. *Lessons from Nature, as Manifested in Mind and Matter*. New York: Appleton, 1876.

———. *On the Genesis of Species*. New York: Appleton, 1871.

———. *On Truth: A Systematic Inquiry*. London: Kegan Paul, Tench and Co., 1889.

Mondin, Battista. *The Popes of the Modern Ages: From Pius IX to John Paul II*. Pontifical Academy of the Sciences, Vatican City: Urbaniana University Press, 2004.

Moore, Gerry, James Macklin, and Lisa DeCesare. "A Brief History of Asa Gray's *Manual of Botany*." *Harvard Papers in Botany* 15, no. 2 (2010): 277–86.

Moore, James R. *The Post-Darwinian Controversies: A Study of the Protestant Struggle to Come to Terms with Darwin in Great Britain and America, 1870–1900.* New York: Cambridge University Press, 1981.

Morrison, John L. "A History of American Catholic Opinion on the Theory of Evolution, 1859–1950." PhD diss., University of Missouri, 1951.

"A New Theory of Evolution Applied to Man." *Catholic Fortnightly Review* 13 (1906): 137–38.

Nichols, Aidan. *Conversation of Faith and Reason: Modern Catholic Thought from Hermes to Benedict XVI.* Chicago: Hillenbrand, 2009.

O'Brien, John. *The Origin of Man: Light from Modern Science.* New York: Paulist, 1947.

O'Collins, Gerald, and Edward G. Farrugia, eds. *A Concise Dictionary of Theology.* New York: Paulist, 2000.

O'Connor, Thomas F. "John A. Zahm, C.S.C.: Scientist and Americanist." *The Americas* 7, no. 4 (1951): 435–62.

O'Malley, John. *What Happened at Vatican II?* Cambridge, MA: Harvard University Press, 2008.

O'Meara, Thomas F. *Thomas Aquinas, Theologian.* Notre Dame, IN: University of Notre Dame Press, 1997.

O'Reilly, Bernard. *Life of Leo XIII.* New York: Charles L. Webster, 1887.

Paul VI, Pope. *Integrae Servandae.* December 7, 1965. In *Acta Apostolicae Sedis* 57: (1965): 952–55.

Perrier, Joseph Louis. *The Revival of Scholastic Philosophy in the Nineteenth Century.* New York: Columbia University Press, 1909.

Pius IX, Pope. *Ineffabilis Deus.* December 8, 1854.

———. "Pius IX on Liberal Catholicism." *Dublin Review* 26, n.s. (1876): 489.

———. *Quanta Cura.* Encyclical Letter. December 8, 1864. In *Acta Santae Sedis* 3 (1867): 160–67. http://www.vatican.va/archive/ass/index_sp.htm. English trans. updated from Pope Pius IX, "Text and Translation of the Encyclical and Syllabus," 500–511.

———. Syllabus of Modern Errors. December 8, 1864. In *Acta Santae Sedis* 3 (1867): 167–76. http://www.vatican.va/archive/ass/index_sp.htm.

———. "Text and Translation of the Encyclical and Syllabus." In *Dublin Review* 4, no. 56 (1865): 500–529.

Pius X, Pope. *Domum Delectis.* November 8, 1908. In *Acta Apostolicae Sedis* 11, no. 2 (1909): 137–38. http://w2.vatican.va/content/pius-x/la/letters/docu ments/hf_p-x_let_19081108_domum-delectis.html.

Pius XII, Pope. *Humani Generis.* Encyclical Letter. December 8, 1950. http://w2.vatican.va/content/pius-xii/en/encyclicals/documents/hf_p-xii_enc_12081950_humani-generis.html.

Pottmeyer, Hermann Josef. *Der Glaube vor dem Anspruch der Wissenschaft: Die Konstitution über den katholischen Glauben "Dei Filius" des 1. Vatikanischen Konzils und der unveröffentlichten theologischen Voten der vorbereitenden Kommission.* Vienna: Herder, 1968.

———. "Der wissenschaftliche Charakter der Theologie nach dem I. Vatikanum." *Catholica* 24 (1970): 194–204.

———. "Die Konstitution "Dei Filius' des 1. Vatikanischen Konzils zwischen Abwehr und Rezeption der Moderne." In *Wege der Theologie: an der Schwelle zum dritten Jahrtausend,* edited by Günter Riße, Heino Sonnemans, and Burkhard Theß, 73–86. Paderborn: Bonifatius, 1996.

Pritz, Joseph. *Glauben und Wissen bei Anton Günther.* Vienna: Herder, 1963.

———. *Wegweisung zur Theologie.* Vienna: Wiener Domverlag, 1971.

Roberts, John H. *Darwinism and the Divine in America.* Notre Dame, IN: University of Notre Dame Press, 1988.

Sachs, J. "Kleutgen, Joseph." *Kirchliches Handlexikon* 2 (1912): 411.

Salis-Seewis, Francesco. *Della Conoscenza Sensitiva.* Prato: Giachetti, 1881.

———. "*Evoluzione e Dogma* pel Padre J. A. Zahm." *La Civiltà Cattolica,* 16th ser., 10, no. 1118 (1897): 201–4. https://babel.hathitrust.org/cgi/pt? id=ucl .a0003520319;view=1up;seq=137.

Schmidt, James M. *Notre Dame and the Civil War: Marching Onward to Victory.* Charleston, SC: History Press, 2010.

Sheehan, Michael. *Apologetics and Catholic Doctrine: A Two Years' Course of Religious Instruction for Schools and Colleges.* Dublin: M. H. Gill and Son, 1937.

Silliman, Benjamin. *Principles of Physics, or Natural Philosophy.* 2nd ed. Philadelphia: Theodore Bliss, 1866.

Sloan, Phillip R. "Bringing Evolution to Notre Dame: Father John Zahm, C.S.C. and Theistic Evolutionism." *American Midland Naturalist* 161, no. 2 (2009): 189–205.

Tanner, Norman P., SJ, ed. *Decrees of the Ecumenical Councils.* 2 vols. Washington, DC: Georgetown University Press, 1990.

Tenney, Sanborn. *Natural History: A Manual of Zoology for Schools, Colleges, and the General Reader.* New York: Scribner, 1866.

University of Notre Dame. *Annual Catalogue of the University of Notre Dame.* Vols. 21–31. Notre Dame, IN: Ave Maria Press, 1865–75. Digital Collections, UNDA. http://archives.nd.edu/bulletin/.

———. *Annual Catalogue of the University of Notre Dame.* Vol. 35. Notre Dame, IN: Scholastic Press, 1879. Digital Collections, UNDA. http://archives.nd .edu/bulletin/AC_35.pdf.

Virchow, Rudolph. "Anthropology in the Last Twenty Years." In *Annual Report of the Board of Regents of the Smithsonian Institution,* 555–70. Washington,

DC: Government Printing Office, 1890. https://books.google.com/books
?id=Ons3AQAAIAAJ.

Vorzimmer, Peter J. *Charles Darwin: The Years of Controversy; The Origin of
Species and Its Critics, 1859–1882.* Philadelphia, PA: Temple University
Press, 1970.

Walz, Angelus. "The 'Angelicum' Celebrates Its Fiftieth Anniversary." *Dominicana* 44, no. 3 (Fall 1959). http://www.dominicanajournal.org/wp-content
/files/old-journal-archive/vol44/no3/dominicanav44n3romanjubilee
angelicumcelebrates.pdf.

Weber, Ralph Edward. "The Life of Reverend John A. Zahm, C.S.C.: American
Catholic Apologist and Educator." PhD diss., University of Notre Dame,
1956.

———. *Notre Dame's John Zahm: American Catholic Apologist and Educator.*
Notre Dame, IN: University of Notre Dame Press, 1961.

Weisheipl, James A. "The Revival of Thomism: An Historical Survey." Lecture,
Mount Saint Bernard Seminary, Dubuque, IA, 1962. http://opcentral.org
/resources/2014/02/17/the-revival-of-thomism/.

Wetzel, Franz Xaver. *Dr. Otto Zardetti, Erzbischof von Mocissus.* Einsiedeln:
Benziger, 1902.

Windle, Bertram C. A. *The Church and Science.* London: Catholic Truth Society, 1917.

Wolf, Hubert, ed. *Römische Inquisition und Indexkongregation. Grundlagenforschung: 1814–1917.* 3 vols. Munich: Schöningh, 2005.

Wolf, Hubert, et al., eds. *Römische Inquisition und Indexkongregation. Grundlagenforschung: 1701–1813.* 3 vols. Paderborn: Ferdinand Schöningh, 2009.

Yzermans, Vincent A. *Frontier Bishop of Saint Cloud.* Waite Park, MN: Park
Press, 1988.

Zahm, John A. "Age of the Human Race." *Review of Reviews* 7 (1893): 605–6.

———. "The Age of the Human Race According to Modern Science and Biblical
Chronology." *American Catholic Historical Review* 18 (1893): 225–49,
562–87, 719–34; 19 (1894): 260–75.

———. *The Age of the Human Race According to Modern Science and Biblical
Chronology.* Notre Dame, IN: Ave Maria Press, n.d. Pamphlet.

———. *Alaska, the Country and Its Inhabitants.* Notre Dame, IN: University
Press, 1886. Pamphlet.

———. "Allegorism and Literalism." *Ecclesiastical Review* 10 (Mar 1894): 176–87.

———. *Along the Andes and Down the Amazon.* New York: Appleton, 1911.

———. *The Antiquity of Man According to Astronomy and History.* 1893. Pamphlet.

———. *Bible, Science, and Faith.* Baltimore: John Murphy, 1894.

———. "Catholic Church and Modern Science." *Ave Maria* 19 (1883): 241–48, 261–68.

———. *The Catholic Church and Modern Science.* Notre Dame, IN: University Press, 1883. Pamphlet.

———. *Catholic Church and Modern Science.* Notre Dame, IN: Ave Maria Press, 1886.

———. "Catholic Dogma and Scientific Dogmatism." *American Catholic Quarterly Review* 15 (1890): 434–67.

———. *Catholic Science and Catholic Scientists.* Philadelphia: H. L. Kilner, 1893.

———. "Christian Faith and Scientific Freedom." *North American Review* 157 (1893): 315–24.

———. *Colorado, Its Past, Present, and Future.* Notre Dame, IN: University Press, 1883. Pamphlet.

———. "A Distinguished Orientalist, Monsignor Charles De Harlez." *Rosary* 5 (1895): 262–71.

———. *Evolution and Dogma.* Chicago: McBride, 1896.

———. "Evolution and Teleology." *Popular Science Monthly* 52 (1898): 815–24.

———. *Evoluzione e dogma.* Translated by Alfonso M. Galea. Siena: Presso l'Ufficio della Biblioteca del clero, 1896.

———. "Faith and Science." *Donahue's Magazine* 30 (1893): 265–74.

——— [H. J. Mozans]. *Following the Conquistadores: Up the Orinoco and Down the Magdalena.* New York: Appleton, 1910.

———. "The Forerunner and Rival of Pasteu." *Rosary* 4 (1894): 433–50.

———. "The Friends and Foes of Science." *American Catholic Quarterly Review* 15 (1890): 630–57.

———. *From Berlin to Bagdad and Babylon.* New York: Appleton, 1922.

———. "A Galaxy of Catholic Scientists." *Donahue's Magazine* 32 (1894): 595–610.

———. *Great Inspirers.* New York: Appleton, 1917.

———. *The Great Southwest, Its Attractions, Resources and People.* Notre Dame, IN: University Press, 1883. Pamphlet.

———. "Idyllic Homes and Lives of Indians in South American Wilds." *Bulletin of the Pan American Union* 33 (1911): 730–47.

———. "The International Catholic Scientific Congress." *Donahue's Magazine* 32 (1894): 459–67.

———. *La evolucíon y el dogma.* Translated by Miguel Asúa. Madrid: Sociedad Editorial Española, 1905.

———. "Leo XIII and Science." *Catholic University Bulletin* 2 (1896): 21–38.

———. "Leo XIII and the Social Question." *North American Review* 61 (1895): 200–214.

———. *Letters from the Hawaiian Islands.* Notre Dame, IN: University Press, 1887. Pamphlet.

———. *L'evolution et le dogme.* Translated by Abbé J. Flageolet. Paris: Lethielleux, 1897.

———. "Louis Pasteur and His Life-Work." *Catholic World* 58 (1893): 445–63.

———. "Mendacity of Voltaire." *Ave Maria* 38 (1894): 365–68.

———. "Modern Theories of Cosmogeny." *Ecclesiastical Review* 10 (Mar 1894): 210–27.

———. "The Mosaic Hexaemeron in the Light of Exegesis and Modern Science." *Ecclesiastical Review* 10 (1894): 161–76.

———. *Moses and Modern Science.* Philadelphia: Gallagher, 1894. Pamphlet.

———. "A New System of Writing for the Blind." *Catholic World* 61 (1895): 32–43.

———. "The Observatory of the Vatican." *Cosmopolitan Magazine* 18 (1895): 599–607.

———. "The Omar of the New World." *American Ecclesiastical Review* 7 (1892): 81–101.

———. *The Quest of El Dorado: The Most Romantic Episode in the History of South American Conquest.* New York: Appleton, 1917.

———. Review of *The Buccaneers of the West Indies in the XVII Century,* by C. H. Haring. *Bulletin of the Pan American Union* 33 (1911): 517–21.

———. Review of *The Incas of Peru,* by Sir Clements Markham. *Bulletin of the Pan American Union* 32 (1911): 300–309.

———. "Roosevelt's Visit to South America." *Review of Reviews* 58 (1914): 81–86.

———. *Scholastic.* Selected articles.

"Bible, Science, and Faith." 28:39–40 (1894).

"Catholic Science and Catholic Scientists." 26:643–64 (1893).

"The Church and Science: Text of a Lecture." 22:414–15 (1889).

"The Cosmogony of Moses." 27:477–80 (1894).

"A Great Experiment." 25:639 (1892).

"An Important Work by Father Zahm: *Sound and Music.*" 25:586 (1892).

"John Tyndall, Scientist." 27:363–66 (1894).

"Lecture in Science Hall." 9:457 (1876).

"Leo XIII and Science." 29:361–65, 378–80 (1896).

"A List of One Hundred Best Books." 20:588–90 (1887).

"Notice of a Lecture on the Teachings of Some Scientists." 20:540 (1887).

"Philosophy of Sounds." 24:507 (1891).

"The Reckless Skepticism of Modern Scientists." 19:146–47 (1885).

"Science and the Church." 30:245 (1897).

"The Study of Science and Religious Beliefs." 26:266–68 (1893).

"Substance of a Reply to a Toast to Fr. Sorin." 21:596 (1888).

"Synopsis of a Lecture on Astronomy." 10:251 (1876).

"Thoughts on Science and the Age in Which We Live." 4 (19): 1–2 (1871).

"What the Church Has Done for Science." 18 (26): 405–11; (27): 421–26; (28): 437–40 (1885).

———. "Science and Religion, Five Lectures by Zahm." *Catholic Reading Circle Review* 3 (1893).

———. *Science and the Church.* Chicago: McBride, 1896.

———. *Scientific Theory and Catholic Doctrine.* Chicago: McBride, 1896.

———. "The Site of the Garden of Eden." *Ecclesiastical Review* 11 (1894): 241–71.

———. "Some Lights of Science and the Church." *Rosary* 5 (1895): 239–350.

———. *Sound and Music.* Chicago: A. C. McClurg, 1893.

———. "St. Augustine and Evolution." *Ecclesiastical Review* 10 (Mar 1894): 194–210.

———. "St. Gregory of Nyssa and the Nebular Hypothesis." *Ecclesiastical Review* 10 (March 1894): 187–94.

———. "Theodore Roosevelt as a Hunter-Naturalist." *Outlook* 121 (1919): 434–36.

———. "The Warfare with Agnosticism." *Donahue's Magazine* 32 (1894): 265–76.

———. "What the Church Has Done for Science." *Ave Maria* 21 (1885): 191–98, 212–16, 233–37, 247–52.

———. *What the Church Has Done for Science.* Notre Dame, IN: Ave Maria, n.d. Pamphlet.

———. [A. H. Solis]. "Who Were the First Bishops and Archbishops in the New World, and Where Were the First Sees Established?" *American Ecclesiastical Review* 48 (1913): 385–92.

——— [H. J. Mozans]. *Woman in Science.* New York: Appleton, 1913.

——— [A. H. Johns]. "Woman's Work in Bible Study and Translation." *Catholic World* 95 (1912): 463–77.

Zardetti, Otto. *Pius der Große: Immortellenkränze auf den Sarkophag Papst Pius IX.* Frankfurt: Fösser, 1879.

———. *Special Devotion to the Holy Ghost: A Manual.* Milwaukee: Hoffmann, 1888.

———. *Westlich! oder Durch den fernen Westen Nord-Amerikas.* Mainz: Verlag von Franz Kirchheim, 1897. https://archive.org/details/westlichoderdur00zardgoog.

Zigliara, Thoma Maria. *Summa philosophica in usum scholarum.* 3 vols. 12th ed. Paris: Briguet, 1900.

INDEX

JOHN P. SLATTERY

is a senior program associate

with the Dialogue on Science, Ethics, and Religion Program

of the American Association for the Advancement of Science.

Lightning Source UK Ltd.
Milton Keynes UK
UKHW020330130220
358654UK00005B/416

9 780268 106096